I0521712

Children of Bipolar Parents
from pain and confusion to hope and love

Children of
BIPOLAR
PARENTS

from pain and confusion to hope and love

Ya'el Chaikind, MA, LPCC   Barry Panter, MD, PhD

Children of Bipolar Parents:
from pain and confusion to hope and love

Copyright © 2022 by Barry M Panter, MD, PhD and
Ya'el Chaikind, MPH, MA, LPCC. Co-Editors

All rights reserved.

Printed in the U.S.A.

No part of this book may be used or reproduced in any manner without written permission from Ya'el Chaikind, MPH, MA, LPCC.

Every effort has been made to locate the copyright holders of the illustrations and quotes reproduced in this book. Omissions brought to our attention will be corrected in the subsequent printings.

Published by:
AIMED PRESS, a division of the American Institute of Medical Education
Rancho Mirage, California
and
Ya'el Chaikind, MPH, MA, LPCC
PO Box 9266
Santa Fe, NM 87504
www.yaelchaikind.com

Cover Illustration:
Linda Hawkins

Production Design:
Ken Rubin

ISBN 979-8-9867321-0-7 (paperback)
ISBN 979-8-9867321-1-4 (eBook)

Acknowledgements

We are most grateful to the authors for sharing their stories, insights, pain, and perspectives with us. With great compassion, we also acknowledge our bipolar parents and the ancestral stories that paved the way for all of us to arrive, at this moment, in this time.

A very special thanks for the help, suggestions, and patience of Ken Rubin, who provided such wonderful assistance with the formatting of this book. We also thank Linda Hawkins for her creativity that is so beautifully depicted on the cover of this book.

Authors:

Ya'el Chaikind • Pat Connors • Maid Čorbić • Megan C.W.
Noah Day • Sally Husch Dean • Susan Delphine Delaney
Trish Eisman Paula Fayerman • Naomi Golda • Elizabeth Goldman
Debbie Schlesinger Greenwood • Leslie Hendrickson-Baral
Helen Hudson • Lisa Kenwyn Lax • Ann B. List • Rena Maas
Myra McKenzie • Veruschka Normandeau • Mark Parker
Sarah Pobuda • Mardi Storm Clewett Von Ronne • Cassandra Sagan
Barbara Schwartz • Gabby Leon Spatt • Julie Strong • John Tavares

Praise for *Children of Bipolar Parents*

"For those who wish to understand, empathize, and connect with the deep well of compassion within them, look no further than the stories that grace the pages of this most profound and important book."

- Keith Carlson, BSN, RN, NC-BC, *The Nurse Keith Show*

"Having the courage to face our own darkness, go through the difficult and painful healing process, and then share our stories with others, is redemptive and cathartic. Whether you have direct experience with bipolar or not, many people will relate to the resilience, life force, love, and creativity of these authors. I highly recommend this book!"

- Nina Ross, PhD, Author,
The Art of Depth Psychology: Intimacy With Images

"These stories will break your heart open with compassion, even as they are educating you to the realities of growing up with a bipolar parent. And, if you are the child of a bipolar parent, they will also give you hope, with examples of people growing beyond their traumatic and painful childhoods."

- Rabbinic Pastor David Daniel Klipper

"The traumas and memories of these personal stories become as indelible to the caring reader as they clearly are to the authors. This material takes us into the world of bipolar with invaluable realism. As one whose own life has been impacted by the bipolar personality, *Children of Bipolar Parents* is a vital reference.

- Reverend Ann Rea, Senior Minister,
Everyday Center for Spiritual Living

"This intriguing and revealing book bravely wades into the bipolar ocean of emotions that creates traumatic waves of shock and struggle for children of bipolar parents. We find amazingly honest examples of heart wrenching behavior and volatility combined with gratitude, acceptance, and hope for change."

- Bob Hoffman, Poet and Attorney

Praise for *Children of Bipolar Parents*

"The complexity of how bipolar symptoms can manifest is captured in this collective telling. These poignant depictions help the reader distinguish between understanding the true self and what was ascribed by unpredictability and abuse from the past. Throughout this perceptive and engaging book, the message of strength, hope, and healing prevails."

- Brenda Jaffe, LCSW (retired)

"Heart-rending yet heart-warming stories of what the human spirit can endure and overcome. Common threads of sadness, triumph, pain, and joy bring forth the reader's empathy for both parents with bipolar and their children."

- Sol Lederman, Software Engineer

"These personal narratives portray the confused, unstable, and painful reality of what it's like as a child to be living with a parent challenged by mental illness. If your childhood experience resonates within these stories, know that you are not alone. Know also, if your past still troubles you—with guidance, you can overcome it."

- Deborah Gallinger, CCHt, Clinical/
Medical Support Hypnotherapist

"What first stands out is the terrible impact on these children of the uncertainty of daily survival and what version of a parent will show up in any moment. Just as clearly, this book offers sensitive insights and proof of the power available for healing and transformation for those born into similarly tragic childhoods."

- Mark Perry, CHt, C-NLP, Certified Clinical Hypnotherapist

"These stories evoke deep empathy for humanity and the challenges many have faced with loved ones. A facet of nearly everyone's experience exists inside this compilation to show we are not alone in our journey. This book deeply resonates and will bring healing we didn't know we needed."

- Kiki Vance, Registered Somatic Movement Therapist

Introductions

Silence isolates us and perpetuates the false sense that we are alone in common feelings of guilt, anger, sadness, and shame often associated with being a child of a bipolar parent. The weight of holding these family secrets often was unbearable, but who could we tell? We were little kids depending on our parents for emotional and physical survival. If they left, what would happen to us? In the minds of small children, it is far easier to believe we are the source of the problem than to ask questions and risk reaction amid the obvious struggle of our parent. So, most of us learn to live with the fallout of our bipolar parent, creating all sorts of brilliant strategies to survive.

Yet, shared stories heal us, validating our experiences by demonstrating not only the difficulties of our childhoods, but ever-better ways to cope and thrive as adults. By writing, telling, and reading stories, we witness each other and discover more about ourselves. After all, my story is our story, is their story, is your story.

This anthology shares the vulnerable and poignant stories of twenty-seven authors who are either children of bipolar parents or bipolar parents themselves. Though the stains of our bipolar family legacies may never completely fade, sharing our stories helps dissolve the shame and secrets in the sunlight of truth: We are not alone and no longer need to remain silent.

Individually and collectively, this book exemplifies how we have turned our stories of survival into stories of thrival. Telling survival stories, and owning the truth of our own experiences, is a vital first step of our healing journey. Equally important is empowering our choice to actively change our life's trajectory. How? With well-earned wisdom, we explore the old stories and choose new perspectives that work better. By living a new story, we create different meanings and outcomes, transforming not only our lives, but our families and communities as well.

May all readers with similar stories find a path to thrival and stand strong with us. May these stories help absolve you of the shame and secrets inscribed into your hearts by your bipolar parentage. May this book inspire you to share and heal your own story!

Ya'el Chaikind, MA, LPCC, Co-Editor and Contributor
Santa Fe, NM

Introductions

Ya'el and I both had mothers who suffered and struggled with bipolar disorder. We know the journey.

We also know that, although there are painful similarities, the journey of each child of a bipolar parent is unique. The following twenty-seven stories are vulnerable, honest, and respectful tales describing the distinctive experience of growing up in a bipolar home and the adult consequences of a bipolar childhood.

What are some of the challenges and tasks of a child living with a bipolar parent? In his 1950 book, Childhood and Society, Erik Erikson describes eight life stages. Each stage has a challenge – a task. The individual is better prepared for the next stage and challenge if successfully passed. For example, the first stage is infancy, and the challenge is to establish trust. If the challenge is not met successfully, the infant develops mistrust. In adolescence, the challenge is between a sense of identity versus identity confusion. In early adult life, the challenge is intimacy versus isolation.

In the same way, being the child of a bipolar parent brings challenges for us in additional ways, and most of us spend our lives trying to decipher the most functional way of meeting these life tasks. For example:

Guilt versus Self-Esteem

The challenge of the parent's depression is guilt ("What did I do to cause this?") versus self-esteem ("It's not my fault!").

A sense of guilt, with its accompanying shame, remorse, and low self-esteem, is nearly impossible for the infant and child to escape. "It's my fault" is a frequent thought for a child of a bipolar parent. Why else would Mommy suddenly erupt in anger, hurtful language, and sometimes physical abuse? The child searches for answers and this thought often comes to mind. Paradoxically, it has a soothing effect. "This is not random. I have some control over it. If I only could be good enough, Mommy wouldn't be this way." So the child unconsciously has power and control

But the damage goes deeper. "It's my fault" becomes, "I'm a bad person. I'm unworthy. I deserve to be treated this way." Carrying these unconscious beliefs into life takes a heavy toll: Self-sabotage, dysfunctional abusive relationships, and other failures. Only later in life is it possible to

Introductions

have the maturity, perspective, and ability to understand what was happening intellectually. Only then can the individual have compassion, forgiveness, and tolerant love for the mother who has given and suffered so much and also caused so much pain and suffering.

Attachment versus Separation

In the challenge between attachment versus separation, it is difficult to maintain a close relationship with a parent who, at times, is lovable, enjoyable to be with, and nurturing, and who, at other inexplicable times becomes angry, emotionally unavailable, and cruel. One path is to remain attached and endure the pain, anger, and ups and downs of being loved and then being hurt.

Another path is separation. "I can't deal with this, I am better off without you. I will see you occasionally or not at all. I have to protect myself from you to survive." Children of bipolar parents likely have the lived experience of both of these challenges throughout their lives.

Being Cared For versus Being the Caretaker

Sometimes the bipolar mother or father is sad, suicidal, confused, and needy. It is not unusual for the loving child, who needs the attention and love of the parent, to become the parent's caretaker. This happens because of the child's love for the parent and the need for the parent to be well and functional in order to take care of the child.

I believe this is why many children of a bipolar parent become mental health professionals.

Without knowing any offical studies, I am sure that the percentage of children of a bipolar parent who become mental health workers is high. This definitely is true for both Ya'el and I.

Trust versus Mistrust

The effect of a depressed, emotionally unavailable mother is the child develops mistrust instead of trust. You cannot trust a relationship with anyone. The lifelong effects of this are illustrated in the life of Vincent Van Gogh.

Introductions

Van Gogh's mother was not bipolar, but she did have a depressive disorder. She had lost a newborn son exactly one year before Vincent was born. She had named that first son Wilhelm Vincent Van Gogh, the exact same name as Vincent. Van Gogh was a replacement child. Vincent's mother was depressed for most of his childhood. In his letters to his brother Theo, he referred to her as "mater dolorosa," the mother of sorrow.

As a result of his childhood experience, Vincent suffered from feelings of isolation, rejection, and a yearning for closeness to others. Yet, his failure to meet the challenge of that first stage, trust versus mistrust, contributed to the creation of some of the world's greatest masterpieces. He wrote to his brother, "I send my paintings out to the world hoping that they will touch the hearts of others and that they will know what lies in the heart of this miserable, irascible, unpleasant man." Vincent's sense of guilt prevented him from being able to be in a loving, comforting, life enriching relationship.

It also prevented him from allowing for financial success. Vincent's works were exhibited only once during his lifetime. Maurice Aurier, a leading art critic of the day, wrote a favorable review of Van Gogh's paintings. Vincent wrote to his brother, "Please ask M. Aurier not to write any more about my work. Success is the worst thing that could happen to an artist."

Vincent's wounds and scars, his desperate yearning for closeness, his longing for a loving and comforting intimacy were sublimated into the creation of his art. His hands, through his paintings, at last, touch the hearts of others.

Being the child of a bipolar parent is, at times, painful, demanding, and mind-bending. But it's not all bad news. There are benefits. For self-protection, one develops empathy. (It is to my advantage to read my parent's moods. If I can, perhaps I can ward off the coming storm.)

Sharing in the euphoria of a manic or hypomanic episode is exciting and fun. A sense of optimism might develop. (Yes, there are times of misery, but they usually are followed by happy times. The depression does lift. The good mother or father does return.)

Perseverance can be learned by observation and by absorption. (If I can ride this out, things will get better.)

Introductions

With time, even after wounds heal, scars remain. While scar tissue may have lost its function, it also can be stronger than the healthy functioning tissue it replaced.

Thank you for your interest in this book. May you find it helpful along your journey.

Barry M Panter, MD, PhD, Co-Editor
Rancho Mirage, CA

Table of Contents

Table of Contents

Table of Contents

SHMATA – A LOVE STORY
BY YA'EL CHAIKIND

Ya'el Chaikind, MPH, MA, LPCC is a licensed psychotherapist in private practice and certified practitioner of Brainspotting, a brain-body trauma healing system. She holds a Master of Arts in Clinical Counseling from Highlands University and a Master of Public Health from Rutgers University. To date, Ya'el has published eight nonfiction books and numerous poems, essays, articles, and short fiction in various anthologies and literary journals. As a psychotherapist, Ya'el supports clients in re-writing the stories that no longer serve them to create a life of more connection, meaning, and belonging. As a book consultant, she shares her craft with aspiring authors to help them achieve their writing and publishing dreams. She lives in beautiful Santa Fe, NM. Visit her website at www.yaelchaikind.com.

SHMAH·ta | \ shə-mä-tə \
n. Yiddish, meaning: A rag, head covering, or garment. Remnants of cloth. A person or animal treated like they are worthless. That old, torn, and/or stained piece of clothing that you cannot bear to throw away because it means so much to you.

Are you born bipolar, shaped by life circumstances, or both? Was my Mom born with her rages, depressions, productive bursts, and suicide threats? Was it the bad luck of birth in an era when women were packaged as wives instead of freethinking artists? Maybe it was the mandate of her Jewish immigrant parents and family roots in pogroms and the Holocaust. With both eyes on survival through gendered roles – don't make waves, don't stand out – in various non-malicious and well-intentioned ways, my grandparents tamped out the incredible creative light pouring from my mother.

When the compulsion to create is silenced and negated, might that be enough to drive anyone crazy? Mom embodied the eponymous *shmata* she wore, a muumuu waving loose around her 250-pound form, stained with oil paints, furniture varnish, and maybe last night's ice cream. Mostly she felt like a *shmata*, useless and worthless, and took to her bed for days as her artist's glow revealed shadows that seemed like real life monsters.

Other times she was vibrant with ideas and painted a new landscape, built the picture frame, reupholstered the couch, dug holes for the fence, or sewed my store-quality prom dress from her own pattern. Usually while raging, slamming, screaming, and breaking things. Or she concocted another get rich quick scheme with willful independence that ignored sage business advice, ultimately failing, again, and returning to her bed.

Between these polarities, when I was a young girl and teenager, Mom threatened to kill me while chasing me down the hallway. Ripped up a phone book, saying, "I wish this was your head." Screamed at me full volume in stores. Smashed the phone against the wall after a fight with her friend. Slammed kitchen cabinet doors. Threw dishes against the wall. She was also hilariously funny with a boisterous laugh, super intelligent and adventurous, a brilliant wordsmith, an avid reader, an unbeatable scrabble player, and made the best chocolate chip cookies…with enough to feed an army.

When Mom was ten, she discovered her mother's head and torso deep into the opening of the gas oven in their tiny walkup apartment in Brooklyn. One cannot dispute that genetics, family culture, and family history all played a role in shaping Mom's bipolar dis-ease.

In turn, her dis-ease shaped my own life. I was the *shmata*, the rag used to clean up my mom's messes, literally and figuratively. She was an eccentric hoarder who did not hesitate to leave food and dirty dishes out for many days and let the garbage overflow. She left sawdust and power tools on the kitchen table. Containers, clothes, wrappers, and more littered the floor until you had to wade through the mess. She filled every inch of counter space with coins, opened glue, bags spilling Hershey's Kisses and cough drops, hammers, novels, broken pots, and tons of other stuff, instead of putting things in their place or throwing them away. I became a neat freak at an early age.

I also gathered the *shmatas* of my mom's collapsed dreams and built them into the mosaic of my own life. It was, perhaps, a futile effort to alleviate her lifetime of regret, guilt, and shame. I was the *shmata* who dusted her words "I'd rather be dead" from countertops and bedroom dressers, fixing her problems so that she would get out of bed once more. As a result, I lived my life to tell her story and claim life for both of us, since she would never claim hers for herself.

Although we spent months or even years with little communication beyond conversations about the weather and obligatory dinners together, Mom and I were a mainstay in each other's lives, particularly in her later years. This is our story, remnants of memories that tell the tale, weaving rags of exile and redemption together into a ratty *shmata* that, with all reason, should have been thrown into the garbage without a second glance. Despite holes in the fabric and permanent stains, I could never bear to toss Mom aside. She meant too much to me. From the way she looked at me, especially in the last decade of her life, I know she felt the same.

This was our love story.

When you are born an artist, the mandate to create is the pulse of life flowing through your veins. No matter how often you get knocked down, you have no choice. My mother was an artist through and through and her creativity permeated my entire life.

A few years after my parents' divorce, I was about nine when she bought a tiny summer shack across the street from a large lake. The house had no walls, ceilings, running water, electricity – nothing but bare bones. I spent my childhood in Rickel's, a New Jersey version of Home Depot. Without any prior training, my mother bought the Reader's Digest book on how to build everything, some power tools, and voila, I became an expert in sheetrock and spackle, the one thing I could do as a kid to help out.

Except for the heat, water, and electricity, she built everything, including all the furniture. I mean beautifully crafted beds with drawers, dressers, a drafting table, a stained glass wall unit, you name it. She was so naturally skilled, it all looked like it was purchased. She painted landscapes (in acrylic, pastels, and watercolors), designed and sewed clothing for us, and came home with chairs with "good bones" left on wealthy curbsides and turned them into masterpieces.

Over the course of her entire life, my mother vacillated between wanting to create and wanting to kill herself. Carl Jung said, "The greatest burden a child must bear is the unlived life of its parents." Starting when I was a child, I grabbed hold of my mother's sadness, loneliness, and regret and did not let go until she finally released life. I held her unfulfilled dreams smashed down as a young woman, from which she never recovered. I tried to fix these broken parts, to help her feel happy and worthy, ultimately to make me feel safer.

This was my lifelong practice, separately and together with my mother. It was a journey of putting down those burdens that were not mine to carry while learning to love her for exactly who she was. And, of course, learning to do that for myself and for others. It remains a lifelong practice, as a gift from my mother.

PERMISSION TO SOAR
I dance for my
mother so her spirit
can feel the freedom

of movement she craves
and can no longer
access in her 87

year old form, and
and as I leap and spin
my body rejoices,

thrilled to stretch
through space,
connected to time

without borders, and
in those few hours
I declare permission

to stop living life afraid
of getting caught,
learning from Mom's

earthly missteps in
her own life dance,
and in response my

mother's spirit takes
my hand and
together we soar

across the floor,
dancing in random
tandem, playfully

following the other's
lead while humming
our own tunes.
- by YC, age 53, for Mom, age 87 -

My sister moved out of the house when I was ten, and the hurricane of my mother's rage turned east toward me and blew the roof off my house. Soon I understood the cycle. Eventually the winds would die down and stagnate as my mother took to her bed and ranted endlessly about killing herself. I would sit on the side of her bed and stroke her hand, developing mastery at empathy, listening, and reflection skills. My career as a therapist was born.

It was solution-focused therapy at its best. However, instead of achieving my mother's goals, I had goals of my own reckoning: I wanted my mother to live so she would get up and make me dinner. I was ten after all! Intuitively I tried to outmaneuver Mom's negative thoughts, applying a type of cognitive behavioral therapy before I even knew what that was. Somehow I knew that if Mom changed her thoughts, she could change her life and stop wanting to die. I spent decades trying to convince my mother that her life was worth living, as did others in her life.

HURRICANE SANDY
She was the hurricane of my childhood,
a class 5 superstorm Sandy,
trying to rip off the door to my shelter,
Kali unleashed, rocking my foundation
with her screaming winds
until her swath of destruction veered off
and dissipated into a gale of tears.

Decades later, I weep at the shore
of the Florida Sea, grateful to Hurricane Sandy
for my resiliency in riding the rough waves
of chaos and for teaching me to harness
my tempestuous creative winds that allow
me to travel to distant shores,
a force of nature in my own right.
- by YC, age 47 -

I grew up with loud, startling, apocalyptic noises, notably my mother's very loud voice. Even her whisper was loud. With adult eyes I understood how her thwarted creativity led to feeling unseen, unheard, and unacknowledged in soul-crushing ways. Thus, her volume was always on high, like a misguided attempt to communicate with a deaf person. Perhaps, after decades of self-silenced dreams, she became deaf, and could no longer hear herself, no matter how loud she spoke.

During my formative years, Mom's pent up frustrations exited her body in fast and furious ways. I learned to predict potentially dangerous outcomes three, five, even eight moves ahead to prepare myself to take appropriate action and save my hide. Immediately, the tenor of her voice alerted me to danger and my entire body went on alert. From a young age, I was a soldier guarding the perimeter of my tiny life, as both my savior and my enemy lived within the same person in my home.

THE SLAP

I am eleven when my mother slaps my face on Mother's Day after screaming at me for hours about what an ungrateful and selfish daughter I am because I have not given her a card and a gift. I awaken that morning with the excitement of actually buying my mother a real card and box of her favorite chocolate-covered cherries, like a grown up, instead of making her something childish from clay or cardboard. She cannot know the promise my sister makes, to come and take me to the store many miles from our rural home. She cannot know that my sister does not keep her promise, though stubbornly I wait and hold out, hoping she will appear.

In the beginning hours of my mother's tirade, she slams the cabinet doors while making breakfast, muttering under her breath. Periodically she takes to her bed which creaks under the weight of her large *shmata*-covered body, the thin cotton barely covering her gigantic embodied rage. I hear her cries and then her screams into her pillow. Periodically she storms into the living room, surprisingly adept at moving fast despite her weight, to shake her paw and scream accusations while I am watching a sci-fi Creature Feature movie on TV. I sit mute as always, cowed and curled into myself like a shell, the better to withstand her onslaught.

I jump as she slams the phone in its cradle after a call. My heart races as she slams a pot on the stove. The steam in her internal pressure cooker escalates as the day progresses, with scalding sprays of hot water intermittently spurting out from under the lid that eventually burn my face. I know this baby is gonna blow, but I endure, because at this age I am eternally optimistic in the face of this mother of adversity. I am betting the outcome will erase what is becoming a huge debacle and misunderstanding, but I cannot tell her because it will ruin my surprise. I am counting on the big ending, the one where I am loved and cherished because I am Such A Good Daughter.

I hold onto my elusive prize of giving her my gifts and try to ignore the clattering inside my chest as pieces of my heart break off with each scream, threat, and torment hurled in my direction. My mother's slap across my face finally breaks me, and I explode, crying and screaming right back at her. That I asked my sister to take me to buy Mother's Day gifts. That my sister she said she would come and never showed. That I wanted to buy her my own gift. That I was sorry I didn't have anything to give her.

My mother stares at me, finally silenced. She grabs me into a swaddled hug, pressing my face between enormous boobs that stifle my crying, along with my breath. My mother strokes my hair and tells me everything is all okay.

- by YC, age 47

I was thirteen when I realized that I did not love my mother and I vowed to learn to love her before she died. Thoughts of my mother's impending death were a constant reminder, spurring me to "get it right" with her. Like a boxer in the ring, I kept getting up after being knocked down. All told, I spent forty years fulfilling this declaration. It was a neo-Biblical journey, crisscrossing the deserts of both our hearts to finally arrive at the same place we began, wholly transformed.

THE WAY THINGS ARE

The foundation of life is death, I surmise
while walking my aged dog, worrying constantly
about her last breath, and god tells me it's
The Way Things Are.

Doesn't he remember that I've been practicing
my mother's death since I was 13,
doesn't he recall how I knew then
that she couldn't die before I learned
how to love her?

You cannot fix This, my daughter, god says,
but I protest and say: I learned how to love
by trying to fix all the broken places
in myself,
in my mother,
in my world,
so that no one
would leave me, by surprise, ever again.

Just then god nudges us and my dog's wet nose
pushes against my hand, urging me
forward into the morning's promise,
pink and radiant.
- by YC, age 51 -

By the time I was fifteen our home had degraded into a battle zone. Both Mom and I were on losing sides of the war. Hindsight could only reveal the buildup of anger and resentment I bore after years of enduring my mother's dragon breath upon me. She passed along the genetic and cultural legacies of dysregulated attachment and neglect, with both of us burying our yearning for connection and love behind bickering and slammed doors. This conflict worsened over my teenage years. I was old enough to admit that it felt impossible to love and honor my mother. I remembered feeling like a failure because Operation Love My Mother was backfiring badly. I was so empathic by this point, I could feel all her emotions on top of mine and it was just overwhelming.

Still, I felt caught. On one side was a bottomless pit of grief and self-reprobation, thinking that my mother's behavior was a direct result of my actions. I believed that I deserved her rageful accusations. I believed that she would abandon me if I did not shape up. I felt unlovable, but was that my feeling or hers?

On the other hand, I despised and did not respect my mother. I ended up taking care of her when she was supposed to be the mother. Instead, she was my abuser whom I was supposed to love and who occasionally stepped up and acted like a mom. This dichotomy was very confusing for me. I yearned for love and had no way of bridging to my mother, to get across to her.

CHOCOLATE MILK

Clumps of powdered chocolate cling to the baby blue wall of my bedroom like a child clings to her mother's leg. I am too shocked to realize that the brown milk dripping off my hair and nose recently has been in the glass in my mother's hand, too dazed to be grateful that the glass missed my head by an few inches, and too enraged to be happy it didn't shatter but bounced off the wall behind me. Her eyes glare at me, oval red demons spitting fire.

The room is tiny, about five feet wide by eight feet long in our renovated shack where we live on Lake Hopatcong. I am on my bed and her heaving 250 pounds block my escape route. She is wearing a flowered *shmata* dotted with schmears of tan furniture staining. I glance at the closed window, assess the pain level of hurling myself through the glass the short distance to the pavement below, and choose to press up against the chocolate-coated wall. Within seconds, I am firmly supported, my legs jacked up protectively, when she grits her crooked teeth and lunges for me.

Instinctively my strong fifteen-year-old legs clock her, one leg on each shoulder of her stained *shmata*. Bull's eye, a direct hit! The intruder goes crashing back against the opposite wall, and I am not sure the crackling sound is the beams taking her weight or the response of her bones. With a dull thud she groans and my immediate thought is, "I've killed her, oh shit, I've just killed my mother!" I scramble over to her, and with a roar, she rises from the floor, spittle flying from her lips, tears spilling from her eyes.

"I won't forget this," she says, jabbing her finger in my face before she leaves.

- by YC, age 45 -

I was not an angel. I inherited the genes, marinated in the family culture of regret, rage, and resentment…and I was a fifteen-year-old after all. I was trying to lend my mother as much benefit of the doubt, yet someone once reflected, "Maybe she didn't do the best she could. Maybe she could have done better."

ROAD TRIP

As we get into the car, the driver's side of the '75 Plymouth sinks with the weight of my mother. I slide into the passenger side and slam the door shut. With an exhaled sigh of exertion, my mother leans her girth to the left and stretches for the door handle. Reaching it, she propels her body to the right, overflowing onto the gear panel that sits between the driver and passenger seats. The door slams shut from the sheer physics of the event and the door hinge creaks in protest. She decides to wear her purple polyester pants under her *shmata,* never intending to get out of the car or be seen in public.

I ask her what time we are supposed to be at my dental appointment, but she doesn't answer.

When new, the outside of the compact car was a shiny maroon, but a few years of lead foot Momma on the back roads of Lake Hopatcong had aged the car to a dull scratchy color of clay dirt. The salted roads in the winter also contributed toward maturing the car before its time.

Inside the car, I sit on the seat with my butt perched on the edge of the balding tan upholstery that is worn away more from neglect than time. My back is rigid and my hands gingerly alight upon the dashboard, careful not to touch any surface with more than a fingertip. The back of my seat is filled with a medley of ancient doughnut and bagel crumbs, black and white cat hairballs, a chewed-on straw, an empty can of Diet Pepsi, and a pile ofsunglasses, coins, and pens.

Tucking the back of my blouse into my jeans, I eye tmy mother peripherally to make sure she isn't looking.

I squeeze my knees together for balance to avoid touching the thick drops of hardened Pepsi that dangle from the silver window crank on the side of the passenger door. The front dash panel is precariously close to my knees, and, should the car stop suddenly, I know my knees will get bashed. With the side of my Keds sneakers, using my ankle as a pivot I wave my foot to surreptitiously push the orange Burger King wrappers away from my feet. The paper crunches and my mother glances my way.

"How the hell are you going to wear your seatbelt sitting like that? What am I, a leper?"

I tell her in a jumble of words that the seatbelt is twisted and digs into my neck since I am too short and that I'm not going to wear it.

"Whatever." The day is young and she is already pissed off. My mother pulls on the gear stick to her right, and without looking back to see if anyone is behind her, steps hard on the gas pedal. Our bodies jerk forward from the sudden surge of gas, and I gasp as my knees smash the dash, damning myself for not thinking about this possibility. In response I push myself back, inadvertently sitting against the motley assortment of food and garbage. I quickly move forward again, looking at my mother peripherally to see if she has noticed my movements. The narrow gravel driveway spit rocks at our house in front of us. Our cat napping on the front steps leaps away suddenly from the commotion.

As I turn my rock station, loudly I ask my mother if she minds if I turn on the radio. She doesn't answer and we speed away toward my dentist's office. As we head up 46 East, I remember that I forgot the damn directions. She is gonna kill me, I think, clenching my hands. My left knee starts to bob anxiously and bangs into the dashboard. Biting my lip, I groan and pull my knee up toward my chest, leaning back against the seat. The position pushes my neck into an uncomfortable bend as my chin wedges into the ribs of my upper chest.

"What now," my mother says through clenched teeth.

Staring straight ahead while clutching my bumped knee to my chest, I tell her nothing is wrong.

"Then why the hell are you sitting like that, huh? Where is the turn off? After the jug-handle by the Nathan's?"

I reply quickly, with false assurance, and say yes, though I'm really not sure. I ask her again what time the appointment is.

"It was at ten, and if you had gotten your ass out of bed we would be there by now. I've got a life too, you know, not just driving all the hell over the place for your benefit."

We make the turn by the hot dog place and wind up on an unfamiliar street. My mother pulls over abruptly, breaking so fast that my knees crash into the dash again but I stifle the pain. She asks, "Where. Is. The. Fucking. Place. At?"

As I stare at her cursing lips, I see she is due for her own dentist appointment. My mother turns the car around.

She loops around the block four times when at last I tell her about the forgotten directions. I tell her, I think I remember where the office is, though, can we try one more time?

"You what?" she screeches, gritting her teeth and setting my heart into stone. I am preparing for the worst. She leans on the gas pedal and I see it touching the floor of the car.

"That's it, we're going home! What a goddamned waste of my time, you are so selfish, oh, fuck it!"

The storefronts zoom by me, faster and faster. I grip the door handle and feel something sticky under my fingers but I don't let go. My face hurts from clenching my teeth.

"Let me out, I'll walk." I say to my mother. There is no response.

"Let me OUT, I'll walk!" I yell, as the speedometer rises steadily above the recommended limit for this local side street. My mother stares straight ahead, her shoulders hunched. We turn onto the highway, moving faster and faster.

I open my door as the speed escalates, threatening, "I'm getting the fuck out of this car!" In my assessment, I can't wait any longer. I need to get out before the car is moving so fast that jumping would cause serious injury. Or that staying would cause serious injury. I'll show her! I'll hurt MYself before I let her hurt me again!

"Shut the door, you'll get us killed!"

"YOU are one getting us killed, stop the fucking car!"

"You're crazy!" my mother screams.

"I'm crazy, fine, that's right, I'm crazy! You're a fucking asshole!" I curse and insult her as much as I can to shock her into stopping the car. I'll do anything to make her stop.

Her foot lifts off the gas pedal and I leap out of the car, falling once and scrambling out of the lane. The force of my mother pulling away from the side of the road yanks the passenger door shut. She speeds away. Miles from home, I shove my hands in my pockets and start walking down the shoulder of the highway.

- by YC, age 34 -

The rebellion continued, with a new mission: Get out of that house as soon as possible. Nearly sixteen, I got my work permit and spent most of my days at Burger King. I saved money for a beat up car. By seventeen I got a job at the mall selling shoes and made decent money.

One day I arrived late for dinner and my mother stood in the front yard, berating me with high-pitched screams. Neighbor heads turned in our direction, and since I was the teenaged target of this tirade, I assumed they thought I was the devil incarnate. Because by now I believed I was the devil incarnate. A horrible daughter. Though I fought against it mightily, I internalized the accusations, criticisms, and rebukes that sowed seeds over the years and blossomed into ugly flowers within me. Wordlessly, I turned around, got back into my car, and left.

My mother's negative words soaked me like a power hose for so many years, they drowned out her supportive words to me. When she so often admired my accomplishments in school. How she rocked back and forth on the couch in her *shmata*, laughing and clapping her hands in glee when I presented funny skits in the living room. How she would write rhyming, farcical poems about my dinner on the stove or when reminding me to feed the cats; I'd find them stuck to the door with a slash of duct tape.

I learned silence and non-reaction was the best way to hurt my mother. And by this time, I wanted to hurt my mother as much as I wanted to love her.

SILENT SCREAM

When I turn into a teenager, I stare at my mother's mouth when she screams at me. Despite her close proximity to my face, I learn to turn the volume of her voice down with the twist of an imaginary radio dial. Have you ever watched someone's mouth move without hearing them? It is like watching a Japanese monster movie where the lips move at different speeds than the dubbed English. And the monster is wearing a *shmata*.

With fascinated detachment, I read her lips with precision. I know the details of her mouth with a curious intimacy. How her lips curl like a coiled snake, spitting words and spittle at me. The number of teeth left, stained from a former three-pack-a-day cigarette habit. The redness of her skin tone as rage pushes her blood pressure beyond her control. How her nostrils flare in tune with the wild machinations of her mouth in this soundless melody.

I am adept at sitting motionless before her maniacal rantings, as if separated by thick, protective glass. My simple act of defiant non-reaction lights her fire higher and higher. It amuses me, in a black comedy kind of way, to see how easy it is to fan her flames without saying or doing anything.

Not getting the reaction she hopes for, she bites her tongue and stamps around the house. She shakes her fist and threatens me. Is that the couch quaking or my body? I never let her see my fear, and smile instead, a beautiful, beatific, fuck you smile, while I cross my legs and pick absently at my cuticles.

Predictably, a switch is thrown, and I feel the electromagnetic forces of the room generate a circle around us, faster and faster. I can almost feel the energetic tornado that is my mother pull chairs, cats, and empty Diet Pepsi bottles into her destructive whirlwind. I feel the cyclone in my body, feel it tugging my insides, and my leg begins bobbing, readying myself for just the right moment.

Wait for it...now! I run for cover, zooming past her with a speed that seems to make me invisible for a few seconds. The volume of her voice always returns at this point, and I hear her yell, "I'm gonna kill you!" The fever pitch screams of my terrified heart match my mother's shrieks as I reach the inside of my tiny bedroom in the nick of time. I slide on the carpet and slam the door shut just as her heavy breathing and fat paws pound on the door. My mother is strong! She builds furniture, hauls two by fours, and hurls heavy objects at walls!

I wedge my body at the bottom of the door and plant a leg on the edge of the dresser. The top of the door bends inward from its frame from the pounding of her fists. Each assaulting blow blasts my body like a rocket, jolting me forward and back. The door's integrity remains. I am not breached. Tired, the beast stalks off in search of other prey.

- by YC, age 45 -

My mother worked her butt off but never at a paying job. She claimed it was not worth working because she could make more money on welfare. I ate lunch courtesy of the free lunch program at school. We received Salvation Army food baskets. When we ran out of oil for the furnace, Mom wrapped me in blankets and sat me in front of the open door of the electric oven.

As a result of her poverty, my mother received several offers to go back to school for free. A "women over fifty go back to work" sort of thing. I remembered her attending a graphic arts program, short-lived because any expectations to produce on a deadline threw my mother back into bed, bemoaning how terrible her life was. I stopped convincing her otherwise and went about my teenaged days.

When I was eighteen, I tried mightily to drop out of high school by missing fifty-five days of my senior year. It only dropped my ranking from third to fifth in my class, which spoke loudly to either my inherited intelligence or the quality of my school. I was born Jewish but raised without even a secular Jewish identity, so I picked Jewish holidays out of the encyclopedia, saying at random that Hanukkah was in October and Rosh Hashanah in March and therefore I must miss school for religious reasons. Since I was one of maybe three Jewish people in my high school, no one realized that the signed absence notes I produced were forged.

I had no adult guidance to help me steer my course. My mother had no idea I was cutting school or working more hours at the shoe store in the mall. Since childhood I had been trying to figure a way out, a way to leave this family legacy of crazy-making anger while drowning in despair. Yet I craved a sense of belonging. For better or worse, this was my family. I ran more slowly, sometimes glancing over my shoulder to see if anyone noticed or showed any desire to join me in moving forward.

Until the school called one day to check. My mother cornered me that evening and pleadingly yelled, "You're doin' so good, don't screw this up! Go to college, I wish I could've gone to college!" She had no idea how I should accomplish this and neither did I.

However, crisis is an opportunity and, back then, poverty meant I qualified for all sorts of funding. Despite my best efforts to find symmetry with my family, I went to college and moved ahead without them. We were not on speaking terms when my mother drove me to my new school. We had not visited the school and I had no idea what was to come. This freedom was exhilarating and terrifying: I felt my desire to fly competing with the gravity of my failure to connect with my mother. I pulled my few boxes from the car to the sidewalk and shut the door. Without a word between us, she drove off.

MY OWN CLOUD
The freshly bleached clouds
soften my footsteps
as I climb to where I'd love to be.

Forever searching,
yes, I know.
But whatever I do,
will be accomplished
by me.

And whatever I find,
will be found
by me.

And whoever I meet,
will be loved
and shared,
with no one else
but me.
- by YC, age 16, one of my first poems -

I was twenty-five and Mom was making dinner. I walked into her messy office and could not resist the urge to clean, just a tiny bit. I settled for cleaning the floor. I threw away random empty boxes and picked up papers to organize them. I found several overdue bills, a refund check dated months earlier, last year's birthday card from me, and the poem below, among other things. I examined everything about the words in this poem, searching for clues to my mother. I ached to know who this woman was! Her poem revealed self-awareness and magic. Turmoil and conflict. My empathy felt her pain in my body, yet I saw my mother from an adult perspective for the first time.

Like the sighting of a rare animal in the wild, I approached her cautiously. I shook the paper in my hand, saying, "Mom, this is really good!"

She took the paper, scanned it, and handed it back to me. Resuming her slow stir of the pot's contents on the stove, my mother scoffed with pursed lips, "Oh that? That's crap, throw it away." I typed the poem into my computer and sent her a copy. She repeated this pattern with her art, and after I retrieved two amazingly good pastel landscapes from the floor, I asked her to sign them and had them framed. They hang on my living room wall today.

PEBBLES AND BREAD AND ENGINE OIL

A poem, says she, on any thought
to solve the complex rhyme of you.
Glimpses of light
wavering then caught
blackened skies and seas of blue.

My indecision looms great and tall
while ideas jump around my feet.
Popcorn bursting large and small
delectable morsels, salty and sweet.

Envelop me, profound and dumb –
take me traveling, feed me truth
mind to you I now succumb
Merlin's wand will wave and poof!

Wonders of stars and butterfly wings
pebbles and bread and engine oil
speed and sleep, voices that sing
Hey Sam, did the kettle boil?

I take my leave, drifting away
close the closet and push the door
empty and fall, curse and pray
now I stop and write no more.
- by Mom, age 59 -

The scene: In my mid-30s, in an Italian restaurant in Pennsylvania near my mother's home. As usual, I brought a friend as a foil to avoid the burden of conversation with her. While they chitchatted I participated absently, with eyes glued to the television on the wall. Out of the corner of one ear, I heard my mother speak about a recent Dr. Phil show. The guests were a middle-aged woman and her teenage kids.

"Apparently, this woman screamed at her kids their whole lives," my mother said quietly as the waiter brought us tiramisu.

"Uh-ha," I said, still watching the television above her head.

"Suddenly I realize, that was me, and that was you, and your sistah," I heard her say.

My friend kicked me under the table, and I suddenly awakened to the conversation. "Go hug her!" he said under his breath for all to hear. He badly mimed his head in her direction.

I stood up shakily and asked, "What are you saying, Mom?" By now I was standing by her chair with my hand awkwardly on her shoulder. I had not touched my mother for many years.

My mother looked up at me with tears in her eyes and said, "I'm sorry is what I am saying. I'm really sorry."

My confused heart was unsure but I hugged her anyway. "Thanks?" I replied, testing the word in my mouth. Still loosely hugging her, I had the insight to understand the opportunity. I cleared my throat and repeated, "Thanks, Mom, that means a lot to me."

LET LOVE
Reclaim loving kindness
with radical acts and majestic pacts.

Believe in fairytales like a magical child
and never forget the power of a wish.

Lift your head and watch the horizon
approach you with open arms.

Let yourself be loved,
Let yourself be love,
let love be.
- by YC, age 49 -

When I was forty and on the brink of divorce, I spontaneously called her because I needed a mother. Not the earth that was a spiritual pseudonym for mother. Not my inner mother that nurtured my motherless inner child. I needed an actual mother. MY mother.

After our usual chatter I asked, "Mom, I gotta ask you a question that might piss you off. Do you...do you...um, love me?"

She was seventy-five and yelled at me in her ever-present Brooklyn accent, "What the hell kinda question is that? You're my dawtah! Of course I love you!" I did not pull the phone away from my ear to diminish the sound of her voice.

And she heard me cry for the first time in my adult life. Then she started crying. Suddenly I decided to drop all the old stories. I began to draw nearer to my mother to see if she could draw closer to me.

Still on a mission to learn to love my mother, I spent the next thirteen years rededicated to the task. I traveled to Florida two to three times each year to develop and sustain this new relationship with my mother. I called her at least once each week, asked real questions, and we started an authentic life together. During this time, Mom still played the roles of both protagonist and antagonist in my story and I was hellbent on writing a better ending. This bold decision on my part opened space for new stories to be written and told.

To be truthful, the old stories did not just vanish. They haunted and tormented me despite herculean efforts to dispel them. There were many instances when I called my best friend from my mother's disheveled and moldy doublewide, pacing and wailing in frustration and condemnation, as my past became my present again. It was a long, challenging road with many potholes...and with plenty of peak connections that rewrote our collective traumatized histories into a love story.

REVELATION

Tonight the clouds will rise
from the mountain and fire
will burst from our hearts,
burning off any excess ego

or arrogance that blocks
our arteries, clearing the path
to open hands, receiving the
the teachings to love, first

ourselves, and when you can't
love yourself, love another,
and when you cannot
love another, stand still

and plug your ears, and listen
to the roar of your pulse
flood your head with sound,
and speak your name out loud

3 times, maybe more, not less,
and bathe the majestic animal
of your body in the calling
of your own voice, calling you

to your self, leading you
home, again and again, and
in that flash of fire and brilliant
light, receive the imprint of

your most noble self, stand
tall, unclench your fists, and
with full conviction simply
say, Yes.
- by YC, age 49 -

An important part of learning to love my mother before she died was making sure I could remember her fondly after she died. I had hardly any positive memories of her as an adult and we never did anything together but go out to eat. I was forty-two and she was seventy-six when I said while visiting her, "Mom, let's start having some fun together!" We began to travel throughout Florida and occasionally out of state.

It became a pattern for us to have one big fight during each trip. When she yelled or blamed with a loud, terrible voice, my inner fourteen-year-old's anger triggered and I lashed out by yelling back, usually bringing up her old travesties from my childhood and pushing them hard against her face. Then my old mother cried and I felt like crap. After storming off for a few minutes, I would pull up my big girl panties and apologize. I tried to explain what happened for me and we made up. Invariably we got ice cream, the universal balm for my family.

SANIBEL SUNSET

Once we are in Sanibel Island and, after a blow up, get on a sunset cruise. Mom loves the water as much as I do.

We are both still raw. I sit in front of her and she starts stroking my hair, singing the lullaby she sang to me as a child. In a low, quiet voice she says, "I know how to soothe the savage beast in you! When I pet you, you calm down." I turn around and smile with genuine love.

Then her eyes cloud and she asks quietly, "I've apologized for your childhood, when are you evah gonna fagive me?"

I face her and reply, "I have forgiven you, Mom, I just can't forget is all. And that bites me in the butt sometimes."

"Turn around," she commands, and I lean against
her chest as she strokes my hair. Her 81 years calm
the hackles of my inner fourteen-year-old as the boat
gently moves us into the sunset.

- by YC, age 47 -

Mom struggled her whole life to feel any sense of belonging and I
inherited this trait from her. I felt exiled from my family, in my struggle to
separate from their legacy, yet was damned to follow some of my mother's
footsteps despite my best intentions. Though I spent my lifetime
overcoming this, we shared a bond feeling separate and alone, detached
from family, each other, and ourselves.

Continuing this theme of exile, I grew up with stories from my mother
that Jews did not want us because we were poor and everyone else wanted
to kill us because we were Jewish. To assuage Mom's need for belonging
and avoid her fear of death because of our heritage, growing up we
celebrated Christmas with presents and Easter with ham and chocolate. I
always felt like a fake but I did not know what was real either.

In our rural town, antisemitism prevailed. The kids tossed pennies on
the school floor and called you a Dirty Jew if you picked one up. The lady
on the checkout line mentioned the big noses of the rich Jews while looking
at Barbra Streisand on the cover of People magazine. Despite my mother's
best efforts at hiding our identity, a cross was burned on our lawn one
evening. I did not want to believe people could be so ignorant or cruel, even
with this evidence in front of me. I did not want to believe my mother could
be right.

I had no Jewish friends, did not participate in Jewish holidays, and
never attended synagogue or Jewish religious services. I did have Yiddish,
blintzes, and Jewish immigrant grandparents who never spoke of their
pogrom and Holocaust pasts. I longed to be part of the Tribe and felt
rejected by everyone. Check! I internalized Mom's *mishigash*.

When I was forty-two, I chose the path of my Jewish ancestors. I
became a Bat Mitzvah and a Jewish educator and lay leader. Judaism
became a central facet of my life, in an earthy, ceremonial, and deeply
spiritual way. When Mom flew to Santa Fe to visit me, I led a Shabbat
service at my house for about ten people. We gathered around the challah

and I asked everyone to link arms, intertwining in community like the bread. I invited everyone to go around and offer gratitude for this sustenance of the earth. With tears in her eyes, my mother looked at me and said, "I think the reason I was born was'ta have you, because the world needs you. I can't believe you're my dawtah." Mom was seventy-six.

Some days later, a woman who attended that Shabbat contacted me to say, "Do you know how much I'd pay to hear my mother tell me that?"

ON THE EVE OF MY BAT MITZVAH

dear daughter, as you know i am not much on this e-mail stuff but i am doing it now. i just saw your invitation and i just realized what an important step you are taking in your life and i can't tell you how proud i am of you and how moved i am. i hope that i don't screw up what ever you have in mind for me but i will do my best. somehow i am always a little surprised that you are a part of me with all of your accomplishments. anyways enough. i look forward to hearing you do your thing...love mom

- from Mom, age 76 -

Mom's health was never good. Her three-pack-a-day cigarette habit culminated in double pneumonia when I was ten and she was forty-four. "Quit right now or die, those are your choices," said the doctor next to her oxygen tent. She quit but had chronic and debilitating hacking coughs, bronchitis, and pneumonia for the rest of her life.

By the time she was seventy-eight...oy, her weight, her heart, her edema, her diabetes, her cancers, her cholesterol, her breathing, her cough, her shakes, her bronchitis, her pneumonia, her lungs! "The doctahs, all these damn doctahs, all I do is see doctahs!" she complained. Her ongoing depression, threats of suicide, and bouts in bed remained constant. Yet under her stated desire to die was obviously the fierce desire to live, evidenced by her living for decades longer than predicted with this plethora of serious medical maladies. Diabetes be damned, maybe the constant flow of Hershey's chocolate kept her going, who knows? Maybe the endless gallons of Diet Pepsi coated her insides with enough corn syrup to protect her vital organs? Who knows.

Eagerly she looked forward to my visits and pulled out all the stops when I arrived. She was mostly upbeat and would rouse herself from bed, exchange her *shmata* for real clothes, and be ready for adventure with me. As negative as Mom could be, she equally was spontaneous and fun loving. As we began to make our new memories, and as long as I arranged for a wheelchair, we traveled many places together fairly easily.

MUIR WOODS

When Mom is eighty, we meet in San Francisco. In advance of visiting Muir Woods, I reserve a wheelchair for her. The wheelchair is old and rickety, and as I push her she bounces up and down, holding down her large breasts and giggling as we go over roots and get stuck on lumpy parts of the asphalted trail. Heading back to the car, the trail has a slight decline not noticeable going the other way. As her weight causes the wheelchair to pick up speed, suddenly the plastic handles pull off in my hands and I watch in black comedy horror as Mom's chair escalates down the bumpy trail without me. I race after her silently. She has no idea this is happening and thinks I am pushing her faster as I occasionally do to tease her. I finally catch up and grab her chair before she topples, stick the handles back on the chair, and continue down the trail.

"Why are you breathing so heavy?" she asks.

"Just having some fun, Mom, just having fun with you."

- by YC, age 48 -

UNIVERSAL STUDIOS

Mom is eighty-one and wants to go on the rides at Universal Studios. I rent her an electric wheelchair but we do not know I will need to push her about one mile in a regular wheelchair to get to the electric one. The gentle rise of the walkway becomes palpable when pushing my mother in a wheelchair. She weighs at least one hundred pounds more than me and sometimes I struggle to get her chair moving.

Concerned, my mother reaches up and grabs my hand. She asks, "Honey, how the hell can you push me up this hill?"

I reply with a grunt, "Weight training, Mom. This is my reward for doing squats for twenty-five years."

As we crest the top of the pavement and move downhill, I ride the back of her chair as we pick up speed. She shrieks, half in delight and half in fear, "Stop it! Get offa dere!"

- by YC, age 47 -

MISSOURI

She flew from Florida and sat there in baggage claim
sitting in a standard airport wheelchair, holding her
cane, her 85 years patiently waiting for her dawtah

to whisk her away to nearby Branson, Missouri, misery
as the locals pronounce, to spend a long weekend seeing
shows and eating, a shared love for both of us

in this Christian version of Las Vegas and in preparation for
Operation Take A Trip With Your Mother Before She Dies,
I decide to manage the risk factors from spending

an unusually concentrated time together by saying YES
to everything, who knew that giving up the fight
without words would soften both our hearts

and from the airport our first meal is, natch, sushi,
and I remember to say YES to everything
so I unfold the origami of my heart in front of her

and speak freely for reals about my life and
maybe she had decided to say YES too or
maybe her heart had unfolded too,

and in my 50 years I had never experienced
her, listening, rapt, and empathic,
round hazel eyes bright with attention,

and I felt the wounded animal inside of me
melt under the tender attention of the source
of my life, and suddenly I knew

what it meant
to feel at home
for the first time.
- by YC, age 54

I was about forty-eight when we decided to go south for a spontaneous adventure to Ft. Lauderdale, about three hours from her house. I was driving, after an extended argument ending in my refusal to go if she did not let me drive. She was practically blind in either rain or the dark, and her ability to drive the wrong way on highways was renowned. She could kill herself, but not me in the process. Hadn't that been my motto since I was a child?

Both of us relaxed, while driving I held her hand like I always did, wanting its tactile memory embedded in my nervous system. The skin of her hand was soft and soothing to stroke. Typically I held her hand in the movies, the theater, the restaurant, and the car, whenever I could.

"Love you, Mom!" I smiled.

She pulled her hand away and scoffed, "Why do ya always havta tell me you love me? You're grown up! I should tell you all the time I love you? Feh!"

I laughed, "Oh right, I forgot, after a certain age, we don't like hearing people tell us they love us. Thanks for reminding me."

Mom pursed her lips together in a silly way and mock pinched my arm. "Very funny, funnybones.

"Speaking of funnybones, what do you call a line of rabbits walking backwards?" I waited a second and said, "A receding hareline!" I guffawed and she sighed loudly but smiled as she played her favorite CD, Scheherazade.

Hours later, it was raining when we stopped at a light very near our hotel. Mom turned off the music, touched my arm, and said quickly, with big saucer eyes, "I love you more than my breath."

Uncharacteristically, I was mute. Tears welled up in our eyes as we looked at each other in silence. "Thanks, Mom, that's one of the best things any daughter can hear. It means the world to me."

THE OTHER EMAIL I RECEIVED FROM MY MOM

love your web site. if i was 10 years younger i would try it. it must be an experience that you would not forget, either good or bad. anyways luck in any endeavor that you do. where there is love any thing can be overcome. just look at us. i'm hugging you, m

- from Mom, age 82 -

Mom was about eighty-four and we were in a Florida restaurant waiting for a "Music of the 50s" dinner show to begin. It was four in the afternoon, prime dinner hour for octogenarians. I slid my chair close to hers, rested my head on her shoulder, and held her hand. She squeezed my fingers. Although I was fifty years old, there was something deeply satisfying to sit with my mother this way. I never felt too old for it. She sipped her ever-present Diet Pepsi, no ice, no lemon.

"You know, my fathah took me on the subway to this office. Without telling me anything, they put this picture of a dress in front of me and tell me to draw it. The guy turned out to be a designer, pop knew I wanted to be a fashion designer. But I was so nervous and he didn't tell me so I could practice ahead …and I blew it. No second chance. We never mentioned it again. That was that."

FENCED IN

she tells me a story about Pepe the neighbor's dog,
when she is six and walks barefoot to a one room

school in lynchburg virginia and he follows her home
each day when no one wants to play with the Jewish girl

and she loves that dog until the neighbor gets jealous
and puts Pepe behind a fence and then she says how she

took apart her father's typewriter and then put it back
together fast after he got mad, she was always good

with machines though her brother is the prince to immigrant
parents of that generation and he goes to engineering school,

and with eyes bright with eighty seven years of tears she says
I wish I could have gone to college and I say

you were cheated, Mom, and she sighs
and says yep, and I hold her hand
- by YC, age 53 -

My mother was eighty-five and the familial tremor that began a decade earlier now escalated to the point that she could not hold a fork or a glass without spilling the food they contained. Noncompliant, she refused to regularly take the medicine that could help her improve, but purchased it each month and stockpiled an army of prescription bottles that eventually expired. She grumbled that nothing she did could help "her shakes."

This was her basic pattern. Noncompliance, refusal of medication, rejection of help from others that could ease her suffering, and then complaining that nothing worked. This way, she stayed locked in her defiant stance, "No one helps me, I'll just do it myself, I do it myself anyway."

Mom had a knack for creating lose-lose situations that re-victimized her over and over again. Her weight and her loud voice made her larger than life, impossible to ignore, but she never felt validated and fought anyone who tried. My mother could not let anyone love her, maybe except for her cats. She spun her own web, fought the entrapment, and blamed everyone else for her misery. Of course it was self-hatred and fear that were the real culprits ruling my mother's life.

Since my teenage years, most of my mother's life had served as an example of how not to live. By fifty-one I was even better at holding my boundaries with my Mom, with kindness, love, and plenty of deep breathing instead of fear and anger. I knew I was safe, with or without her.

ALCHEMY OF LOVE
I try to calm my fluttering heart when
my mother's knife hits the plate hard

in a rapraprap as her tremors decide
how much food will miss her mouth

today and this time she screams in
frustration as the fork clatters out of

her hand and I stop to catch my breath
and wait until she catches her breath

and then ask may I cut your food for
you in a nonchalant undertone and

most times she growls no and I remind
her that it's ok to eat with her hands

and I will too who cares if we are in a
restaurant and she mutters

goddamned shakes
nothing works nothing works

and a few years ago she asks what
am I going to do if I can't feed myself

anymore and I know she doesn't want
to hear my reply so I say nothing

because she rarely makes choices to
make her life easier and now we all

are living with the consequences of
her actions and I practice the alchemy

of love, transforming my resentment
into compassion, one minute at a time.

- by YC, age 53 -

I told you this was a love story. Mom was seventy-five and I was forty-one at the start of our life together, our real life together, and though we never directly discussed this shift, we both experienced miraculous changes. We both grew up, proof that age is never a barrier to change. Mom and I won the game, against all odds.

Each trip had at least one mountaintop victory of connection with my mother. I accomplished my mission: I learned to love my mother. Despite the fights, the triggers, and those moments when our history beat my love down so that I was unable to open my heart to her, we always found some path that left both of us feeling satisfied. Honest feelings were honored between us. We recovered ever more quickly from our fights. She let me help make her life easier - sometimes.

We both said, "I'm sorry" more often, and meant it. We played cards with her friends, attended Red Hat luncheons, watched her favorite zombie shows, snuck into a second movie at the theater, went to comedy shows, ate at endless restaurants, and went to endless doctor appointments. She asked me to read her some of my poems and then gave her candid appraisals, opening coveted doorways into my mother's wisdom and her brand of truth. Everyone we met told me how my Mom talked about me all the time, how proud she was of me. I could finally reply to those who asked, "Yes, my Mom and I have a good and close relationship. And…it's complicated, like all mothers and daughters!"

FALLOW
Let the fields of my heart
lay fallow amidst the ruins

of this awful beauty

harvested over decades past
and rest in the composted tears

that watered the seedlings
when rains never appeared.

I remember the smell of dirt
when I buried my burdens

and turned over the soil of
each season as a labor of love
to begin again,
and begin again,

and as I inhale the fertile
remains of my life, the clouds

pin me to the ground and ask:
Are you done punishing yourself
at last?

Uprooted, my striving bones
finally melt into winter's dormant

inspiration as I await springtime's
revelatory uprising.
- by YC, age 53, for Mom on her 87th and last birthday -

Writing this essay has been a rite of passage for me, and an ultimate act of individuation. I have written, told, and performed stories about my mother for decades, creatively and therapeutically processing the trauma and conflict of my formative years. I have wrestled with understanding where I begin and end as my Mom's voice and our history lives inside of me. Mom has been the beginning, middle, and end of nearly every thread of the *shmata* tapestry of my life. There are so many more fun, agonizing, and poignant touchstones that I hold dear from these past thirteen years with my Mom that I could share. Yet this telling feels complete. And with this telling, I am freed from living her story.

I have inherited and expressed so much of the same emotional *mishigash* of my mother, naturally, and by now I feel the decades of my hard work have paid off. I let go of my *shmata* security blanket and integrate the gifts of the wounded healer in service to others and myself. I let go of the past and take Mom's love with me, because her love IS me. From *shmata* rags to riches, my mom and I no longer are exiled because we belong to each other. I am her legacy. *Hineni*! Here I am, carrying all this transformed goodness of her in me, to shine light into the world.

ONE MORE, PLEASE

One more hug, please. Let
me feel your arms pull my
body back in time. Oy! I can
feel your bones, you'd say,
Here, have some nice soup.

One more laugh, please. Let
me hear your shrieking delight
and clapping hands at my joke,
you'd say, *You have a dirty
mind…like me!*

One more card game, please.
Let me watch your face light
up as you triumphantly collect
your chips, you'd say, *You win
some, you lose some, ladies.*

One more movie, please. Let me
stroke your soft hand during the
show, you'd say, *You're always
touching me*, then squeeze my
fingers and not let go.

One more dumb fight, please.
Let my inner teen rage with yours
until we heal each other, you'd
say, *Let's get ice cream*, and we'd
watch the sun set in the Florida sky.

In Loving Memory of my Mom,
January 4, 1932 - December 20, 2019

Ode to my Dad:
What I Am Left With
By Patrick Connors

Pat Connors first chapbook, *Scarborough Songs*, was released by Lyrical Myrical Press in 2013, and charted on the Toronto Poetry Map. Other publication credits include: *Spadina Literary Review*; *Tamaracks*; and *Tending the Fire*, released last spring by the League of Canadian Poets. His first full collection, *The Other Life*, is newly released by Mosaic Press.

www.facebook.com/patrick.j.connors.3
twitter.com/81912CON

❦   ❦   ❦

Walter Gretzky died two days before my Dad.
They were both born in 1938. Other than that,
they had almost nothing in common.

My Dad and me also had very little in common
except our first names
and our last

the propensity to drink
as a means of dealing with anxiety
and a deep and abiding love in Jesus Christ.

My childhood was a hopeless struggle, founded
on pleasing my Dad, protecting my Mom
and becoming the next Wayne Gretzky.

My Dad was deeply damaged.
He was torn between trying to save us
from this damage and sharing how it felt.

Finally, we became
a family, found the courage
to leave the source of our abuse.

I started to live my life
and make my own mistakes
and then, eventually, become sane.

Decades later, after
a few vain attempts to make peace
I found out my Dad was very ill.

I couldn't go see him.
In the times of Covid, 5 provinces away
it just wasn't possible.

From decades gone by
the distance may as well have been
a million miles, even in the same room.

My Dad died.
The pain he felt and the pain he inflicted
cannot be reconciled.

I never got to tell him how much he hurt me.
I never got to say I forgave him.
I never got to say goodbye.

Emotional Depression of a Manic Mother
By Maid Čorbić

Ambassador Maid Čorbić is from Tuzla, Bosnia and Herzegovina and 22 years old. His award-winning poetry is recognized across the globe. He also is moderator of the World Literature Forum dedicated to humanity and peace in the world.

www.facebook.com/xcelendge
www.facebook.com/globechampion

Never again, I swore to a long time ago
that I would be a happy man, no matter the situation,
because I know I'm worth more than anyone in the world
and I believe that behind every misfortune
I must discover joy as soon as possible.

My emotions are mixed every morning
when I wake up from hibernation and stay alone
because I am the child of a manic mother, unfortunately,
and I can't erase my memories so easily
because these feelings have not changed at all.

I am aware that I cannot waste any more time
for I am the child of a manic mother who has dementia
and also psychological tics, which gives me a sense
that I am not worth a percentage in this world
yet I know my life is really my thing to own.

Time moves forward now for me, for I seek
only an honest account of myself when I look in the mirror,
yet all I see is my wounded self
as I perish slowly but surely without error,
since I failed to gain self-confidence when it was most needed.

And it does me no good to have such a childhood,
since I am different from others because I am silent a lot,
as if for me the world stopped
and I give coexistence to someone else to experience it
but I deserve some good and deep love.

I endure all adversity with certainty, and emotions burst
every night when I go to bed and cry
because I can't imagine myself a happy man
for the most beautiful years of childhood are ruined
because I failed to make some wishes come true.

I would run into someone's arms if I could
but the difference in value between us
keeps my emotions to myself as tears, blood, and sweat
fly in all directions from this emotional collapse,
and I am no longer sure if I am important.

Is it my fault I'm alive
or is it fate itself
without an answer?

Some People's Children
By Megan C.W.

Megan C.W. is from New Mexico and has spent the past decade working in social services to advance opportunities for people living with HIV in the Gulf South. She regularly writes heartfelt content about day-to-day life with themes ranging from nature to spirituality, sexuality, yoga, parenting, mental health and wellness, peacemaking, and the quirks of life in New Orleans.

In the predawn darkness, I sip coffee on the porch and watch a caterpillar inch his way across a series of late October leaves.

He must not know what time of year it is, I think to myself, and then, *but it's 2021, nobody does.*

The whistling ducks fly over, one frantically noisy v-formation after another. The wind chimes, tuned to C, smoothly hum out a sustained low note, like a breeze-coaxed *Om.* My mind is briefly still in this rare moment of urban placidity before a car zooms by blasting a Coolio hit from the '90s and I'm irked into recollection of the toils of my life.

My heart quickens: Anxiety. For sanity's sake I reframe my to-do list, breathe, and spend a second acknowledging my fortitude.

"It's a list of opportunities," I laugh aloud to myself in the morning breeze. One such "opportunity" being someone else's waste clogging the toilet so completely in the space I'm renovating that if today's dislodging mission is unsuccessful, I'll be forced to hire reinforcements. Of course, this happens the same week I empty my savings replacing the roof I sacrificed to Hurricane Ida. Of course, none of the local hardware stores have toilet augers during the compound hardship of COVID and disaster recovery. Of course, I'm stressed by the prospect of intimacy with a disgusting object and I also see the opportunities to learn, grow, and make peace with shitty situations. Acutely, I am also conscious of my current good fortune: A strong roof, a healthy family, a home with an extra toilet for clogging, and a garden where confused caterpillars live.

I laugh again that this inconvenience is my current Most Pressing Problem. Thanks be! Life bestows a quirky blend of humor as it guides us towards our truths that are maybe eighty percent funny bone, seventeen percent belly laugh, and two percent remarkable serendipity. The remaining percent is relegated to the realm of comic ineffability.

The year 2021, for all the icky disorientation of continued existence in Pandemia, has shown us that humanity is shifting towards greater self-understanding and deeper truth. In the stripped-down version of modern life, even the most privileged among us have new cause to reflect on what is essential, what never actually mattered, and other realities obscured in the era before this rite of suffering. For me, the viral pilgrimage actualized something that I'd been quite resistant to accept: In spite of my intense and often-dysregulated moods, *I am a good mom.*

Like any parent, I'd love to pretend that the best of my kid's attributes and habits come from me and the others come from elsewhere. Anywhere elsewhere. Lightheartedly, I'm called to recognize, accept, and tactfully respond to the next generation manifestations of what I've modeled, in good moods and bad, for the kid who looks up to the only mother she's got.

Some people's children… I say it to myself, shaking my head when my four-year-old retorts with a certain sharpness of tongue. It'd be a stretch to say her father is faultless, but given his generally mild nature, there are no disputes in this co-parenting setup about which branch of the family tree Kiddo plucked her occasional curtness from.

On a good day, I catch my urge to scold and instead might ask, "Is there another way to get what you want, Honey?" Other times, I struggle to find grace and my irritation ends up bubbling outward. After I've taken a minute to breathe, attend to my guilt, and consider the hypocrisy of becoming frustrated upon seeing my behavior in her, I apologize.

"It's not because of me that you get angry, Mama."

"That's right, Baby. I've been dealing with strong feelings my whole life."

"Yeah, and you're really old! Can't you just stop, already?"

Honestly, I don't know, but I tell her that I believe that things can always get better, a little at a time. I also don't know how this candid discussion about feelings and responses might be perceived by the mind of such a young person. Her presence extends miles and miles beyond her tiny frame and I have to remind myself that she's just escaped babyhood by an order of months.

Still, life experience compels me to make explicit to myself that I must account for my behavior just as I ask her to learn to account for her own. There's nothing she can do to make me fly into a rage. These behaviors, flying and raging, are my inheritance, and though passed-down and well worn, they indeed are mine to ignore, attend to, or use for good.

It's been a year and a month since I first sat in front of a therapist (by way of Zoom) and said that I was committed to becoming the mother that I wanted my Kiddo to have: Patient, attentive, responsive, loving, and securely imperfect. He responded that I might not have seen it then, but that the process of showing up for help, vulnerably, likely meant that I already was that mother. Anger, he assured, emotional dysregulation, and intense mood swings result from biochemical processes mediated by our genes and experiences. Habits employed, often to assure survival in our families of origin, engrained as they may be, are still susceptible to reprogramming. In giving ourselves the love and compassion that we feel we've missed out on elsewhere, we can learn to redirect even our most destructive emotional energy into thoughts and actions that promote peace and resilience.

To better understand the things that trigger unpleasant cascades of feelings and reactions, it helps to recognize that our insecurities are not innate. These triggers are installed at some point in our lives, or quite often gradually through many interactions with caregivers and others. As children, we look to other (hurt) people for clues about who we are and how we should be. We move from intrinsic self-assurance, towards questioning, uncertainty, and obstructed views of our unending magnificence. It is curiosity, and generally, pain, that ultimately lead us back to the knowledge of our inherent sufficiency to survive and joyfully thrive through a lifetime of sequential surprises.

At some point, everyone strays far enough from their own true spirit to feel the call to reconnect with it. Sometimes we find the strength to honor the call. Other times we use vices to mute what we're not ready to hear. It is always true that our basic good nature never actually abandons us, even when it feels as though the connection's been severed.

A beloved yoga teacher recently pointed out that the Higher Self (our most peaceful version) tends to speak in a whisper, not a scream. There's a degree of inner quietude that allows for it to be heard. Each person's path to stillness, acceptance, and peace may be distinct, but ultimately, we're all on the journey to reacquaint with the best of ourselves. Some days it feels impossible.

Jane Goodall shared her favorite biblical quote from Deuteronomy in her book *Reason for Hope: A Spiritual Journey*, "As thy days, so shall thy strength be." Somehow, miraculously, we survive every day of our life, no matter what it brings. The capacity to persevere is universal in all things, living and nonliving. *Don't believe me?* ask the rocks. *Ask the Universe, as she's busy recycling every molecule there ever was into something brand new.*

The Northwoods adjacent to Lake Superior in Wisconsin is where my boyfriend spends much of each year. Late summer, he texted a picture of sugar snap pea vines in his garden, each of their stems bisected at a height coinciding with the reach of a rabbit mouth. "C'est la vie," we commiserated. Three weeks later, he texted a picture of a snap pea pod that had since developed, despite the plant's complete disconnection from its root. "C'est la vie!" we jubilated.

To understand how we got to where we are in a given moment, it's helpful to consider where we came from. Identifying beliefs about ourselves that no longer serve us helps change our thinking patterns to align with a more optimal experience of life.

My favorite memory of my dad is an odd one. As an adult, I appreciate its symbolism and obscurity. However, I have no idea why my childhood self found this incident so significant that I prioritized its memory over more profound experiences.

It was around the time I was eight when Dad was sporting an offensively hideous rat-tail haircut. Most of his hair was short, but he left one piece on the back, bottom and center, to grow out like the thin tail of a rodent. He was sitting on the couch with a hand resting behind his head, tired from a day's work on his feet. I suppose his plan was to get up for a beer, but as he leaned forward to stand, the tail caught in his own resting hand abruptly halted him.

"Help! Meg, I'm stuck! Help me!" He pantomimed trying to escape the couch, unsuccessfully, against the grasp of his own fingers ensnaring the ugly part of his hair. I suppose the farce was for both his amusement and mine. The moment was an absurdity and I remember the situation prompting immediate internal inquiry:

What on Earth is Dad doing? Is this what he'd be like always, if he were happy? Is he on drugs? How am I supposed to respond? What self-respecting barber would facilitate this predicament?

This is one of the few times I recall my dad seeming genuinely joyful during my childhood.

From my youthful, self-focused, perspective, I naturally concluded that his intermittent rage was the result of my presence in his life and all the ways in which I wasn't a good enough person to have a happy parent... *Duh!* It never occurred to me, never ever until my twenties, that Dad's misery was just one spoke supporting a multi-generational wheel of trauma, propelling itself forward through one human life after another.

Always prone to verbal expression, I employed vocal outbursts as a child. Assuming the position of family scapegoat came naturally to me, hopping between opportunities for drama, like a frog in a lily pond. I could reliably be counted upon to distract my parents from the toils of their own healing work and the needs of my brother, which were at least as great as my own. As long as I acted out, there would always be an obvious cause for our domestic dysfunction. This was a convenient deviation from the far more complex reality involving wayward ancestors, the social taboo of mental illness, personal horrors of all sorts, and pain, multiplying like a virus, through human life cycles.

Did I consent to the role of scapegoat? *Yes and No.* Did I consent to being useful to the people with whom I shared love? Yes. Have I willfully promoted discomfort in people around me? *Yes, repeatedly.* Still, I feel that a child could not consent to struggling the way I did while feeling unsupported by her folks.

My parents did the best they could for me. I truly believe it and I know that I want much better than that for my kid. Two seemingly distinct realities can harmonize: I can respect and honor my parents' endowments after also having been hurt by their parenting. I am a more reliable guardian for merits earned in the experience of working to heal congenital wounds. I hope that in striving to replace destructive and well-practiced emotional-behavioral patterns with more optimal ones, I will resource my child and myself with tools for continuing resilience. Given my long-standing confusion about the origin of my dad's frustration, that I was born unworthy to experience his loving joy, being explicit with Kiddo about my emotional processes makes sense.

"Mama goes up, Mama goes down."

"That's right, Baby, and it's not because of you. And guess what else?"

"Huh?"

"I love you no matter what mood I'm in."

"You already told me that, Mama."

Some lessons are best taught by repetition. Some are better taught by reduction, subtraction, and loss.

Dad died sick and young, and for once in his life, at peace with the world. I was twenty-four and verbally spited him for his abandonment. "Oh. You're bummed that I'm leaving the world early? How do you think it makes me feel, Meg?" He had a good point. He'd rapidly become a much better communicator in the days after he realized there was no more time for bullshit.

By the most unlikely stroke of serendipity, life provided our family advanced knowledge of Dad's early expiration. For eighteen months we knew that Dad would be gone any day now. He softened a lot in the face of his finality, calmed down, and became more pleasant and inspiring company. Our family shifted, too. We came to honor more deeply our time together and things like shared meals adopted a new sacredness.

The last time I broke bread with my father was the last meal of his life. Too sick with cancer and chemotherapy to digest anything else, bites of cheeseburgers and bagels went down all right during those final weeks. He was small in the passenger seat next to me on the way to Mr. K's, a burger joint in Charlotte, North Carolina.

Tumors in his eyeballs had taken much of his outward vision but his electric blue gaze was sharpened by the urgent crispness of his terminal introspection. We ate in greasy commune on a sun-warmed outside table. The sound of passing traffic rooted us in the present amidst our keen awareness that the value of each moment inflated as it zoomed past with the cars.

"Meg, you must find a way to make peace with life," he implored with unusual calmness. His bony hands trembled as he pushed his fries through the glob of ketchup on the greasy paper liner serving as his plate. The paper would have blown away, were it not for the weight of his barely nibbled burger. As its corners flapped in the late-December breeze, I found myself hoping that meal would also spare the gravity required to hold Dad to Earth, just a little longer.

The effort employed to move fry to mouth was remarkable, given how well practiced Dad was at the endeavor of eating. An astonished witness of the perseverance of his mind and body through years of intense sickness, I intently marveled in his struggle and simultaneously prepared myself to respond lest he become suddenly nauseous or too weak to sit up any longer. Defensive about his impending abandonment and his insinuation that I had a hand in my own experience of tranquility, I squeezed in some final snarkasm.

"Listen to me," he insisted with rare authority, "I spent my life unhappily and now it's over. Don't waste your days in misery."

Quiet for a moment and determined not to betray my vulnerability, I was suddenly desperate for an opportunity to busy myself through the process of goodbye. "Wanna take the rest of your burger home, Dad? Here, I'll wrap it back up for you."

For all the moody discontent Dad modeled for me since before I was old enough to make memories, he marked his leave with a lesson he'd learned late. Our experience of misery or joy in life, to a remarkable extent, is a matter of choice. Into a painful, blind, and shaky death the following day, my dad moved with a last minute and self-created sense of peace.

I am decades into my own process of dealing with chronic confusion and emotional pain when it occurs to me that my dad was afflicted by unacknowledged and untreated mental illness. Retrospectively, it seems like one of those No-Shit-Sherlock realizations, but considering time, context, and social taboo, it's unlikely that Dad's blue-collar life would have afforded much opportunity for him to consider that he was symptomatic of anything beyond being a slightly odd professional artist. Given his behavior towards me and his responses to normal parental stress, I wondered if he erroneously believed his unsettled moods were created by external causes… like his moody daughter.

Could he see himself in me? If he did, did it make him angry? Did he ever feel ill equipped to provide the best for the kids he loved, and lash out against us in response? I've done that, and I wish I could ask him now that the stakes are lower, since I'm grown, stable, mostly shameless about the quirks of my mind, and pretty much disinterested in blame.

More times than I care to admit, I've intimately re-created this original family drama. The array of permutations of this theme that I've found time and time again in my romantic life with very different men is a testament to the human capacity to find our way back to where we started. This psychic "homing" instinct is almost uncanny, and I've discovered myself recreating the Daddy Dynamic even when I've intentionally sought not to.

What. The. Hell.

When I catch myself permitting "his" bad behavior and blaming myself for making him that way, I hear the taunting of a tiny-bodied and huge-spirited friend of mine echoing inside my skull, *Mirror, mirror on the wall, I am my mother after all!* Thirty years later and I'm still the child who wrecked the family. How is this possible?

It's not. It never was, but we buy into the dynamics of our youth with steadfast commitment to their veracity until, eventually, we realize they've entangled themselves while nesting snugly… around our throats. Patterns in families arise within broader social contexts that impact the roles individuals assume within their families and later as adults.

This context also matters when it comes to the resources people may access for solidifying or redefining themselves. I have come of age in the Google generation and part of my process of revolting against installments from my family of origin involves YouTube searches for things like "re-parenting" and "self-sourcing tools for healing." These things are helpful and I've benefited greatly from their ready availability.

Still, when I consider the ways in which I was injured in the process of growing up in my family, I must not take for granted that these are tools that my parents, and their parents, didn't have. That such resources exist, aside from marking digitally savvy times, is evidence of a culture in which mental wellness is more broadly discussed. My experience in developing an understanding of my own mind has been vibrantly colored by life in the information age.

I've wondered often about the behavior of the relatives who came before my immediate ones, particularly on my dad's side. Never having been close to this part of my family, I know little about the characteristics of anyone ahead of my dad's mom, who was a key figure in my childhood. Grandma Rita, with her fiery red hair, mastered the perplexing art of simultaneously being the most generously fun and intermittently, nasty-spirited person I'd ever met. I feel both pride and apprehension to be as alike her as I am, dyed hair and all!

Shortly after the raw days following Dad's death, I voyaged to the depths of Middle America for a Dad's-side family reunion. I'd never known "These People" and found them to be particularly generous in their casserole preparation - no expense spared on the good cheese - and their whispered tales of this grandma or that uncle who had "mental problems."

"Oh, so we're all nuckin' futs? That's oddly comforting, Barb," I said to a distant cousin while I crammed my mouth with macaroni. She seemed unimpressed with my cavalier insight, or perhaps, table manners.

The trip was life changing, though. Dad had never told me that madness was our birthright, and I came to wonder if he'd ever even known. Given how much had changed in the capacity for understanding such things in the chasm between my dad's generation and my own, I wondered if moods discussed over dinner today would have had any airtime at all at an earlier potluck. Even at the table of my youth, the elephant in the room was Dad's mood-du-jour. At best, we jested at his expense, shielding ourselves with humor by telling diminishing jokes about him. At worst, there was screaming involved or toxic silence mercifully broken by the scooting sound of the chair of the first brave person to exit the tension.

Things are MUCH better now. Except for an occasional unhappy meal, I strive to make opportunities for my kid and I to discuss our feelings and behavior openly. Still, my mood is a bit of a wild card, and as I continue to grow towards self-regulation and consistency, I know that everyone I'm close to wonders which version of me they'll meet on a given day.

My Kiddo has devised tests to ascertain which Mom Variant she's dealing with, and to affirm that my love for her endures through my shifting mood states. When I'm even slightly depressed, preoccupied, anxious, or disassociated, I often notice her behavioral response to me before becoming aware, myself, that my discontent is outwardly appreciable. Her instrumentation for perceiving me is more sensitive than anyone else's, built and fine-tuned to aid her survival in our home. It's a tool from which we both benefit as it informs the harmonizing of our shared life and a penchant for peace that, ideally, will continue to come more naturally to her than it has for me.

Everyone develops survival apparatuses, because the ability to adjust is a characteristic of all things living. Ideally, an apparatus is used in the context of relationships, healthy and adaptable enough to eventually make it obsolete. Today, my mood informs her actions, and then her response informs my need to parent us both through the moment. Tomorrow, perhaps our balance will come through a less complex process. In this line of thinking, I can also see how my own tendency for emotional lability was installed. Some time ago, I needed it to survive at home. Though it's long since outgrown its usefulness, I've only recently become sure enough of my own capacity to cope without it that I can begin to let it go.

The growth process is subtle and powerful, a steady trickle of water to build the most majestic of canyons. My Kiddo's signals to me that I'm drifting into mental rapids are not subtle at all. She finds my gaze. Will I look her in the eyes now? She performs or acts out. Will I laugh? Will I attend? She waits for her effort to catalyze my response.

Kiddo calls for me to give what I may believe I don't possess in a moment of emotional depletion. It can't matter to her that all my energy and focus is consumed in the perpetuation of some sort of mental anguish. She is a child, and she needs to be cared for and nurtured anyway. She's hungry now, for assurance; my tableside pup suddenly begs for even a scrap when something about my state tells her she should prepare to go without.

Sometimes, I feel helpless in the task of helping her build a strong sense of self and belonging when mine's been so often compromised. Still, in even the worst of moments, I know the truth is that the best of me is what she deserves. I may not be able to mother her faultlessly, but I can mother her consciously. That I am called to do so won't skip past her mega-radar unnoticed.

Whatever button she's chosen to push, her performance is my cue, a signal that my Higher Self has apparently exited stage left and is needed front and center for encore. Forever, I've suffered alone and it feels unnatural to pull anyone towards me when I start to hurt. Still, I know that each time I allow her to remind me of my capacity for compassion, each time I reach for her, hold her, look at her, and assure her of my solidity and her safety, we purchase stock in a future in which she doesn't have to test people to know that she's worthy of their love.

We both grow when I'm able to choose an intentional response to finding myself in the experience of impatience, frustration, sustained sadness, or crippling anxiety. In fact, the desire to be a good mother for her has catapulted my healing in a way that nothing else could have. I'm not sure that I ever actually respected myself before seeing my reflection in the face of someone else, someone whom I could so easily regard with deep and unconditional love. Through her natural need for guidance and reassurance, one earnest moment after another, I find myself striving to meet her in the soft and vulnerable places that I'd long ago learned to avoid with others.

Sometimes, we discuss the process of choosing a favorable response to an uncomfortable sensation, and she charms me with her innocent insight.

"Wow. I feel myself starting to get nervous, but I bet I can take some deep breaths and calm down some. Do you think I can teach myself to be calmer?"

"Probably."

"Me too, Baby. You know, we can teach ourselves to do anything, with practice."

"Yeah. Well, we might not want to teach ourselves to swim into a shark's mouth."

"Good point!" I laugh at the imagery and the irony of having willfully steered myself into precarious situations more times than I care to remember.

Though I still daily feel the gravity of my practiced wretchedness, I notice that it loses its power when I'm able to perceive alternative ways of being. I still find myself in the tank with the shark, and perhaps always will, but I'm no longer automatically swimming toward the jaws. Some days, I may, but other days, I may curiously check the roughness of the scales, give the creature space to move elsewhere, or I find the ladder and climb out of the water altogether. My Kiddo has helped me to believe that there's always another way. My writing, time in therapy, learning about the mind, and yoga practice have all helped me along a bumpy path of reconfiguring my response to thoughts and feelings that have historically triggered destructive behaviors.

In the early days of parenting, the inadequacy I felt for the task of meeting my child's needs, emotional and otherwise, was intense. Looking back with a lighter heart now, I assume that most new parents feel a version of this, and also that adding guilt and self-disparagement to the sleep-deprived emotional tsunami of a first child's infancy does little to improve the wellbeing of anyone involved. I found it difficult to relax into the role of mother and harshly questioned my ability to provide anything well, with the exception of intellectual stimulation. I read to my baby constantly: novels, Pema Chödrön books, Scientific American, parenting guides, and New Yorker articles. Whatever I was reading at the time became the bedtime story in the background of her perpetual infant slumber.

When she was a month old and I was comfortable enough with breastfeeding to be away from her for a couple of hours at a time, I returned to pottery classes at a neighborhood studio. The first thing I made was a gigantic piggy bank, adorned with spots and a tutu. My classmates assumed correctly that it was a gift for Kiddo, and I deflected every one of their compliments as I labored diligently to create a beautiful, handmade thing. Ten or fifteen hours in, the pig had taken form, was fired, painted, glazed, and a character to behold.

"Oh. This? This is the Therapy Pig. Kiddo's gonna need to start saving soon to be able to work through all the trauma of being *my* daughter!" I joked, fending off tears with a huge smile, because I didn't know how to be honest with anyone about the awful feeling that my failure as a mom was certain.

❧

The experience of becoming a mother accelerated a personal growth process I'd been on, really since I was ten and started having mood swings. In the early days of feeling and healing through the tumult, I turned strongly to mysticism, perhaps because it was the thing most available to me without external support, or perhaps because the intensity of my lived experience felt naturally mystical. In the following decades, I pursued loads of therapy, earned mental health degrees, studied voraciously, had many years on different psychotropic medications, fell into the depths of dysfunction and pulled myself out repeatedly, lost and rediscovered art, found yoga, became a mom, and ultimately, have returned to where I started: Intent on uncovering a deeper sense of spirituality.

Looking back, it's clear now that my certainty of maternal failure and my early-accepted role as the Family Burden were rooted in the same basic thinking, that I was inadequate, insufficient, and unworthy. This belief has been so fundamental to my ethos that it's had a role in every relationship, every adverse incident, and every fit of rage or stint of depression. Swings of elation on the more manic end of my bipolarity have offered brief reprieve from that way of thinking, and it is now my goal to centralize self-adequacy so that I no longer need to visit one of the poles to experience it.

In regards to the therapy pig, there's a matter of discernment that can be used to tint the memory of its creation. Was all that hard work really motivated by my desire to offset inevitable parental failure or was it actually an expression of the deep love that I feel for my child? The logic can be extended to the healing pursuits. Would I have quested after growth opportunities so voraciously if I honestly believed I was worthless or that things would never get better? The answer is so obvious now. I'd be dead already if I didn't trust that there was a purpose for all of this, even the part that feels like insanity.

Motivation, like every other mind-thing, is somewhat fluid, though we tend to think of it as being static over time. A person may begin an exercise regimen because they desire to modify their physical appearance, stick with it upon discovering that it improves their outlook on life, and ultimately, incorporate it as a ritual in their day-to-day spirituality. In the process, they may be able to relinquish focus on the external benefits for the sake of being more finely attuned to the internal ones.

Eventually, it doesn't matter how they got into the habit of this beneficial practice, or when they started. Through doing it regularly, they are afforded the experience of unanticipated rewards, regardless of what they initially assumed they'd reap from their pursuit and in what time they'd hoped to reap it. When it comes to "Right Action," habits that equip us to be our best selves and thus, participate meaningfully in the world, no motivation is more righteous than another. Whatever call to heal we're capable of hearing is an opportunity to begin engaging with life in a way that is stable and eventually, beneficial beyond our expectations.

There is merit in intentionally fine-tuning our motivation. It is also true that motivation can both precede and follow action, and that it develops somewhat naturally in the wake of habits that support the emergence of our best selves.

What's *best*? I hesitate to use the word here because it is both subjective and implies the existence of a single right way of being. In that context, it tends to connote shame or guilt around anything other than some ideal standard. That's not my intention, as I aim to explicitly honor all life experiences for their validity and completeness. When we're at our personal best, we know a sense of wholeness and integration, we have comfort with the limits of our comprehension and control, we experience a degree of peace with mortality, and we have capacity to share ourselves with the world for the sake of improving things *for others*. The process of integrating is different for each person. Each of us has both native and potential strengths that can be realized through effort.

As mentioned, intellectualism and creativity have come very naturally to me, and it is those talents that I'm most inclined to share. On the other hand, I struggle to find peace and presence, especially within personal relationships. For the sake of experiencing balance and wholeness, I work to cultivate the attributes that I believe would improve the quality of my interactions with others. Thank goodness I've been blessed with the loving company of a few people in my life who are patient as I work on honoring myself enough to allow for true vulnerability and presence with them. Clearly, I've also been resourced in other ways, like being privileged to access school and therapy, having the good fortune to pursue hobbies and opportunities for personal development. I have both the skills and flexibility of time to articulate these ideas in writing, for the benefit of myself, and hopefully, at least one other person.

I fully acknowledge that such opportunities are not equitably afforded to all people and that my position of privilege is helping me to mitigate the most challenging consequences of my experience with bipolarity. I am most grateful for all the ways in which insight and opportunity have gifted me on my journey. Ideally, the sharing of these experiences will catalyze hope for others to grow, not by my influence, but by recognition of their own innate worthiness to realize the benefits of their gifts and to share those gifts with others.

All people possess the ability to create, share, heal themselves and others, and experience resilient growth. In fact, humanity is naturally inclined towards generative processes and collaborative endeavors within the context of community, though we can also interfere with these processes by habituating self-limiting beliefs. Like my silly dad, impeding his own mobility with the grasp of his hair, we all have moments of trapping ourselves and begging for external liberation. "Help me, Meg! Help! I'm stuck!" Perhaps, we get lucky, and a barber shows up to shear off our misfortunes with a single lop. More likely, we begin to develop habits that allow us to gradually discover more optimal states.

The ability to self-source the tools for our healing processes are facilitated by practice and gratitude and compassion for others and ourselves. There's a cascade that starts when unpleasant thoughts give way to uncomfortable feelings to which we respond with defensive behavior. Ironically, behaviors that are unconsciously rooted in self-protection tend to perpetuate the very conflicts that they're *supposed* to safeguard against. In this way, our insecurities are almost comically (or tragically) self-fulfilling. From childhood, I've carried beliefs about being burdensome and unworthy of love and can see how these beliefs have amplified urges to act out and to push people away when I'm feeling unwell. Consequently, I've ended up alone when the closeness of others would have helped me to restore my sense of safety and stability. The isolation, at times, has reinforced the initial painful thought that I am burdensome and unworthy.

Therapy has helped to excavate the core beliefs, buried in the ashes of so many burned bridges, responsible for a cycle of discomfort and destruction in my life. Now that I've identified them, it's easier to notice when they're sowing seeds of havoc in my psyche. Starting with the moment in which I realize I'm out of balance and working backwards, I consistently find those thoughts, snickering into their muddy little palms, right at the place where my mood took a turn for the worse. No longer believing in their truth, I see my toxic little thoughts now as a pair of sneaky tricksters, coaxing me into growth with their mischief. Each time I pull myself back towards peace upon noticing they've diverted me away, I strengthen my commitment to a reality in which my life is no longer driven by my moods.

How have I come to believe that I am worthy after decades of believing that I was not? Some days, sufficiency is the baseline and it's easy to see all the ways in which I've been gifted to meaningfully engage in life. Other days, it takes a lot of faith to believe that I'll ever feel worthy again. On those days, I perceive even my breath to be a wasted resource that'd be better spent supporting the life of something else. There's a line from a *Satsang* song called *I Am* that I use as a mantra for good days and bad ones: *I am holy, and sacred, and righteous, and True, and I deserve to be here, and so do you.*

The first half of the line feels lofty at times, but the implication of the second half, that all beings are inherently worthy, reminds me of an oddly placating truth. My wacked out nervous system and I do not exist at the locus of the universe. In fact, there are many, many beings, all having unique experiences of life while navigating the sentient trials of survival.

A very funny friend of mine used to quote *Dream Girls* to let me know when my complaining was getting out of hand by saying, "Effie! We all got pain!" If nothing else, the reminder is a call to gratitude. In a life in which suffering can be immeasurably intense, again, I am blessed by the relative insignificance of that which currently inconveniences me.

It's easy to get wrapped up in our own living, as though everything else isn't simultaneously happening, and as though we aren't electron-microscopic in our influence within the totality of life. At the same time, Satsang is right, that despite being minute compared to the immensity of everything else, each of us retains an almost divine significance by way of our existence. Is it not a miracle that against monumental odds, each of us was born and is surviving as a unique and tiny being in a boundless universe? Isn't it incredible to be a participant in the collective human experience, the experience of life, right now?

The table on which I write and I, are, molecularly speaking, made of the same stuff, yet I happened to come together with a consciousness. And, consciously, I am compelled to mention that my table is made from materials that were once alive. There's a cycle, an order to everything, and at the same time, everything is randomly interacting with everything else. Somehow, each of us has made our way into the mix of things and each has come equipped to perceive the experience from a unique perspective.

Wild.

Consistent practice of the things that help us to feel centered and complete in our sometimes-chaotic lives enhances our efficiency in returning to peace when we find ourselves at odds. Over time, reducing the degree to which we struggle with even our greatest challenges happens when we've repeatedly met our trials with grace. Day-to-day, we're provided ample opportunities for cultivating the will and skill to remain in balance when faced with emotional or literal adversity: In the checkout line, in the midst of an ugly mood, at the dry end of a plunger, or through more major struggle. From this perspective, we can see that which challenges us as a gift, a reason to develop ourselves beyond the bounds of maladaptive patterns that we've learned and practiced to destructive mastery.

Living intentionally, and repeatedly choosing behaviors that override the worst of our habits naturally leads us down a gradual, but revolutionary, path towards a better world. It is true that refining oneself towards a more peaceful state has an impact that extends beyond one's own experience. Immediately, those around us benefit from our harmonious engagement with our lives and ourselves, consciously or unconsciously. Beyond that, this process of refinement interrupts the transmission of hurtful tendencies through our lineages by replacing those tendencies with ones that promote growth and healing. Through the willful weaving of our life's tale into the familial tapestry, we can bring focus to the threads of resilience that existed before us. Consequently, these threads are more readily incorporated into the ancestral fabric that's created through the lifetimes of all subsequent generations.

The time and energy I've invested in making sense of my experience with bipolarity makes it, in some ways, my life's work. Looking back, the big choices impacting my trajectory have mostly been motivated by a desire to "get better" or to create circumstances to buffer the impacts of my worst days. I see now that many significant choices were made while I was afraid: Afraid of the risk of instability, afraid of being discovered by my peers as being "insane", afraid of letting people close enough to eventually grieve them when they die or give up on me. A significant endowment of a bipolar mind that flips between realities is the ability to see things from multiple perspectives. While my path has been influenced by fear, it has also been influenced by a depth of self-awareness that has grown out of the process of managing life amidst the shifting of moods.

There was a time in which I struggled against my own mind, thinking I could educate, discipline, or will myself into a state of constant emotional neutrality or some baseline of happiness. For decades, I thought that healing meant no longer having symptoms, and I'd flagellate myself for having the type of complex and inconsistent emotions that all humans have. Today, the struggle has mostly given way to acceptance that my experience of life will be colored by moods and that I have a responsibility to strive for centering compassion in my interactions with others, even during the days in which I feel miserable. Ultimately, I hope to feel it all, the good, bad, ugly, and intense, and to trust that I don't have to initiate fallout in my relationships when I perceive myself to be less than lovable.

For the insight it's provided, I'm grateful for the many gifts I've gained from what I once referred to as "mental illness" and have since come to see as a non-pathological process. I have deep appreciation for the variety of ways in which humans can move through their lives, navigating triumphs and struggles. Watching my dad in his process helped solidify the reality for me that people are complex in their resilience and that our most difficult tendencies are repurposed in our experiences of life at its best. Hours and hours every day, for decades, my dad labored at the easel, sometimes moodily, but always with an intensity of focus that made him appear to the world as a natural master of his craft.

Indeed, my father was a phenomenal artist, and I wish I could ask him now about his motivation and about how it felt to show up through all the ups and downs, every single day, to create beautiful things. His dedication to the practice of art was undoubtedly therapeutic, and it resulted in an enduring body of creations that have ultimately enhanced the world for others, despite the fact that his actions were sometimes sparked by pain. Great things often come out of unpleasant experiences.

As a parent, I strive to articulate such nuances for Kiddo's benefit and because I have great faith in her capacity for coming to terms with them. I'd be lying to say that I don't feel a measure of pride to watch her interact with the world and see that she possesses a bit of the Familial Fire, the spark to illuminate a room with her presence or burn it down with her discontent. She's big, bold, and tiny, all at once, and I think she's somewhat aware that her influence extends beyond her physical body. I work diligently to model the benefits of selecting for illumination, as much as possible and emphasize repeatedly that return to peace matters more than any deviation from it.

"Holy smokes! You were having some strong feelings for a minute, and then you chose to calm yourself back down! High five!"

I teach her to feel pride in the wake of an emotional event when she might otherwise feel shame, while also holding her accountable for her role in the outcome. In enthusiastic reciprocity, she teaches me about forgiveness, love, and other things that, through the practice of giving to her, I become more comfortable sharing with myself. She also shows me that it's okay when things aren't perfect and that in truth there's joy in every moment.

When we're present in the here-and-now, no matter our history, we can discover that joy at will. Now on the porch, early in the morning, at the onset of another laborious day, I remember my blessings, give thanks for the experiences that shaped me, and enjoy the minute company of a caterpillar, dedicated to healthy existence in the shifting of seasons.

GREEN GLASS BOTTLES
BY NOAH DAY

Noah Day was born and raised in Massachusetts and is now a sophomore at Texas State University pursuing a degree in neuroscience. While conquering every task that comes her way, Noah loves expressing herself through artistic skills such as painting, photography, and writing. Writing is a passion Noah has had since she was young and plans on releasing a book of her own one day.

Until the age of sixteen I lived in a small scale apartment that I referred to as a house I simply stayed in, never as my home. To me a home was a structure where one could unwind emotionally and connect with others in an area they value as their own. This was not my home. This area consisted of three bedrooms, a poorly half decorated living space, and one small shared bathroom for my mother, my brother, and I.

There were days when the house was as still as the dead and as stale as the saltines sitting in the back of the cluttered pantry. Never being completely full, I still remember the dusty white refrigerator that seemed as though a twenty-four pack of Heineken beer came incorporated into the purchase. Beside the refrigerator was the home of boxes filled with empty green glass bottles that stacked tall until it was time to grip the sides of the boxes, load them into the trunk, and turn them in at the neighborhood liquor store for a cycle of replacements.

At one point my mother tried to turn the loading of the bottles into a racing game for my brother and I. It angered me. How could she do this to me? Why am I being forced to attend and participate in an addiction that is not mine?

All I thought was how alcohol was integrated into our house finances as if it was the electric bill. I choked on my words the very next day as I told my teacher I could not participate in the scholastic book fair. I told her that I simply forgot the money my mother left me on my nightstand. Joke's on her. I didn't even have a nightstand.

Excuses were something I learned to come up with quickly because whatever happened at the house was supposed to stay in the house. I never wanted anyone to judge my mother for her faults, flaws, or her present yet absent behavior. I felt as though it was my job to protect her, and as far as everyone else could tell, my home life was perfectly fine.

It wasn't fine. I knew the moments my mother was having a manic episode by the smell of cigarette smoke lingering in the house for a few weeks. I can still picture her sitting on her bed as she sucked the light of her cigarettes down to the nub.

During these times I craved her attention yet my mother focused on everything but me. Her mania did not involve me as much as her rare couple of friends. I was hardly around for these moments. I remember being shipped away to my grandparents house during her mania and coming home after her euphoria party crashed, along with her mood.

The fall of my mother's mood meant the fall of all of our moods. The atmosphere of the house could be felt instantly as I stepped through the door. I knew immediately that she was coming down from her high. Her emotions seemed so intense they filled the room with gloom. Even with the blinds open, the house was still dark.

Embarrassed that she was once so exhilarated my mother would begin to frantically clean while hoping we wouldn't notice the mess. I always noticed. Although it killed me, I missed the thought of seeing her happy, even if that meant it wasn't with me. But what goes up must always come down.

"You are the greatest gift God has given me," my mother would always tell me when she was in a mania. I was the greatest gift because her pregnancy with me saved her life. But when she was depressed, I was the reason for everything wrong that ever happened to her. This laid the foundation for my black and white thinking. I never felt neutral about myself, either I was superior and great or a complete failure.

Today, I've reached exactly seven thousand four hundred and ninety nine days old. I like to mention the specific number instead of the year because every day something new is being learned and, though I promise to follow through and constantly work on myself, often it can feel like I am still not doing enough. Sometimes the small accomplishments can go unnoticed, but in reality I am grateful every day when my lungs take a breath and my heart continues to beat.

Because of my upbringing with a bipolar mother, I had to rewire my brain into positivity and kill who I used to be, in order to become who I wanted to be. I started thinking that life is not so complicated. Every second that we are alive we are just simple, yet complex, beings experiencing life. Creating reactions, making meaning, and attaching emotions to experiences to make us feel alive, ultimately giving us emotional connections.

What we as children don't realize is as we are growing and understanding these emotional connections, so are the adults around us. I had to realize that although my mother watched me physically grow up, I watched her grow up as well. There were many concepts that my mother had to learn while raising me due to her lacking her own mother's emotional connection. She was never taught to express her feelings but instead to compress and explode.

I never thought of my mother's pain from having to do it alone, with no role model of how things should be. How can one do for another what was never taught to them? I used to blame her for making me feel alone, but the truth was that my mother was never used to having someone stay. Except for me, I was permanent.

Now that I am older, I fight the similarities between us. The lack of motivation to do even the simplest of tasks. The urge to distance myself from everything and everyone for no apparent reason. The random anxiety attacks in restaurant bathrooms that cause me to leave events early.

I used to get so angry at my mother as I watched her throw everything good in life away. Now I understand her better and in return understand what I need to do. I can see my mother as my role model of what not to do.

I am the change.

TWO MOMS
BY SALLY HUSCH DEAN

Sally Husch Dean is the founding artistic director of The San Diego North Coast Singers Youth Chorus. Since retiring in 2019, she has devoted herself to writing. Her forthcoming memoir brings readers into her Midwest youth during the 1960s and '70s. Dean shares personal stories, some humorous, some tender, some dark, as she seeks a way of life different from the chaos and worry she knew as a child.

Two Moms

I don't remember a time when my mother's mood swings didn't dominate my life. Mom must have been in her seventies when she confided in me that she'd always felt she was two persons in one body. This made sense to me.

One night when I was only eight or nine, I crouched outside my bedroom door, looking down at Mom as she sat very still in the green leather chair in the den. A dimly lit lamp gave off the only light in the room. Smoke curled up from the burning tip of her cigarette. She wasn't reading or knitting. She just sat there, smoking.

I didn't approach this mother. I snuck a good long look, though, my face pressed between two posts in the upstairs railing. I could feel my heart beating against my chest.

Please get up, Mom. Can't you see I'm scared? Why are you sitting there in the dark? Why are you smoking? You detest cigarettes.

"Even the smell makes me sick," she always said.

My small hands held on tight as I stared down at Mom from my vantage point, where the railing curved toward my bedroom. At last I stood, slipped into my room, and closed the door.

Two days later, the other mother emerged like molten lava erupting from within my still, cigarette-smoking mother. This mother never sat down, much less still. This mother talked incessantly, seemingly never sleeping. I listened to her rattling around in the kitchen in the wee hours of the night. She practiced her recorded Russian lessons while washing dishes. This mother laughed a lot, but a bit too loudly. She let the world know that she abhorred clothes shopping, and she dressed eccentrically. If you ask me, she dressed funny, oddly, nothing like other mothers.

"I dress for comfort. I don't care about fashion trends." She was wearing plaid pedal pushers and a flower-patterned shirt as she pulled on tennis shoes, jumped on her bike, and headed to the store.

As a child, I did not know about the deep hole of depression. I learned the term manic depression in my teens. It was a relief to finally have a name for what I'd grown up knowing. Mom's moods impacted me. When Mom was depressed, I lived with a hollow ache. I felt helpless and afraid. When she blasted into mania, I kept a nervous eye on her. Anything might happen.

The Husch Family

My brothers and sisters described their early childhood in the forties and early fifties as chaotic. Peter, my Dad, drank nightly and became strict, bordering on abusive. His only parenting model had been his mother, who, they tell me, tied a rope around little Peter's leg if she felt he was misbehaving, then tied the other end around a tree in the backyard.

Ann, my Mom, was the eldest of three daughters. Her parents hired a full-time nanny and a cook. The three Rubinstein girls remembered their mother, Blanche, dressing them in matching frilly dresses and parading them before her bridge group. After being admired, they were returned to their nanny. The sisters hated being on display, like fancy dolls. They imagined caring for their own children, and knew they did not want to parent from the sidelines like their mother.

Pete and Ann fell in love when Ann was just seventeen, Pete twenty-six. A year later, they became engaged. Ann's father, Wilton Rubinstein, died suddenly of a heart attack at age forty-eight, shortly before Ann and Pete's wedding day. We grandchildren never met this grandfather, yet he existed vividly for us as the hero of endless stories told by Mom and her sisters. We imagined gleeful neighborhood children gathered in the Rubinstein front yard as Wilton launched colorful kites from the upstairs deck of their house. He'd built the kites himself. As the girls were falling asleep most nights, they heard their father at the piano, playing his favorite sonatas. Wilton's daughters adored him.

Once Dad mentioned to me that possibly Wilton had exhibited mood swings. A genetic curse? My guess is that Mom's first depression pulsed through her while she dealt with the grief of her father's death. I doubt that my young parents understood Mom's increasing mood swings, the uninvited, invisible invaders of their new marriage.

My oldest sister, Peggy, was born in 1942 when Mom was only twenty-one. Tony came two years later, followed four years later by the twins, David and Joan. The family was complete, my parents thought. However, according to my sisters, while on a romantic trip away from their four small children in 1954, Ann and Peter drank a few too many Stingers, a sweet cocktail composed of cognac and crème de menthe. Nine months later, I was born.

"They nicknamed you Little Stinger when you were a baby," my sisters laughed. But Mom and Dad just said, "You kept us young."

Augusta

Our beloved Augusta Grady Black, an angel in human form, found her way to our family in 1945 after Mom answered the ad Augusta had placed seeking work as a housekeeper. She told me later that she and Mom bonded the very first day they met. There was immediate trust between them, as though they'd been close friends for years.

Augusta had grown up on her family farm in Duncan, Mississippi, during the twenties. It was a large, close-knit family. Her parents' deep love and high expectations instilled a strong work ethic, caring nature, and self-confidence in Augusta.

We Husches all felt the strength of Augusta and will never forget the rich, deep sound of her laughter. She cared for my siblings and me alongside Mom. Augusta gave us what she had known in her own family: acceptance and unconditional love. She was always there for our family through easy times and dark times. Augusta was simply there.

The House

Entering Polo Drive from busy Hanley Road was like passing through a magic gate to a charmed realm. The neighborhood provided a warm, safe place when my home life was puzzling. An ever-present gaggle of neighborhood children rode bikes, ran, and skipped along the curving sidewalks. Oaks, elms, and maples offered shade in summer and bare, beautiful, dark branches in winter. Our house was a three-story, white colonial with rose painted shutters. It stood proud and welcoming, like another member of our family. The rooms were spacious with high ceilings. Plenty of light poured through the paned windows.

Looking back, I see myself during my pre-teen years, sitting with Dad on the screened porch, my legs curled under me on the sofa cushion as a summer storm rolled in. Distant at first, the thunder was barely a grumble. As the storm moved nearer, the sky darkened and the thunderclaps grew louder. A sudden crash startled us. We breathed in the damp aroma of the steaming earth and listened as the gentle tapping of the raindrops on the roof became incessant hammering. Bolts of lightning flashed, and I was glad my dad was with me, seated in his favorite porch chair, his feet on the ottoman. Nothing was better than this sense of wellbeing.

And yet, dark memories floated by as well. I saw myself opening the door to the dank basement stairway. The steps were uneven. It smelled like a cave, and the concrete floor was hard and cold on my bare feet.

Thinking about the basement brings a disturbing story to my mind. The twins were still babies when Dad found Mom huddled in the basement corner beside the small cast-iron oven. The oven door was open, and the smell of gas filled the air. Had depression's anguish driven Mom down those uneven stairs, to the gas oven and this unthinkable last resort, this desperate seeking of relief? Mom was admitted to the hospital and remained there for a month. The doctors recommended shock treatment, but Dad refused.

I picture Dad, terrified as he found crumpled Mom. It hurts to imagine Mom's utter despair. Although the twins were not yet three, Joan lives with a strong sense of her abandonment with Mom suddenly gone. Peggy, who was eight, completely blocks out the trauma, with no memories from that month that Mom was hospitalized. The event was a taboo topic in our family. I'm sure Grandma and my aunts grieved and worried along with Dad and Augusta, but children were excluded, and told nothing.

Augusta's Story

In June 1981, my husband Bill and I flew to St. Louis with our toddlers, Laura and Alice, to celebrate Mom and Dad's wedding anniversary. One lazy afternoon while the girls napped upstairs, Augusta and I sat at the kitchen table talking. I asked her to tell me about our family before I was born.

"Even the sad parts?" she whispered.

"Yes." I moved closer to her.

Augusta folded her hands in her lap. She had a faraway look in her eye as she began to speak.

"Your mother used to hide sometimes when the four kids were expected home from school. She had difficulty facing the loud shouts and chattering of all of them bounding through the door together. I remember one afternoon she walked over to the curtain by the living room window, about to hide behind it. I felt so sad for her."

Augusta said that she locked eyes with my mother, squeezed her shoulder, and said, "Don't you worry, Mrs. Husch, I'll go fix the snack."

Augusta turned her head and looked directly into my eyes. "Your mother joined us not five minutes later, ready to greet the children who'd settled down some and were eating their sandwiches. She thanked me with just a look from her dark, sad eyes."

Augusta looked down then and shook her head slowly. "Hmm, mmm, mmm. Those were some hard days."

The Yin and Yang of Mom

As I grew up, I became finely tuned to Mom's mood changes and could tell with the utterance of a single word which mother she was from day-to-day. My world changed according to her mood swings. As she morphed from her exciting self, verging on madness, to her limp, sad self, my emotions rode along, as though I was seated behind her, hanging on tight as she rode her bike uphill and down. I worried about her unceasingly.

Mom was one of the original "New Agers." She rode her bike all over our conservative town. She baked crunchy granola and taught yoga classes in our backyard. She studied Transcendental Meditation and worked for a local social health agency teaching sex education to Girl Scouts.

Always, following a few months of a high, Mom would plummet. She stopped listening to her Russian lessons, and her bike leaned lonesome against the garage wall. Her voice changed from confident and musical to timid and dull.

A yin and yang resided in our house. There was laughter and singing. Stories were read aloud. We five kids were expected to study hard and do well in school, and we did. Yet, there lurked a dark undercurrent. Mental illness bumped up against the security of privilege and plenty. Mom and Dad's frequent loud arguments were upsetting to us kids. Dad shouted and slammed doors. His tightened jaw and gritty words spoken through clenched teeth were scary to me. Mom appeared frantic in response to Dad's anger.

Tension built between them, and the fight always ended the same way, with Mom sobbing, in a voice not motherly, but like a hurt child. A few times, she ran straight out the front door and down the sidewalk, swinging her arms as if they wanted to punch something, or someone.

We loved our parents, but this was embarrassing and deeply unsettling. What would the neighbors think? Grownups shouldn't act like this, not in a large white wooden house on a circular road where tall leafy trees canopy the street and children play freely for hours on hot summer days.

Mom's Kitchen

Mom's kitchen was the life-breath of the entire house. It was full of goodies, like homemade granola and yogurt, or maybe some lentil soup with a fresh salad and homegrown beansprouts. There were mysterious items as well, especially in the fridge. Mom had trouble tossing anything, probably rooted in her Depression-era childhood.

"Don't waste food!" she emphatically told us.

"Hey, Mom," my brother Tony once joked when we gathered in the kitchen as adults. "I just found the tuna sandwich you made for me in fourth grade." We had tried sneaking rotten, moldy stuff out to the trash when

Mom wasn't in the room. But she inspected trashcans too, so this wasn't easy.

Back to Mom's granola. Most St. Louisians had never heard of that hippie cereal. This was back in the day of Corn Flakes and Wheaties. Somewhere, somehow, Mom discovered a recipe for "Crunchy Granola," and she began to roast oats, seeds, coconut, and wheat germ in the oven. She added a bit of honey and some raisins and gave anyone who passed through the house a small batch to take home.

"This is good for you, very healthy." No one refused her gift.

People felt welcome in our home, and that feeling flowed from Mom. In her kitchen she felt free to be her authentic self. She prioritized not fitting into expected social norms. She was known as a character, a beloved character. The kitchen had a lot of traffic with five children, our playmates, and Mom's people, friends she'd met in yoga classes, encounter groups, and human potential gatherings. These new friends of Mom's might as well have been from some exotic land, so different were they from the usual suburban company we were accustomed to. Dad usually went into his den and closed the door to read, but sometimes he was drawn to the kitchen and the lively conversation. I'd see him smile then. I think he needed this side of Mom to pull him out of his comfort zone of solitude.

The table was the center of the kitchen. It was covered with this and that: salt and pepper shakers, small vases with pansies, or whatever tiny flower snippets Mom found on her bike rides or walks. She placed her Daily Word booklets upright in a small box. Guests might read a page and let go of some needless worry.

The shelves above the low radiator were filled with unmatched mugs. The matching cups and saucers in the cabinets were rarely used. Instead, everyone selected a mug from the shelf that fit his or her mood. Maybe the round one with bright flowers, or the engraved peace-sign cup, or the pink one with "Breathe" printed in large letters.

Mom loved listening to Cardinal baseball games on summer afternoons while putzing about in the kitchen. Harry Caray, the famed baseball announcer's voice poured from her transistor radio perched on the shelf above the sink. Mom cheered along with the crowd at the game.

There was a wide picture window above the sink. It looked down the curved driveway where the old linden tree's curved branches offered appreciated shade on hot, humid summer days. Mom hung wind chimes from branches and placed a bird feeder on a stand. She loved feeding seeds to the birds. She was horrified if a squirrel shimmied up the stand to the feeder. She'd bolt out of the house, shouting and clapping her hands, shooing it away. She sometimes added kitchen scraps to the feeder, tossing the rest onto her compost pile behind the garage. Composting was another undertaking my mother began decades before it was mainstream.

Shattered

David made us laugh. Teachers, friends from school, everyone adored David. He was fifteen years old that June day in 1963 when he and two friends were riding bikes through the Missouri countryside. An inexperienced driver slammed the accelerator instead of the brake as David pedaled in front of her car. I was eight that summer day when I came face to face with the death of my big brother. For Joan, losing her twin felt like a part of herself had been torn out. We all missed him so.

I tried hard to protect Mom from becoming too sad. I threw away any pieces of mail or catalogs that arrived for David. Being a kid with lots of interests, he had signed up for magazine subscriptions and mailing lists. I thought it best that Mom not be reminded of David by seeing these envelopes with his name on them.

Our family shattered the day we lost David.

Mom and Yoga

After David died, Mom sank lower than low. A thick cloud settled in the house. Even the house itself had trouble breathing. We moved like zombies through the rooms. Mom didn't cry. Unlike her frequent sobbing during manic swings, depression left her numb. The rest of us joined her this time. David was gone. Every day felt worse than the one before.

Aunt Peggy came by almost every day to sit with Mom. One day, weeks after David's accident, Aunt Peggy said in her gentle voice with its melodic lilt, "Annie, I've found something that I think might help you.

There's a yoga class offered through St. Louis Community College. Let's try it. I'll go with you."

Mom met her sister's eyes. She dug deep for some semblance of strength and nodded.

That Wednesday evening, Aunt Peggy came by for Mom. They dressed in loose fitting cotton clothes and carried a towel under their arms. Walking down the front path side by side, Aunt Peggy gently wrapped her arm around Mom's shoulders. The following week they returned and did not miss a session all semester. Mom began moving around a bit more at home, making a cup of tea for herself and a peanut butter and jelly sandwich for me.

When the morning came that I saw Mom sitting outside on the shady brick patio, I breathed more deeply than I had since David's accident. I went out the back screen door and down the two wide wooden steps to where Mom sat on the green wicker chair on the patio. I climbed up and nestled into her lap.

One evening I joined Mom for her yoga class. We took off our shoes and laid our towels down on the mats provided. The adults in the room smiled at me, as adults do when a child is present in an otherwise adult scene. I crossed my legs into a double lotus position and got hearty appreciative comments about my flexible young legs. They then laughed at their own rather stiff attempts.

After a year or two, Mom trained to be a yoga teacher, and she never stopped teaching. She taught at the community college, on the grass in our backyard, weather permitting, or in the living room when too cold or wet to be outdoors. Practicing and teaching yoga helped Mom heal her sorrow.

Hi, I'm David. Don't You Remember Me?

I wasn't feeling well, so I stayed home from school one day in 1971, my sophomore year of high school. When my friend Mary finished her last class, she walked to my house. Mom wasn't home. It was around four pm when the doorbell rang.

"I'll get it." Mary shot out of the room and down the stairs.

When she returned, she wasn't alone. A young man was with her. He seemed around Joan's age, twenty-one or so. He strode into my room as if he belonged in our house. I was shocked.

He jammed his hands into his pockets and looked right at me as he paced back and forth.

"Hi, I'm David! Don't you remember me?"

I said nothing.

"I'm David. Joan's twin!"

Who was this person, standing in my room and proclaiming to be David, my dead brother? My heart pounded. Could he be a ghost? It seemed like an episode from The Twilight Zone. A crazy man had pushed his way into our home. But, even weirder, he seemed authentic and sure that he was David.

"Where's Joan?" he asked.

"Joan's away at college." The words caught a bit in my dry throat.

"Oh." He looked devastated. Disappointed and sad.

"I think you need to leave now," I heard myself say. The man turned then, his shoulders slumped. He walked out of my room and down the stairs. We listened to the front door close.

"What just happened?" I looked wide-eyed at Mary.

"I'm not sure," Mary said. "You do know that was Mark Evans, don't you?"

I had heard of him. Words like schizophrenia were mentioned when his name came up.

When Mary had answered the doorbell, Mark asked if Joan was home.

"No, only Sally is home."

"May I come in?"

Recognizing him, Mary opened the door and let him in.

When Mom got home later, I remained shaken.

"Mark Evans came into the house, into my room, claiming he was David. He left when I asked him to, but it scared me."

Mom listened intently. Then she left my room, went downstairs, sat at the little telephone table, and took out her blue book of phone numbers.

"Hello, Mark. This is Ann Husch. I'm calling to thank you for stopping by today to let us know you are thinking about David. It means a lot to us."

I stared at my mother. Branches of respect for her spread through my body. She understood that when he came to our door, Mark believed he was David. He felt compelled to come home, to our house, to let us know he was alive. Mom's assured understanding of Mark's actions impressed me. Her calm, sincere phone call to thank him warmed me.

I wanted no other mother.

I Love

I love you so much, Mom. My love for you hurts. Picturing you, I ache and feel on the verge of tears. Your face is framed by dark curls that later turn silver. I watch you apply red lipstick. No mirror is needed. Somehow you make red lipstick look natural. In summer you wear shirtwaist cotton dresses. You are pretty.

Your voice is lyrical. I love when you read to me. I love going downtown to Kiel Auditorium on Saturday afternoons for the Young Persons' Symphony concerts. You always let me get soda and potato chips during intermission. I love going ice-skating together. We put on our warm jackets, hats, and gloves. We lace up our skates and laugh at the sight of our steamy breath in the cold afternoon air.

Skating

Do you remember the day you took me skating at Steinberg Rink in Forest Park? You were skating ahead of me like a graceful swan. You went faster and faster, leaning forward and lifting your face high in the cool air. Your arms stretched out to either side of your body, your back leg straight behind you. You were flying. But then, Oh no, Mom. You're going to fall!

Now you're sprawled on the ice. Your long legs slide wide open in front of you. Your arms are limp at your sides. Why don't you get up, Mom? I feel so...what? What am I feeling? Scared? Not exactly. Sorry? Yes, I am sorry you fell, sorry that you are not steady on the ice, not steady in your moods.

Moms shouldn't skate the way you skate. They shouldn't fall. A mom should move easily beside her little girl. She should smile down at her daughter and clasp her small hand reassuringly. Anyone watching feels happy and peaceful as mother and daughter glide in sync to the waltz music heard through speakers positioned around the rink. I wish hard for this scene to be you and me. I want this mom with me. I seldom have her, though. I look at you there on the ice. Get up!

But you don't get up. You don't brush yourself off and reassure me that you are okay. You stay on the ice, crying. You have the attention of everyone. I move away from you, out of the way, uncertain what to do. Then a rink guard lends you a gloved hand and helps you up. I want to go home.

Purging My Upset

Home was often a place of comfort. But what was happening to my intelligent, kind parents when they fought? They loved each other. They loved us. But they argued often, and tension was always at bay, ready to fill the house. Mom's mental illness, especially her mania, contributed to the unease, but the impact my dad's troubled childhood had on him also played into the unrest. So we were all swept into the chaos.

I often felt anxiety bubbling inside me when away from home. I worried about Mom if I couldn't see her. Was she okay? What if she got upset and I wasn't there to hold her hand? My worry manifested as nausea. I'd find my way to a restroom, and I'd vomit.

Mom thought my upset stomach was the result of David's death. So, she sent me to see a child psychiatrist when I was in fourth grade. She pulled me out of school early once a week. I was mortified.

"Where are you going?" the other kids asked.

I mumbled something about a stupid appointment my mom made for me. Once I saw a fifth-grade girl from my school leaving the office as I was arriving. We pretended not to see each other.

I do not remember any conversations with the psychiatrist about David's accident, my parents' fights, or Mom's mood swings. I made every effort to answer her questions so that she would think I was cured and no longer needed to visit her.

"What is most important to you?" I remember her asking.

"World Peace," I said.

She must have told Mom I did not need to return. I was relieved.

In the summer following my senior year of high school, my parents hosted a party. I helped Augusta pass trays of appetizers. One of the guests was our pediatrician. We called him Dr. Al because he was a family friend, as well as our doctor.

When I offered an appetizer to him, Dr. Al said quietly to me, "Did it ever occur to you that your upset as a child was related to your parents' frequent yelling matches and the unpredictability in your home?"

My belly did a somersault. I did not answer him.

A Kaleidoscope

Manic depression did not define my mother. Like an ever-changing kaleidoscope, it was Mom's creativity, her love of nature, her quick mind, and her ingenuity that defined her. She and Dad played bridge regularly with friends. While Dad knew the rules and had studied smart moves, Mom was the better player. Like most anything she undertook, her bridge style was outside the box and intuitive. It was these contrasting characteristics, her bright, creative mind alongside her manic spurts that baffled her children.

We knew and loved this warmhearted woman. Why then did we all live with seemingly unnecessary anxiety? Why, as a child, did I feel responsible for Mom's happiness and guilty when she was depressed? Why did my oldest sister Peggy believe that she was a bad little girl? Why did Tony isolate himself in his tiny bedroom as a child, quiet and somber? Why does Joan, to this day, question Mom's love? And if Joan's twin, our brother, David, had lived, would we Husches have had a different experience as a family? So many questions swirl round and round in my mind.

Tony inherited Mom's bipolar swings, and his mood changes were even more extreme than hers. In his late thirties, Tony sold his successful vineyard and winery in California, uprooted his wife and two young sons, and moved back to St. Louis. During a low ebb, he lay curled in a fetal position on the guest room floor at Mom and Dad's house.

He once told me, "The high of mania beats any mood-enhancing drug. Better than heroin!" Was this exhilaration the reason Mom resisted meds that would temper her euphoria?

At age forty-eight, Tony chose suicide, the excruciating pain of his depressions too much to bear.

Detach to Attach

Early in my life, I began closely observing relationships in other families. I intently studied those that seemed effortless, stress-free, and loving. I began to educate myself on the power of choice. I realized I could determine my own life path, and I carefully created ties with steady and accepting people.

As a teen, I was drawn to a boyfriend who was self-confident. He had a calm way about him, was a good listener, and made me laugh. Of course, he had various moods, but they weren't extreme. I married this young man a few years later.

Bill's childhood experience of parent interaction was the opposite of my own. He remembers only one instance of loud shouting. During our busiest years raising children while juggling household management with careers, I instinctively confronted Bill when upset, expecting him to engage in verbally hashing out our differences, face to face, in the heat of frustration, as Mom and Dad had shown me. Bill, however, confounded me by turning his back on me and walking silently into another room.

I made an appointment with a marriage counselor.

"Not everyone is like you, Sally. Bill needs time to digest your upset and process his role in it. He isn't abandoning you, he's sorting things out quietly. Next time, try waiting until a peaceful moment to talk with him, rather than confronting him in the heated moment." This one pearl of advice was well worth the cost of my sessions.

It takes a lifelong effort to change default practices. But I reap rewards today because I decided to change. Now I feel a powerful attachment to Mom. Ironically, the attachment occurred by detaching from her.

Mom's Mania

Years later, as I was tucking my kids into bed, Marcy called. Marcy was Mom's good friend. She'd been living in the house with Mom for a few months.

"Your mom seems wild. She fell yesterday." Marcy sounded panicked.

I thanked her for contacting me, and we strategized about Mom and her extreme manic swing. I knew how erratic and unpredictable her behavior could be. She often lost her balance and fell. She frequently cut herself while cooking. Then she'd wail and jump up and down, holding her sliced finger in the air. I knew the toll the manic phase was taking on Marcy.

After we said goodbye, I made myself a cup of tea, pulled down my books on mood swings, and started to read. When I woke the following day, my stomach was in a knot. I called Mom and listened to her incessant, egocentric chatter. I asked if she had been sleeping. She dodged the question.

"I sleep at unusual moments."

I asked about her Lithium. "Are you continuing to take it?"

"I think I'll stop," she said. "Don't need it anymore. But I'll continue the antidepressants."

Oh wow. She's revving her engine. Doesn't she know this will bring her crashing down into that sinister dark hole?

I Hate

Mom, I hate feeling that I'm responsible for your wellbeing. I hate that we aren't easily close to each other, especially now that I am a married woman with my own children. I hate that you cried so often during my childhood. You wailed, really, like someone badly injured. I hated the times you ran crying down the street, embarrassing the whole family. I hate that your feelings were hurt if I spent time away from home, away from you. Your hurt feelings negated the time we spent together.

Even now, when I call you from San Diego, I hate that I'm listening not to what you say but listening instead for which mother you are today. Are you Up-Mom or Down-Mom? As a child, I tried to protect you from your depression. I hated seeing you in so much pain. I did not understand what caused you to plunge. So during my twenties, I read everything I could find on manic depression.

Speaking of those manic episodes, did I hate those too? They, too, were upsetting but in a vastly different way. You weren't in the painful depths of the black hole. But you were over-the-top, in every way: too energized, too loud, cried too easily, and laughed too wildly. It was as though you never slept. These highs shook me. What's wrong with you?

I always longed for you to still yourself at the midpoint of your swing. Stop there, Mom! Not too high, not too low. Just right in the middle. Please remain Middle-Mom. I wanted to shake you. I hated the ever-present cloud hovering over me, the cloud that rained anxiety. It's not fair, Mom. You need to be the grownup.

Hi Mom

Mom rebelled against needlessly throwing anything into the trash. Stapled envelopes from junk mail became shopping lists. She made cutout hearts from saved greeting cards and included them in the frequent letters she mailed to family and friends.

Following her death in 2011, her grandchildren met at the kitchen table to cut out oodles of colorful hearts and tuck them into "Mimi's" memorial service programs. The many who had gathered that snowy February day to honor Ann grinned and were warmed as the hearts tumbled onto their laps.

Shortly after returning home to San Diego following Mom's memorial service, I gathered my mat and towel and headed to my favorite local yoga spot. The studio is on the second floor. Out the windows are treetops and sky. Across the street is the Darshan Bakery and Cafe. Darshan's is as kindred to yoga as a bakery can ever be, as monks from The Self Realization Fellowship down the street run it. They understand, as I do, that buttery croissants and dark chocolate are not simply heavenly but genuinely spiritual.

Shavasana, also known as the Corpse Pose, is the closing pose of every yoga class, performed lying on the back, eyes closed, and relaxing completely. Usually Shavasana became a daydream of pastry and coffee for me. But on this day, so soon after Mom's death, as I lay still, eyes closed in my Shavasana pose, I felt a warm human hand gently take mine. I wasn't startled. I knew this was Mom in the room, beside me, holding my hand. "Hi Mom." I smiled.

Middle-Mom

It's been over a decade since you died peacefully during your afternoon nap. When I look in the mirror at my now sixty-six-year-old face, I like seeing your face in my reflection. I miss you, and yet you live on for all of us through the many memories you gave us. Everyone plays Russian Bank, the card game you taught us, and then, taught to each of our kids. It's as though you are looking over our shoulders when we get together to play.

We imagine your voice saying, "Are you sure you aren't missing a move?" Then we hear you shouting, "Tonk!" if we neglect to notice a move.

Tonk meant our turn was ended. Your turn again. How were you always able to see every possible move with just a swift scan? That brilliant brain of yours. So quick, so complicated.

Honestly, Mom, most of what I care deeply about in life comes from your influence. My love of nature, the night sky, the ocean and mountains, books, and movies. I don't cry as loudly as you did in the sad parts, but I know where you'd cry.

I often think of you and carry you with me during my day, as though you are still alive. You are quiet, though. And, I admit, this is nice. I guess I can now tap into your best essence. Your warmth was overflowing with real empathy and love. When I listen to music, you are there. Symphonic music, piano music. When I see a musical or a play, you are beside me, alert. And of course, whenever I spend time in nature.

"Go outside and play," you insisted if I stayed inside too long. Like you, I now carry a bag on my walks, especially beach walks, to pick up litter.

My favorite photo of you and me together is one taken at the beach in my hometown of Leucadia, California. We each have a hat on. Mine's floppy, yours, Western style. We are standing close, arm in arm. You are the Middle-Mom I always longed to have. Not Up-Mom or Down-Mom. I framed this picture. It sits on my piano.

And so, we are still together.

WHIPLASH:
LIFE WHEN A JOVIAL, HYPOMANIC DAD IS FLUNG
INTO FULL-BLOWN MANIC-DEPRESSIVE ILLNESS
BY SUSAN DELPHINE DELANEY

Susan Delphine Delaney, MD, MS, is a Psychiatrist in private practice. She is a graduate of the University of Maryland; has her MS in Physiology from the University of Wisconsin, 1974; and the University of Wisconsin also granted her MD in 1977. She is a graduate of the Menninger School of Psychiatry and has four years of study in the Topeka Institute for Psychoanalysis. She is the author of two books.

ରୀ   ରୀ   ରୀ

For most of my childhood, my dad was a jovial hypomanic. He'd grab all the kids, five of us, and we'd march up the alley to an old farmstead and harvest blackberries. Back home, he'd make a piecrust and allow us kids to put in the berries, sugar, and flour. Then he'd top the pie and pop it into our gas oven. "Never take a pie out of the oven until the juices run out," he taught us.

He was a joker, loved puns, and never met a person he didn't like.

He drank a six-pack after the children's bedtime of 8:30 pm. Today I understand that when a male drinks more than four beers it's called heavy hazardous drinking. The alcohol did something to him, proven by the yelling and fighting that we kids heard every night between our parents. It was like he became another person. It was terrifying to us kids to hear them fight. They smashed all their china dishes and had to get melamine ones. I know now that the alcohol woke up his daytime-dormant manic-depressive genes and turned his jovial hypomania into mild mania, resolving overnight when he sobered up.

Dad was a medical photographer at George Washington University Medical School in Washington, DC. He worked six days a week. When the three oldest of us kids were old enough, he started taking one of us with him to work on Saturdays, in rotation.

At eleven, I was the oldest when Dad started taking us to work. I hung out with a Japanese female graduate student, quietly watching her as she cut a small square in the top of the shell of a fertile egg, added compounds, and then sealed them up with a fabric patch without contaminating them. This relationship, I believe, gave me the vision to go to graduate school myself, getting a Masters in Human Physiology. I later got an MD from the same school. Later still, I graduated from the Menninger School of Psychiatry and studied for four and a half years at the Topeka Institute of Psychoanalysis. I served five years as a Staff Psychiatrist at the Menninger Hospital. I taught a class to the residents. I supervised medical students and residents.

My brother hung with Dad in the photo lab and he became a professional photographer, serving as the photographer for the Environmental Protection Agency for its first 25 years.

My sister went wherever scientists were working with live animals, and loves all animals and humans to this day. She raised five kids and provided a home to our brother with Down syndrome for eighteen years.

Dad was a fine, happy-go-lucky dad in the daytime, and a loving father to us kids. He was the kind of dad that young men are these days, fully involved in the care of the children. He changed diapers. He cut our fingernails and toenails. He walked the floor with sick kids. It was only at night, when we kids were in bed, when he drank and the yelling began.

In 1964, when I was fifteen, my happy-go-lucky dad, age forty-five, became deeply depressed. No one in our extended family had ever seen him like this. At home, in the daytime, he would watch TV, not moving, even when the picture started rolling, as black and white TVs of that era were wont to do. Enter one of the MD-PhDs at the medical school, a cell researcher not involved in the care of actual human beings. The scientist had prescriptive privileges and he prescribed amphetamines for Dad.

This drug permanently woke up Dad's previously semi-dormant manic-depressive genes. Dad went from being palpably depressed to absolutely manic. Once, he decided we were moving, got a U-Haul, packed up our apartment, and took us from Riverdale, Maryland to Annapolis. Annapolis was the full extent of his planning. We were just kids then, and when he encouraged my sister and I to ride on top of the cab of the U-Haul, we did. There was an amber light above and behind us. I remember how beautiful my redheaded sister's hair looked, blowing in the wind, backlit by that amber light. At the time it was fun. Today, of course, I see the danger for my sister and I.

Before long, Mom got the police involved and had him committed. I'll never forget them coming to get him. At first, they were jokey with him, "no big deal." Then I watched them handcuff my father, throw his wallet on a chair and hustle him away. Although I knew it was necessary, although I knew it was coming, seeing a father I had respected and looked up for fifteen years humiliated, arrested, and hauled away was heartbreaking. He was sent from the State Hospital to the VA hospital, where he would remain for two years. Dad never worked again.

It was early summer when Dad was in the manic part of manic depression and involuntarily hospitalized. My first cousin, my godmother, got her husband to drive the U-Haul to their house and filled their garage with the contents of our apartment. We spent the summer with my cousin's family. She had six kids and was five months pregnant with her seventh. My Mom moved my oldest brother and me back to our old neighborhood to a new apartment while the younger kids in my family remained with my cousin for a year.

Although medicine was my dream, I went to college and majored in chemistry because Dad was still in the hospital and Mom was not well. I knew that I might have to leave school and support the younger kids, and chemistry was my ticket to a government job in the DC area. Hundreds of lab jobs would have been available, if it came to that.

That decision to major in chemistry turned into a huge blessing. There were only sixteen chemistry majors in my year, and we were together in lab twenty-five hours a week. So, I had this wonderful chemistry family within the department. It saved me! Living in the dorm saved me. So much went right to preserve the future of my dreams.

I had no money for medical school, so I decided to work and save half of my income to prepare. I took a job as an adhesives chemist in California. It was fantastic to get away from my still chaotic family. My dad's illness affected the other four kids much more deeply than it me.

Just before I moved to California, I married a Stanford University chemistry major. While he was finishing his final semester, a recruiter for a large computer firm lured me to write operating systems for large scientific computers for twice as much as I was making as a chemist. I said yes. When my husband graduated, I recruited him to sign on too. We banked the bonus I received for recruiting him, and also banked half of our salaries. After eighteen months, he was in love with computers and I was not. We moved to Madison, WI for him to pursue a graduate degree in computer science. And for me to begin my journey to medicine.

I loved medical school. By the time I started I had a full and rich life in Madison. Psychiatry always fascinated me, and a rotation fourth year cinched my decision to become a psychiatrist. I was one of the first Psychiatrists to be Board Certified as an Addiction Psychiatrist.

Dad turned mean when his manic-depressive illness activated, and that never left him. I had been so close to him, and now I felt like I almost hated him. It was very confusing. When released from the VA hospital, he became one of the first Americans to take lithium. It controlled his illness for the most part, but his continued drinking pumped the meanness. He was humiliated at his downfall and lashed out at anyone and everyone. Soon he was blackout drunk every day, although he continued his lithium until his death at age seventy-two.

People have asked me if my father's illness led me to become a psychiatrist. There is no simple answer to this question. I really, really like psychiatric patients. This may go back to the idyllic relationship I enjoyed with my dad, when he was a jovial hypomanic: fishing, hiking in the woods, picking blackberries and making a pie, as well as his equal co-parenting of us. I was viscerally aware that he had a very good side. And that his illness, brought on fully by the ill-advised prescription of amphetamines, was just another side of him.

Today, as a psychiatrist, I have about 50 drugs I can prescribe. Today, I could have had dad well in three weeks. Back then, when I was a junior in high school, there were only had two drugs: Thorazine, an anti-psychotic, and Chloral Hydrate, a sleeping pill.

Now I know how to carefully dismantle a person's complex psychiatric situation, piece by piece. My care in assessing the fullness of a patient's strengths, as well as assessing the presence of every active psychiatric gene, puts me in a position of being able to heal people. If the person has both bipolar disorder and attention deficit disorder, I treat the bipolar first, and if there is an excellent therapeutic alliance, I slowly and carefully add a stimulant. No one knows more viscerally than I do the dangers here. However, if after careful assessment I can trust the patient to understand the signs of increasing manic-depressive activity from the stimulant, trust patient to stop the stimulant; and trust the patient to call me immediately if there are problems, then I can carefully and thoughtfully manage both illnesses.

Having a dad who was a jovial hypomanic, and who was fully involved in caring for me and my siblings until I was fifteen, and then having him become full-blown manic-depressive, mean, and a black-out drunk daily until his death, was a major whiplash. But a variety of miracles followed that allowed me to pursue my education, debt-free, to eventually become a psychiatrist who is a synthetic thinker, able to dismantle complex psychiatric problems, while treating my patients with compassion and respect. I would not be the psychiatrist I am today without my backstory. I am grateful for each of the challenges that led me to this place, and I am grateful to all of those who helped me to become all that I could be.

I Cried When I Learned
By Trish Eisman

Trish Eisman, MEd, LPCC, is a psychotherapist in private practice in New Mexico. She specializes in treating addictions, childhood trauma, and mood disorders. When not seeing clients, she binge-watches surrealist Scandinavian series and teaches her miniature poodle new tricks.

❦   ❦   ❦

When I was twenty and suffering from depression so severe I felt like my bones were full of lead, my therapist said, "Ask your mother if you were ever depressed as a baby."

I didn't think babies could be depressed, and I didn't understand the point of asking for my mother's perspective on anything, given how crazy I was beginning to understand that she was. But I had learned quickly enough that my therapist was much wiser than I was, so in the next phone call, I asked my mother the question.

"Yes, but only when you were alone," she said. I asked for more explanation.

"Well," she said, "You would be playing in the morning, and you seemed pretty happy. Then your dad would go to work and your brother and sister (three and five when I was born) would go to school. And as soon as you were alone, you would get very sad. You would just sit on your rocking horse in the corner. You would sort of come back to life when they came home. So you were pretty depressed, but just when you were alone."

"Uh, I was alone with you, wasn't I?" I murmured. At that point my mother drifted into some subject-changing land, only at this time I was aware enough not to follow her.

I cried so many times over this story. I remember crying when I told my therapist about the answer to the question. I cried while getting my masters degree in therapy when we learned about how babies develop and attach. How they try to sooth their shattered little nervous systems when they are left alone, like I was, with someone who seemed randomly gleeful, or checked out, or raging, with no other family members to witness, buffer, or possibly comfort me.

I cried even harder when I watched the video of the "Still Face" experiment, where a mother was instructed to stare blankly at her baby, who went from happily interacting to confusion to piercing wails. (Look it up on YouTube. "Still Face Experiment." Brace yourself.) My classmates and I discussed how, as the baby became more upset, the mother's blank face felt more and more psychotic to the viewers. If that's what a blank face could do, what about a rage face? And what about a rage face that lasted for more than two minutes?

I cried furiously when, after taking Prozac and suddenly feel "normal" for the first time in my life, I learned that the developing brain gathers its "set points" of neurotransmitters (such as serotonin, the "safety" messenger) from the surrounding environment. When I understood that, as a result, people who are repeatedly traumatized as infants often require antidepressants for the rest of their lives because their brain will never be "normal" any other way.

The trauma response systems of fight, flight, and freeze are programmed into us from birth. Freeze is crucial, especially for toddlers, because prehistoric tiny humans were prey for three motion-based hunters: Snakes, big cats, and birds. I spent another afternoon in an empty classroom in graduate school sobbing after I learned that depression is a kind of extended freeze response. If you just hide in a burrow and stay still all the time, the monster won't see you.

I'm a huge fan of evolutionary biology. In the same way that freeze is an instinctive response to threat, our fight response makes our jaw clench (so we can bite) and our hands ball into fists (so we can hit). I believe that tears, like all emotional expressions, are there to serve a purpose. My parents seriously believed that children's tears were manipulative bids for attention that the child of course did not deserve.

When I was about seven years old, my mother came across me crying and snapped, "What do you want?"

"To see a psychiatrist," I said, having just learned what therapists were sometimes called.

"Why do you want that?" my mother asked.

"Because," I said, "Either I'm crazy or you are." I did not get an appointment with a mental health professional.

Another thing that happens when you are traumatized: Your immune system and gastrointestinal tract shut down. After all, who cares about digesting a meal if it could be your last? Who cares about getting a cold next week when you need adrenaline and blood flow right now to fight for your life? I spent much of first and second grades at home "sick;" I suspect my lack of attendance set off alarm bells, because I was forced to attend daily in third grade. Late morning was the worst time because my stomach would swell with painful gas. I went to the nurse's office, at least once a week, sometimes twice, and she would have me lie down on her paper-covered exam table, to "have a rest."

On the wall by the table was a poster that I read repeatedly. "I am me and I am OK," read the first line over pictures of little kids wearing costumes and playing. This scene etched into my brain so indelibly that I recognized it years later as a poster from Transactional Analysis, one of the first forms of psychotherapy used in the 70's.

You can imagine how hard I bawled when I found those old textbooks as a beginning therapist and recognized those odd little drawings of children in costumes busily being themselves, and OK. I realized that in third grade, I found a way to leave class, go to a cool, soothing office staffed by a quietly nurturing adult, lie on a couch for about forty-five minutes, and read that I was OK. I got to have these "appointments" twice a week if necessary. I creatively found a form of psychotherapy for myself as a child.

When I was in junior high, I met two kids at the roller skating rink who needed a ride home. I was extremely cautious when asking my mother on the pay phone if we could give them a ride. I even said, "I told them we probably couldn't." My mom brightly and cheerfully responded that of course she could do that, she wanted to do that.

Well, by the time she arrived at the skating rink, she had "turned" (is it any wonder zombie movies are so popular with my generation?). She was wearing that face that I later recognized in the movie Mommy Dearest, a sarcastic, vitriolic look that says You Really Should Have Known Better. The ride to drop those kids home was excruciating. But the real lesson happened at school Monday when I saw them and started to awkwardly apologize.

"Oh no, It's OK. Our mom is just like that when she's drunk too." My mother hadn't been drunk, but I was starting to understand.

Probably I learned as much from addiction recovery groups and literature as I did in graduate school. I have heard that everyone cries at their first 12-step meeting. The relief of being recognized and realizing you are not alone, morally deficient, or unique is such an intense experience. I went to an Adult Children of Alcoholics meeting and wept, silently and without sharing, recognizing myself in everyone's stories. I was pretty confident my mother was not an alcoholic, but oh, could I relate to each person in that room. Every bit of perfectionism, self-hatred, imposter-syndrome, fear of anyone getting to know me…it went on and on.

Later a woman from the meeting told me about para-alcoholics, indistinguishable from alcoholics except for the drinking part. After hearing my story, she shrugged and said, "Or maybe your mom was just crazy, you know?" My mother never got an official diagnosis, and Bipolar Disorder fit as well as Borderline Personality Disorder, both of which were as good as para-alcoholic. The result was the same: I was a mess.

When I was 30, I met the man who became my husband. On our first Christmas, after only seven months of knowing me, my guy had me open his gift: A beautiful maroon V-neck sweater that fit me perfectly. I wore mostly maroon and dark blue in those days, and mostly V-necks, or at least a round neck, because anything around my neck always made me feel like I was suffocating. I opened the gift that my mother sent me: A lavender turtleneck.

My guy raised his eyebrows and asked, "is this some inside family joke I don't understand yet?" I cried until I laughed.

I believe that crying serves a distinct purpose in direct opposition to the beliefs of my parents while growing up. Crying lets everyone know, including yourself, that you are grieving, and that the pain and hurt you are suffering is real and true. My eyes well up when something feels intensely true for me, because I worked hard to own my own experience, regardless of what others tried to make me believe.

Now, my eyes will fill with tears when I tell a patient who is despairing of getting better that I have hope, and she needs to hold on and trust me that things will someday be all right. People in every culture weep together when sad to show their sadness is genuine and to share it with others. In this way, tears connect and heal, like a balm to the wound of life's pain. Tears are a wet, salty, snotty reality that we cannot deny in ourselves or others.

Even when you have tears of happiness, you are grieving the fact that the wonderful thing that is happening now has not happened before. You are grieving the past, because it is only now past. You cannot actually grieve something painful until and unless the reality dramatically changes. When I cried with happiness at my beloved's Christmas gift and its contrast with my mother's, I began to grieve all the years of not being seen by the person closest to me. I could only cry with joy when I had evidence that I was truly seen.

I am grateful to have survived and to live in a time when the majority of people see tears as real and would never describe therapy as touchy-feely hippie nonsense. Each time I see a famous athlete or performer come out as a person whose depression has required psychotherapy, I am grateful to live in a culture where healing emotional wounds is a badge of honor. I am so full of gratitude that now my tears usually turn into laughter. And contained in this laughter is the message I live and share daily: Your joy is precious. You are precious.

Summers and Winters
By Paula Fayerman

Paula Fayerman, MD, FCFP, is a Family Medicine Doctor in Calgary, Canada. Currently she works in Sexual and Reproductive Health, and has worked with adolescents with complex issues including homelessness and addiction. Her personal life, growing up with parents with mental health concerns, as well as her professional life, working with patients with adverse childhood experiences, stimulates her continued learning in trauma theory and treatment. She also studies Integrative Medicine and holistic modes of healing including Yoga, Qi gong and meditation. She honours the powers of relationship and compassion for her own healing, and in her work with others.

"Does it hurt?" I asked my father. My hand reached out to point at, but not to touch, his belly.

He lay on his back on the far-right side of the double bed. I stood close at his right. The sheets were off and he lay in boxer shorts, showing his low abdomen. At nine-years-old, I was only a foot taller than the bed. My face was just above his belly. So close to him, I looked down at the patchwork quilt of scars.

Lines crisscrossed his stomach, oozing thick yellow pus. I was most upset that I couldn't make out his belly button, the way his stomach looked was so weird. I wondered why I had never seen his stomach like this before. I had glimpsed his stomach with a thick white dressing that was stained yellow, but he usually wore a brown paisley cotton nightgown, loosely tied. That day the nightgown was open lying to each side of his body.

This was the first time I saw his open wounds and distorted abdomen. The surgery to fix his bowel disease, Crohn's, had almost killed him. The way his nightgown was draped reminds me now of the unzipped body bag that held cadavers I dissected as a medical student. Maybe he had protected me until that moment when I got a glimpse of the seriousness of his illness. Perhaps that day, it was just too painful for him to have something touching the wound. He had developed abscesses that drained for many months.

His bedroom curtains were open, and a weak light came in from windows by the far end of the bed. I can't remember what season it was, nor if there were any seasons that year. I can't remember if the television was on or off. Generally, it was on while he watched hockey or football and slept. That day, I focused on his sores.

"I'm okay, Paula," he said, closing his eyes and turning his thin, tired face away from me to the left. "Can you let me rest now?"

Why did he turn away? My adult self has compassion for a gravely ill parent of a nine-year-old, and how hard it must have been for him to see me so scared. The child in me thought, "Don't bother your father, he doesn't want you to bother him."

I left his room and walked the short hallway back to my own bedroom, all pink and ruffled. The portable clock radio my father gave me sat on my bedside table. It was always tuned to CKXL AM 1010, the station that played the Top 40. I turned the radio on softly and opened the doors of my closet.

On each side, two panels of hinged doors folded open or closed. These doors were painted the light pink of a perfect girl's dream. They had slats running side to side along the whole length of each door. I ran my hand over the slats, poked my small finger into the gap, and tried to wedge it in to get my finger stuck and hurt myself. Crawling into the closet, I scootched up against the back wall, folded my knees to my chest and crossed my arms around my knees. The slats on the closet doors were wide enough to let in just a little light. I stared at the light coming through the slats, hugged myself, and hummed the hits. I spent a lot of time in childhood this way.

Time passed, but I couldn't care less about any seasonal change. The scars healed over and the draining stopped. My father got out of bed one day. I got out of the closet. I left scarred, but amazed by the miracle I had witnessed as my father's body healed.

Those open wounds healed miraculously, with time and modern medicine. To treat his bowel condition my father used the anti-inflammatory medication prednisone. I now know this medication may have a side effect of mood changes. In 1973, after taking prednisone, my father had his first manic episode, and it was terrifying. I was nine, and he would have been forty-three. That was the summer after the surgeries, after the abscesses, after the prednisone, the first summer of his unpredictable and erratic behaviour.

"I won't let you go, you can't sleep over. Don't be so selfish Paula, you have to stay here and do some work. I need your help!" My father slammed the front door. I curled up on the stairs of the front hallway and cried. I just wanted to go to a sleep over birthday party at a friend's.

My grandfather sat beside me and said, "Don't worry, we will find a way for you go to the party."

I lived with my father and my paternal grandparents from five years old, the time of my parent's separation. As an adult, I read that if a child has one ally they can get through very difficult situations. My grandfather was my ally. But I recognize how I needed the comfort of friend's homes, the comfort of safety I didn't feel in my own home. Friends whose two parents simply took care of their kids with no yelling and no unpredictable behaviour, where dinner was made and eaten together, in conversation and happiness with no outbursts or uncertainty.

My father was irritable, not sleeping, and more often than not, dissatisfied with me. He was on a buying spree. He redecorated the whole house and his office. He had the interior of the house repainted, got new carpets, bought new dining room, living room and bedroom furniture. He wallpapered his office and bought new chairs and equipment. He wanted my help and advice about all these purchases and took me to the stores where sometimes he would yell at the sales people and storm out. I was terrified and embarrassed and didn't want to go. If I went to the sleep over, I might not have to go shopping with my dad.

I missed that party, but my father let me sleep over on a different weekend. Marnie was a school friend, blonde and lithe. She took dance lessons and taught me how to spin and twirl. After elementary school, we lost contact with each other. I heard she married and had four children before I finished university. She died in her thirties of the same disease my father had, Crohn's, leaving her young family.

But at age nine, we were great friends. When we played outside in her backyard, we laughed and she would teach me ballet and tap. Her mother made us dinner, and we ate all together at their family table with her mom, dad, and brother. I felt like I was on one of those happy family shows I watched on television in the 1970s, the ones where Marcia's worst problem was giving her friend a makeover.

I stayed at Marnie's Saturday day and night. Sunday at dawn, probably around five in the morning, the doorbell rang. My father had come to pick me up. He rang the bell, then went back to sit in his car in front of the house. Marnie's mother answered the door in her nightgown.

I imagined the conversation.

"Get Paula, I've come to pick her up!" My father yelled from his car window.

"Let her sleep, it is so early."

"No, she has to come RIGHT NOW!"

Marnie's mother came down to the basement and woke me up. Marnie and I were sleeping in a little tent pretending we were camping. I got dressed quickly and left the safety of my friend's home to get into a car where uncertainty awaited. As I walked down the front path toward the car, I turned back to see Marnie's mother in her bathrobe, holding her front door open, looking at me. It was bad enough this whole thing had happened, and now it was worse that someone knew.

My father wanted me to pick carpets for my bedroom, but the store was not open. I don't remember what we did, but I suspect we waited in his car for several hours until opening time. I chose a pink shag with some white and red threads running through it.

My grandfather and I were scared, not knowing how to handle my father's rages. I am not sure if my grandfather recognized the symptoms of mental illness. But my grandfather knew we needed some help, and suggested we call a psychiatrist friend of my father for advice.

My grandfather's first language was not English. He emigrated from Russia with a young family in the late 1920s. Although he spoke English well, with an accent, he often left it up to me to make phone calls or fill out paperwork. I was to make the phone call.

We waited until my father was out of the house. I looked up the name in the yellow pages. I picked up the phone. My hands were shaking as I dialed the number. My grandfather stood beside me.

"Can I talk to Dr. Sarnat please?"

"Who is calling?"

My name is Paula, I'm Jack's daughter."

"Just a minute."

I looked at my grandfather and waited on the line, my stomach was upset and my palms sweaty.

The psychiatrist came on the phone, "Yes?"

"My father, the way he is acting, we don't know what to do?" There was desperation in my young voice, I remember that, even if I don't exactly remember what I said. But I clearly remember his response.

"There's nothing I can do for you."

He hung up. I looked at my grandfather.

"He won't help us," I said.

My grandfather and I looked at each other, we had nothing to say, nothing to do. We had no idea how to get through the next days and weeks.

I know this memory still activates and distresses me because, when writing this passage, I feel my nervous system charge. My chest is vibrating, and my mouth is dry. I feel symptoms that identify anxiety. I have more work to do to settle the past as the past.

I've worked with many of my own traumatic memories in therapy. One of the hardest, but most astounding accomplishments, is to sit with the profound feeling of danger left over from childhood that still seems as alive a threat as an adult. Those of us who have experienced a lack of safety in childhood may feel an ongoing dread that anything terrible could happen at any time. Catastrophes are always waiting to happen.

To integrate the memories of the past, still vibrant in our nervous system, we learn to watch the fight-flight-freeze mechanism in operation. Traumatic memories run our nervous system as if they were happening in the present. To resolve trauma, we learn to recognize the past as the past, by staying oriented in the safety of the present. We learn to experience the feelings of terror and when our life felt threatened, and stay in a zone of safety to just watch it all unfold. We learn to allow the emotions, body sensations, and defensive movements to move through and integrate. Although it seems straightforward, this has been some of the hardest work I have ever done.

Only later in medical residency I pieced together what happened that summer. I recognized my father's symptoms when I worked with several manic patients during my psychiatric rotation. The patients spoke quickly, didn't sleep, were irritable, and made rash decisions. They spent money recklessly, even bankrupting themselves buying cars, houses, televisions and electronics. After they were admitted to hospital, the mania was treated, but these patients had the dramatic changes of a psychiatric diagnosis and hospital stay, medication, and the instability of personal and financial loss.

Did I go into medicine to spite my father who wanted me to study law? Did I go into medicine to help heal myself? When I practice medicine now, I try to remember to listen carefully and respectfully, and to be there for those who were not seen or heard by their parents, or even by their previous doctors.

I remember my nine-year-old self left hanging on the phone line, with no support, no clue what to do. Sometimes I imagine that Dr. Sarnat actually did something to help us, but just couldn't talk to me because of confidentiality. So many years after that phone call, I am still stunned by his response and the lack of support for our family.

My compassion for the child I was grows as I learn more about trauma theory. I am amazed by our nervous system's strategies to create security. I am amazed at the resilience of the nervous system to cope with overwhelm in the most difficult situations.

Summers and winters, ups and downs, highs and lows, gregarious and withdrawn, manic and depressed, my father held it together with the constancy of routine, work and home. He sustained his medical practice in the specialty of otolaryngology for twenty more years, somehow coping with his physical and emotional health problems and difficulties from my mother.

Winter in Canada is cold and can be bleak, as the sun rises late and sets early. This was when my father was isolated, withdrawn, and concentrated on work. It was dark in the morning and dark by the time he got home. Weekdays he was out of the house by six am, home around six pm, when he had dinner and then disappeared to his room to bed or to watch TV.

He maintained this same routine, day after day. Weekends he spent in his room, often did not dress, and just stayed in that paisley robe. His bedroom curtains remained drawn day and night. He emerged from his bedroom to go downstairs to the kitchen to make a salami sandwich and grab a glass of cola. Then up to his room again. Sometimes, if he was feeling unwell, he would ask me to fix him something to eat. Occasionally, Sunday mornings, I went to his bedroom and we had a game of Monopoly.

In summer he took two weeks off work. The sun rose early at 4:30 am and set late after 10:30 pm. He rose early or did not sleep at all. He was endlessly occupied, washing the car, mowing the lawn, playing golf, going out all night. In winter he hardly said a word, he did not engage, he hardly left his bed. In summer he had energy, talked quickly or non-stop, so I could not go to sleep or do my homework. He was demanding and easily upset when I did not perform well.

In winter he never drank alcohol, and in summer his drink of choice was a "brown cow" with milk and Kahlua. As an adult I would become nervous seeing it on a menu. Even now, I can become anxious around people drinking alcohol, since the unpredictability in their behaviour reminds me of my younger self, facing my father. I had to make my father those drinks, brown cows, and make them properly in a short crystal glass with just enough ice. If I didn't get it right, I faced his irritability and anger.

As a pre-teen I was scared to make a mistake, and it was a lot of responsibility to make the perfect drink and to act exactly right. I never wanted to make him mad. Sometimes he yelled at me to wash the car, take care of the yard, clean up the house, and just get to work. I tiptoed around him, trying to appease him, scared to set off a condemnation by my less than perfect behaviour. But I also had to be engaged and happy enough so he would not think I was surly and withdrawn.

Workdays for him seem gruelling to me now, but he never complained. Mornings he did his hospital rounds and surgery. In the afternoons he worked downtown, in his corner office on the fifth floor. The rectangular waiting room had chairs against two facing walls; the third wall had a window that looked to the street, and under the window a planter with artificial plants. Some old magazines, *Time*, and *Sports Illustrated* were available, and a hardcover book, I don't know where he got it, of Children's Bible Stories. Not raised with Christianity, I had a strangely uneasy feeling looking at the pictures of Jesus robed, haloed, with arms outstretched. A pocket in the back cover held mail-in cards for people to order their own copy. Over the years, that book became beat up, the spine damaged, and all the ordering cards disappeared.

The reception desk opened to the waiting area, and the office assistant greeted patients and typed consult letters on what was then the latest thing: the IBM type ball. The ball whirled around, made a buzzing sound, the correction tape included right there on the typewriter, "automatically correcting." Consult letters were typed on white stationary embossed with his name and address in cursive script. A sheet of carbon paper was placed between the white sheet and a less expensive yellow sheet, copying the letter for his files. There were two examining rooms, and a small soundproof room for patients to have their hearing evaluated. My father's corner office overlooked a small park across the street, and held his large desk across which patients received results of biopsies and diagnoses. On the wall, built in wood shelves held school pictures of me from every year, kindergarten to medical school graduation, prompting patients to ask him, "How many daughters do you have?"

I knew that office well. Though I didn't want to, I worked there most summers typing letters and filing those yellow sheets. Children, who live with uncertainty learn very well how to get along, not say no or make their own wishes known and avoid possible outbursts. Researching trauma as an adult, I saw myself in writings that described the fawning behaviour response, also called people pleasing behaviour, conflict avoidance at all cost to keep the peace and avoid a rage.

As a child I just did my best to keep my wits about me and not let anyone hurt me. I was like that IBM type ball, whirling around in fear, automatically correcting everything, or better yet not making any mistakes in the first place. I kept my head down, not causing any difficulty for my father, doing what I was told, working in his office, cleaning the house, and getting good grades in school. I was being good, not just good, but as perfect as possible, causing no trouble to anyone. This method got me through school, medical school, and helped me in my medical practice. But I now see these as coping strategies to deal with overwhelm. Grateful for these strategies of childhood, I've also learned how these arise from feelings of inadequacy, and may create difficulties navigating adult life. I could never achieve the perfectionism I asked of myself.

As part of his medical practice, my father was often on call. The phone rang frequently in the middle of the night. When on call, it could be the emergency room, and then I would hear the garage door open. He was off to pack a bleeding nose, or perhaps deal with swallowing problems due to a severe throat infection. Many weekends were also spent on call, and he was gone at the hospital doing rounds or seeing patients for most of the day.

If it wasn't the emergency calling, it could have been my mother. My mother lived in the United States, and would phone many times a day, yelling and berating my father for imagined infidelities. If my mother called at night, my father would pick up the phone and then immediately slam it down. The phone would ring again, and he would pick up and perhaps yell into the receiver, "Don't call so late!" If it rang a third or fourth time, he would leave the phone off the hook and I would hear the beep, beep, beep until it stopped.

We never talked about my mother. As a child I did not understand what was wrong with her. All I had were her phone calls. Though sometimes we would pick up and immediately hang up the phone, sometimes we would just let it ring. When it rang twenty, thirty, or more times in succession, we knew it was her. When I did pick up, my mother would start her long rant, a tirade against my father and his mistress, using harsh tone and profanity.

"You are a traitor, an outrage, how can you treat me like this, I am still your wife and Paula is still my daughter. Stop seeing that whore, when are you going to change your ways?"

She would go on and on like this for hours if I did not hang up. Sometimes if I answered and she began her diatribes, I would put the receiver on the counter and go back to what I was doing with her voice yelling in the background. At least that way, the phone wouldn't ring again.

To the best of my knowledge, my dad could not have had a mistress, he was too sick and too busy with his office and hospital work. At that time, cassette tapes were used in answering machines. She would fill up both sides of a ninety-minute cassette tape at home and at my dad's office. She phoned the hospital trying to track him down. Some days she probably called several hundred times between home, office and hospital.

She ran up a large telephone bill, and a stop was put on her home phone for long distance calls. After that the calls were fewer, but still frequent. She had to leave her home and go to a pay phone. Often she was out late at night, because we would get calls at 2:00 or 3:00 in the morning. I imagined her standing at a pay phone under a street light near the 24-hour gas station, yelling into the receiver, or yelling at the operator when she wasn't connected or the collect call not accepted. I wished she were safe and that she could just go home and sleep.

I have no idea how my father managed all this. I erased and turned over the cassettes on the answering machine at home. Sometimes I listened, but it was too upsetting. He silently erased the cassette tapes at work. He never mentioned any difficulty about the calls coming to the hospital. What was it like for him knowing a hospital operator was at the receiving end of my mother's wrath, refusing the request to page him time and time again? We did not talk about these phone calls; neither my father nor grandfather explained what was going on.

Once in a while, if I answered the phone, I would try to get her attention.

"Hello, hello, hello, hello." I would softly say over and over again until she heard, and stopped her ranting.

"Oh, hi Paula, how are you, how is school?" She seemed to be lucid and quietened for a few minutes, and then went back to her yelling. I hung up on her many times.

I saw my mother twice by the time I was seventeen. She came to visit once suddenly when I was ten. My father and grandfather were also surprised to see her. I don't remember her coming in the house. I can see her standing on our front step as the evening sun set. She did not stay long.

The second time I saw her was at my high school graduation. In grade twelve I took a psychology course. It was my favourite course and I worked hard making a table comparing and contrasting childhood developmental models. I told my father I loved psychology and wanted to study it and become a psychologist or a psychiatrist.

He dampened my enthusiasm and said, "You don't want to be on the wards with all that yelling."

The teachers went on strike that last semester of high school, and I couldn't finish my psychology course. But I read some of the material we were going to study that included descriptions of mental illnesses.

Mildred, my mother, told me she was coming for my high school graduation. I didn't want her there; I was terrified to see her. My father had no control over her actions and could not stop her from coming. I don't know how she managed to get organized to buy a ticket and get on a plane. But I see her actions as her determination and love for me.

Prior to the graduation ceremony at the auditorium, she came over and talked to me. She was calm, and did not rant or yell. She told me I was beautiful and how proud she was of me. Those few minutes were all I saw of her. It was only then, at seventeen, I got the courage and remember asking my father, "What is wrong with her?"

"But you must know, Paula," he said. "She has schizophrenia."

But I didn't know, or if I knew, I wasn't sure. When he said this, the phone calls that were so confusing in childhood suddenly became understandable. My interest in psychology made sense.

A few days before my twenty-eighth birthday, I got a phone call from my father in the middle of the night. He was having bad abdominal pain, the signs of a bowel blockage. Usually, he was able to cope with his pain and never complained so I knew it had to be bad. At three in the morning, a cold, February night, I went to my dad's house to drive him to the emergency room. My car had a flat tire. My partner, Doug, helped me change it. My father never accepted our relationship. Perhaps, if he had seen Doug in the cold, dark night helping me, he could have developed some appreciation for this man I loved, who provided the support and care I needed.

My father was admitted to hospital that Tuesday morning. On Monday, the day before he was admitted, he worked a full day, seeing his patients. He forgot my birthday on Wednesday because he was so ill. I didn't remind him. The following week, he apologized for forgetting. I found the birthday card he wrote for me at his home, much later.

For six weeks he was in and out of intensive care. I called his remaining family, his brothers and sisters who lived out of town, two different times, and each time I thought that was the end. They came both times and spent time with him at the bedside. He rallied and improved. I remember them laughing and telling old stories from childhood. He was stoical and never complained to me, not about his pain, his hospitalization, his treatment, my mother, or his life.

While he was in hospital, I was in the middle of my family medicine residency and took time off to be by his side, so I visited most days. Once, when he was on the ward, I worried that his fluid output was greater than his input, and that he was dehydrated. He was thin, what we called cachectic, and his heart rate was elevated. He was very thirsty. I called the doctor on call, but it was a Saturday and it took all day for him to be seen and transferred once again to intensive care. This made me angry, but also guilty that I had not pressed harder to get him seen sooner.

The last time I saw him, he was in the intensive care unit, attached to tubes and IVs. The thinness had vanished, as his body was now retaining fluids. He looked about three hundred pounds. His face was swollen and puffy, with every part of his body bloated. He had gone from being a tiny stick figure to the Michelin man.

Although his lips were swollen, distorted by the retained fluids, I saw him whisper, and whisper again. Was this just delusional mumbling of someone close to death, someone on many pain medications? I leaned in closely to hear.

I could convince myself he was saying, "I love you, Paula."

I held his balloon like hand, and restrained my tears. "Thank you for being my father. You are a good father. I love you too, very much."

To myself, I said silently, Despite all our difficulties, this is true, despite it all, I know you did your best, I know you love me, and I do love you.

I saw him open his eyes and nod.

For many years this last image of him overwhelmed me with crying and shaking. Now I write this passage calmly, without anxiety, although I sometimes still feel the tears. I know this memory is integrated in my nervous system as the past.

Trauma theory and trauma informed care has developed significantly in the last several years. These theories, including knowledge about attachment disorders and adverse childhood experiences, inform my life and my medical practice. What we have learned about trauma has helped me tremendously, personally and also with my patients.

Trauma theory has also informed my understanding of meditation. We can better understand our behaviors when we ask with compassion, "What happened to you?" rather than with the judgment, "What is wrong with you?" One of my young patients, a twenty-one-year-old man with drug and alcohol addiction, often lived on the street. With great insight, he once said to me, "When I remembered my sexual abuse at age seven, I understood why I tried to commit suicide at age eight."

My father gave me many strengths, not the least of which was the ability to endure difficulties. What happened in my past catapulted me into healing my childhood traumas as an adult. My own experiences inform my ability to be a doctor, and to develop healing relationships with patients, in ways medical school never taught.

Within each of us is the impetus towards healing. My father's open wounds healed, with time, care, and medication. Seeing this inspired my interest in medicine. But in medicine, I was frustrated by limitations of treating psychological distress.

Contemporary psychological therapies and information about trauma offer new opportunities. I am interested to see what future research says about the role of childhood trauma in the development of bipolar disorder and schizophrenia.

I know I do not have to be defined and triggered by my past traumatic experiences. A part inside of me knows when something is not quite right, and seeks healing and change. Like I trust the changing seasons, I trust this process guides my own flourishing. And I trust we all can flourish in this way.

MANIC DEPRESSION: A REFLECTION OF THREE GENERATIONS
BY NAOMI GOLDA

Naomi Golda is a happily retired certified rehabilitation counselor and licensed mental health counselor. She enjoys spending time with her family and taking time to smell the roses. Her philosophy is best summed up by Vivian Greene, "Life isn't waiting for the storm to pass. It's about learning how to dance in the rain." Also, she likes to think she's a rainbow in someone else's cloud. (Maya Angelou). Ngolda153@gmail.com

Mt. Everest to Death Valley
Soprano to Bass
Penthouse to Basement
Roller Coaster to Merry Go Round
Abusive to Respectful
Overeating to Abstaining
Excessive Spending
Reckless Behavior and Poor Judgment
Suicidal

As a niece, sister, and mother to loved ones with manic depression, I witnessed all of the above experiences. I felt scared, angry, frustrated, hopeless, and helpless. What was wrong with these people I loved?

How could I best help them? Each affected member of my family endured a tremendous amount of pain and hardships with different journeys, yet fortunately had good outcomes based on new medications and treatments.

Having spent most of her adult life in psychiatric settings, my maternal aunt was discharged after decades of locked wards and electroconvulsive therapy, among other treatments that probably was like a scene from One Flew Over the Cuckoo's Nest. Lithium was literally and figuratively the key that unlocked the door to her freedom. She experienced many years of stability and independent living prior to her death of natural causes at the age of eighty-four.

My sister suffered throughout her college years with a major depressive disorder that eventually led to a diagnosis of manic depression after several manic episodes. She had several hospitalizations in the 1980s that were short term and included psychotherapy and dance and art therapy. Her treatment was an effective, comprehensive team approach. Depakote was her salvation.

Unfortunately, a year prior to the coronavirus pandemic in 2020, my sister decided she no longer needed to take medication and went into a seven-month severe depression. At some point she was hospitalized for observation and medical management to obtain stability. She was discharged after two weeks to my care, since she lived alone and definitely needed someone to monitor her medical and mental condition. It should be noted that this also necessitated support from my husband since it was difficult to have a severely depressed person in the household. My sister began anew with a knowledgeable, efficient psychopharmacologist, and after two months on Tegretol she regained her stability and returned to independent living.

At the age of twenty my son was diagnosed with bipolar II. He had classic symptoms that were very apparent to me personally and professionally, as I was well aware of the genetic component of the illness within families and generations. Truthfully, I was heartbroken and very concerned. I had pessimistic thoughts about the life he would lead. After only one brief hospitalization, that was more of a respite for me, he was successfully treated with Lamictal and Lexepro. His early diagnosis, proper medication, and psychotherapy were essential to his mental stability. He is now a professional living a happy and productive life.

It's a major understatement to think that the journeys of my aunt, sister, and son were smooth and uncomplicated. Quite the contrary. As a family member, I experienced pity, fear, and anger. Progress was not linear. Qualified, knowledgeable, and skilled professionals were difficult to find. Medication was adjusted and readjusted. Side effects had to be tolerated. My sister and son often expressed that they felt like guinea pigs. We had to deal with well-meaning but ignorant people.

Reflecting upon my experiences dealing with familial manic depression as a youth, young adult, and senior citizen, I learned that a strong, solid support system is essential for both patients and family members. One needs perseverance and resiliency. As with any illness and difficult life situation, self-awareness, education, patience, acceptance, and optimism goes a long way in meeting life's challenges. Manic depression is no exception.

Snowy Day
By Liz Goldman

Elizabeth Goldman is a poet and artist and has worked as a writer, teacher, and education researcher. She holds a Master's degree in Religious Studies from Indiana University and lives in Dover, NH. She posts on Instagram as zolatov.

Too young for school, my neighbor and I
tunneled all day in Buffalo's deep snow,
carving arches with spoons from home,
the sun a pale dot overhead. When the cold
finally reached our bones, we went home.

I hung my coat and snow pants, settled
my boots and gloves, laid the spoon beside them,
and padded down the dark hallway,
hoping to watch cartoons on our new TV.
Maybe my mother would make cocoa or warm milk.

In the kitchen I found her furious, her face
creased in anger, her breathing broken.
"She would not eat," she said, in a flat voice.
Strapped into a highchair, my baby sister wept
beneath a bowl of chicken soup upended
on her head. Little noodles mixed with tears
and flecks of parsley. The chicken fat
gleamed yellow as the sun dimmed.

My Bipolar Mother, Shoes, and Suicide
Debbie Schlesinger Greenwood

Debbie Schlesinger Greenwood is a long time culinary educator and caterer in Los Angeles, California. She is passionate about food and is a committed Francophile. Debbie credits her literary genes to the DNA of a beloved and departed Grandmother and thanks her own MFA-degreed daughter for the encouragement to write this essay. www.caterdeb.com

I was 25 years old, and my boyfriend said, "Let's go shopping. You need some new shoes." And then he specified, "You need some espadrilles."

"What's an espadrille?" I asked.

He explained the shoe to me, and then a couple of others. I had never learned these fashion-forward terms. I was hurt that he saw imperfections in how I dressed. But the reality was that he just put words to a gap in my education, words normally taught to a daughter by her mother.

My mother died a few months after I turned fourteen. She committed suicide in our home's garage. She turned on the car engine. She left the garage door closed. The autopsy said it was carbon monoxide asphyxiation. She was forty-two.

My father came banging on my bedroom door at 5:00 am that mid-August morning in a panic. He was yelling, "I think your mother is dead!"

"What? What?" I asked. His words made no sense.

"She's lying on the garage floor," he went on, "and I don't think she is breathing…"

I remember saying something to him about needing to try mouth-to-mouth resuscitation. That's what they taught us in school. My brain was on some kind of out-of-body autopilot. I had never actually performed this life-saving procedure, nor had he.

We didn't even know if it was too late. He said he tried to move her and that she was cold. I still remember those exact words. I followed him to the garage at a run and then he stopped me. He had a moment of parental clarity.

"No!" he yelled. "Don't go in. Don't look!"

So, I didn't. I never saw her body that morning. I never saw her dead a few days later when she lay in a closed coffin a few blocks from our house at the cemetery where the service was held, where they buried her on a hillside. I never saw her again, ever. I only saw her in my dreams after that.

This was not my mother's first suicide attempt. Mom had bipolar disorder and she was under the care of a psychiatrist. She was taking Lithium. They thought she was doing so well that they cut her dose in half the very week prior. Today, the medical community knows better. They know not to make drastic changes to medication. They know to wean a person's dose in gradual steps. They know to titrate, to continuously measure and adjust the balance of a given drug cocktail.

During my childhood, there would be months of calm and busy days filled with her being a wife to my father, and a mother to me. And then there were the other times, dark and scary times that filled me with fear, panic, and dread. She said and did frightening things like try to kill herself with pills. She was not like the other moms. She was not normal. She was up and down, and she had so many rules. It was hard to be a kid around her. It was hard to be the perfect daughter she wanted.

I had no brothers or sisters. It was just my dad and I after she left. I learned later that even I had been a negotiation. She didn't really want children, but he did. I think she knew her fragile mental state made having kids a precarious proposition at best. Still, they compromised and agreed to have just the one. Agreed to have me.

The family photos, all smiles, all happy, belied the truth of her condition. The black and white 8mm movies of her joyfully singing through a montage of my birthday parties belied the truth of her condition. How in the middle of a heated argument she could answer the phone with her secretarial voice, calm, syrupy, and in control, belied the truth of her condition. No one knew. Everyone was completely shocked at her suicide. Everyone but us.

The night before she killed herself, we fought. It was a fight about shoes. She was deep into one of her episodes of complete unreasonableness. Well before I turned fourteen I could see that she was, at times, unwell, unreliable, (and) unsound. By age fourteen, I could see that even I thought with more clarity, more logic than she.

The fight that night had to do with me wearing shoes that were black patent leather. It was August 17th, and she lived by rules that could neither be broken nor bent, which I now realize is because they gave her neat, clear-cut boundaries to follow. They protected her. They were her safety net. This particular rule dictated that black shoes could only be worn *after* Labor Day, still some two weeks away. I didn't care. I wanted to wear them right then.

Today, I understand that this was part of the obsessive-compulsive behavior that came with her bipolar disorder. But these mental health words were not part of my fourteen-year-old lexicon or understanding. Yelling at one another was. What did two weeks on a calendar matter to me, a teenager?

Isn't it poetic though? My mother died after a fight over the merits of black versus white patent leather shoes when her entire world was black and white. My world conversely, even back then, allowed for shades of gray. It still does. But those two poles, the rigid *this* or *that* of her, were the manifestation of her bipolar disease. Her gray matter from birth, which controlled her emotions, was somehow compromised. Her brain chemistry did not work like mine, or like my dad's or my friend's.

That night I slammed and locked my door to shut her out. I needed to put a physical barrier between myself and what felt like her "crazy." I needed all that high-pitched yelling turned down. This fight about shoes and how I wasn't picking the right pair.

Ever since her death, talk about shoes triggered me. Because she took her own life on that next August day in 1967, I didn't learn about espadrilles, huaraches, Mary Janes, or sling backs. So when my boyfriend told me what I "needed" insofar as footwear was concerned, all those memories came rushing back. When he asked me about espadrilles, I realized what I really needed wasn't new shoes. I needed my mother.

Now, I am twenty-six years older than she was when she died. I never learned to walk in heels as she did effortlessly in her size 8 1/2 narrow pumps that she owned in every color. She was a stylish woman, but I never had the chance to emulate her style. All I can do is try to put myself in her confused head and her imperfect mind and imagine, for a moment what it must have been like to walk through life in her shoes.

DAY LIGHT
BY LESLIE HENDRICKSON-BARAL

Leslie Hendrickson-Baral, MEd, BCIM, DAAIM, a Neurotherapist, is a thought-provoking published poet. Her literary resume includes publication in "Carbon Culture Review," 'Falling Star,' two editions of 'Wired Art from Wired Hearts,' "California Quarterly," six consecutive "San Diego Poetry Annual's," and "Please See Me Literary Magazine." Leslie loves deep probing both in the form of planting health-sustaining organic foods and exploring our mind's far-reaching questions of Purpose.
linkedin.com/in/leslie-hendrickson-baral-17067a6
www.attention-training.com

What do you tell people when they ask
why your parents never visit? My guess
is you reinvent a truth that isn't really true.

You are very much a balanced adult now,
but you harbor memories you cannot share
mired under betrayal and resentment.

To heal you backed into corners and closets,
windowless light that turned into deep inhalations
of sunlit shafts of soul lifting music.

Beating in joyful tune with your waking heart,
newly revealed highways blossomed within your life's map
that reset the course of your life, a pioneer's path.

Accept your unredeemed medals of bravery and
invest full spectrum intention in your journey now, choose
to open your mind's eye in the fullness of day light.

Growing Up in a Goldfish Bowl
By Helen Hudson

Helen Hudson writes the popular blog "Agefully Aging" with readers in more than 100 countries, and has also been a guest blogger for the American Counseling Association. She is a former Campus Entertainer of the Year, performing all original material and recently placed several songs on TV shows. Helen has a BA from Stanford in Communications and a MEd from Vanderbilt in Human Development Counseling, and is a practicing therapist.

∾ ∾ ∾

As a child, I never knew which mother was waking up that day. She vacillated from having wild and grandiose plans like "We're going to Paris!" to catatonic states where she stayed in bed for days with the curtains drawn. In between, she often became hostile over the most ridiculous things. If I forgot to wear socks on the white carpet, I might get a sudden, swift slap. If I didn't clean the toilet bowl correctly, I might get my mouth cleaned out with the toilet bowl brush itself.

Were we really going to Paris or would I be punished for being unable to eat her dinner of slimy, old onions mixed with hash and marshmallows? Would she show up at school wearing her pajamas and demand to see the principal? Or, would she be deathly silent, lying in bed with a pillow over her head? I just never knew. Mother acted as if everyone were out to get her but it was clear to me, even at six, that most people simply wanted to get away from her, including me.

As if to heighten my fear of her, Mother stood over six feet in her heels and had once been a cover girl. Her blonde beauty and tall stature dazzled others, especially men, for years. It also made my pleas to be heard fall on many a deaf ear. Once, during a party, a friend of hers brought over a plate of cookies. I ate every, single one of them by myself. Her friend thought it was quite funny and said to me, "Goodness, young lady, doesn't your mother feed you?"

"No," I replied honestly. She laughed. I was devastated. I'd hoped she might actually intervene and help me.

For some, memory is a bridge to burn. For others, it is a window to look through. For most of us, it is a little of both. Noted psychotherapist Salvador Minuchin says that our earliest recollection will reflect who we are today. What event we choose to remember, and more importantly, how we remember it, defines the way we see ourselves now. It also closely predicts just how we will deal with our choices and decisions in the future.

If that is true, then self-knowledge lies close to consciousness. It waits in the first memory we call to light, that one tiny, brief moment years ago that has so come to define us without our knowing. That first flash, when our eyes clicked open like a camera and caught the moment that was passing, even as it arrived. It is a picture long overexposed and reprints itself on every roll of film we take.

Herein lies my first photograph, from the summer of 1958.

Summer, like all of the seasons, could not penetrate our house. Though the Arizona sun had baked our small apartment to a stifling stillness, I was shivering. My scrawny, five-year old body was alive with goose bumps. I would have run outside where the sun burned brown holes in the grass, but could not. Whenever Mother left the apartment, she always dead-bolted the door behind her with a key. I was cocooned in a world apart, safely locked from harm into harm itself.

I was staring at my two goldfish swimming in their bowl, imagining how they would taste. A loud growling in my belly startled the eerie quiet of the room. It had been several days since I had eaten and everything looked good to me now.

Goldie was plump and glistening in rich hues of deep orange-yellow. Each scale on her body shimmered like a tiny medallion of gold. Her partner, Blackie, was really a dullish gray, but long, trailing fantails echoed her every move with a quiver of cascading trellises, making her equal in beauty to Goldie.

Both were lovely swimmers. I had watched them for hours, marveling at the way they never tired, tracing lonely loops around and around the water. Their fins would barely flutter, pause, and then propel them forward in a long, smooth glide. Another quick swish and they skimmed effortlessly through the water. Everything about them was quiet, yet they were constantly in motion. I was in awe. Next to them, I felt large and clumsy.

Our lives had much in common. We were prisoners in our respective glass cages. Theirs was a bowl. Mine was a one-bedroom apartment, whose only entrance was a large sliding glass door that ran the length of the living room. Day after day we circled our territory in well-worn patterns. We also counted on someone bigger to care for us.

Mother bought the fish to keep me company on those days I was locked alone in the apartment. Where she was, I was never quite sure. Years later, relatives would confide she was a waitress or an entertainer, but the overriding consensus was that she was, "in the arms of some man or the other."

Goldie and Blackie were my constant, quiet teachers. Their shimmery silence had given me an appreciation for both beauty and solitude. It takes a certain grace to keep moving even when you cannot go anywhere. Sometimes I talked to them. They circled indifferently. Other times, I pressed my face against their bowl trying to get a reaction. If one chanced to stop mid-swim and glance my way, I would be thrilled. It didn't happen often or last long, though, and I was not naïve. These fish were far more excited about seeing their food than me.

Nevertheless, they counted on me for their survival and I took that seriously. Each morning and night I was to give them "a pinch" of food. The moment it hit the water, their mouths formed tiny "o's" and vacuumed the food clean from the surface in a flurry of bubbles. It always disappeared before I could rub the last bits off my fingers. Often, I would give them another half pinch just to be sure they had enough.

Every week I cleaned their tank, catching them one at a time in a small white net so they would not bruise. Carefully, I eased them into a waiting pan of water while I scrubbed their bowl until it squeaked. Afterwards, I gently placed them back in with fresh water and long strands of green algae. Most importantly, I protected them from the paws of Louie, my Siamese cat.

Goldie and Blackie would have remained in darkness had I not risked Mother's wrath to merely pull back the gray curtain a few inches. She demanded the curtains be closed at all times, so no one knew I was alone.

But today would be different. Mother had not come home for several days and the cupboards were now bone-bare. I had already eaten all that was left in the icebox: Two raw eggs. If you chew the shells long enough they taste like granulated milk. I licked the cellophane from an empty bag of bread, to catch the last few crumbs.

As a last resort, I rummaged through the trash and took out all the old yogurt and milk cartons. I chewed their insides until every bit of wax was gone. It was a good taste and left my teeth gummy like a caramel apple. It was fun to open my mouth and bite down over and over again, just to feel the suction as the wax held fast.

Louie and I had already licked his cat dish clean. My hunger gnawed in every hollow of my body, leaving me weak and quiet. His made him yowl in deep, long, dreadful moans and move frantically. He had begun to scratch my bare leg bloody. Then he flicked the red drops hungrily with his rough, fast tongue. I didn't mind. His tongue was warm and kept me from feeling so cold.

Suddenly, Louie leapt to the table where the fishbowl sat. He stuck one paw into the water and began striking at the fish. Each lunge went deeper. Water began splashing all over the table. Goldie and Blackie hit the side of their bowl several times before I realized Louie and I had the same thought: He wanted to eat them, too!

I knew people ate fish and had been wondering if there was a distinction between tuna fish and goldfish. Apparently, there was none for Louie. Perhaps there shouldn't be one for me. I pushed Louie from the bowl and reached into the water with my own hand. Goldie was an easy catch and felt cool and slimy in my palm. I had to put my other hand on top to keep her form flopping out. When she grew still, I laid her down on the carpet.

The second I put her down, Louie went wild. He pawed at her tiny orange body. She flopped and arched, then went still. He pawed again. She flopped and twisted, then grew quiet. I knew something was wrong and quickly put her back in the water. She merely floated along the top. Blackie became distressed and began bumping against her, but Goldie lay limp.

Slowly, I lifted her back out of the water. Before I could bite into her, Louie pounced on me and sank his claws right through my shirt. He hung from my stomach by one front talon, still trying to swipe at the fish. His hind legs scratched up my thighs struggling to get a foothold. The pain was so excruciating that I had to drop Goldie back into the bowl.

It took both hands and all my strength to pull Louie off me. His talon was linked hard into my belly button. By the time I curved the edge of it out, blood was oozing down my shorts. I tossed him into the bedroom and slammed the door between us. His yowls were muted now, but the sound of his claws scratching the door made me shudder.

Goldie was still floating sideways when I returned. She looked much smaller with her fantails flattened. I picked her up by the tail, closed my eyes and slipped her head between my lips. Using my teeth to feel out the plump part of her body, I bit down, just behind her gills. There was a burst of salty liquid on my tongue and I gagged.

She was still in one piece, but slightly crooked when I laid her back on the carpet. Slowly, I walked to the bedroom door and opened it. Louie flew past me and stopped short in front of the fish. With one deft paw, he held her body down and began to eat. When he had finished, only a gristly spine, one eye socket and the edge of her tail remained.

As he licked his paws clean, Louie's head turned upwards to the bowl where Blackie now swam alone. Stealthily, he lowered his ears and began to creep towards her. Afraid he would eat her too, I grabbed him from behind and shut both of us into the bedroom. His heart was beating as fast as my own now. The rapid thumps from his furry breastbone shot out like tiny bullets against my fingers.

Just as I thought I had calmed him, Louie sprang from my arms, leapt to a painting on the wall and sank his claws into the canvas. Helplessly, he hung by his front paws while his hind legs struggled to get a grip on the slick surface. His silken, Siamese body stretched lengthwise down the wall, like a skinned tiger mounted in a hunter's trophy room.

I ran to the bathroom and cranked open the bubbled glass window, like I had seen Mother do before. Then I rushed back to Louie. Standing on the bed, I held his body close and pulled each of his front claws out of the painting. The instant he was free, he started to bolt. As he did, I caught him fast and ran back to the window. Before I could push the screen completely out, Louie lunged through the small opening and was gone.

For the moment, I was relieved but strangely flushed with heat. I returned to the living room. At first glance, everything looked the same: Curtains drawn, pillows on the couch just right, books shelved neatly along the wall, and the chair angled slightly towards the fishbowl. Only now Blackie was swimming alone. Goldie was unrecognizable; a tiny pile of debris on the floor that a vacuum could suck with barely a rattle.

I picked her remains up with my thumb and finger and placed them in the cup of my palm. It was hard to imagine only moments ago these little bits of chewed up scrap had shimmered with life. I flushed them down the toilet, watching until they swirled into a tiny cyclone and disappeared.

The evidence was gone, but the perpetrator could not escape. She lived at the scene of the crime. Strangely my hunger was also gone. In its place only two emotions remained. The first was sadness for the loss of my pet. The second was far more consuming and fraught with terror. How would I explain this to Mother?

When I was born in 1953, there was no such thing as "Child Protective Services." It wouldn't be formed for another twenty-seven years. In those days, there was a deeply held belief that a child should always be with the mother, no matter the scenario. In my case, this wasn't such a great idea because, according to my family, my mother "wasn't quite right in the head." No one had a real name for what her problem was then other than, "crazy" or "nuts." Nowadays, they would call her, "bipolar" or "a paranoid schizophrenic."

Bipolar disorder is "an illness that involves mood swings with at least one episode of mania." It may also involve repeated episodes of depression. These issues were clearly evident in mother's behavior and began during her teenage years. By the time I was twelve, I was very used to the fact that mother would either be in bed when I readied for school or she'd be maniacally cooking something inedible while excitedly insisting I run for class president.

As time passed, however, another fault line emerged and her paranoia and psychotic tendencies evolved into a different beast altogether. Schizophrenia, the disorder that affects one's ability to think, feel, and behave reared its addled head. Everyone was after her. The bank charged her twelve cents more interest, "On purpose because they're trying to manipulate my funds for their benefit." So, she took her money out of the bank. A woman on the subway "glared at" her. "I thought she might be a lesbian so I didn't dare go back to my apartment in case she followed me." Her landlord, "purposely released rats into my apartment so I would move out. He wants to raise the rent! But I fooled him," she said delightedly. "I've loaded the place with rat poison."

On the other hand, she often made things seem far better than they actually were. Her imagination knew no bounds. Her sometimes paramour, a Mafioso who carried a revolver in a shoulder harness and once held me at gunpoint, was to her, "a charming raconteur and fabulous opera singer." The one room shack where she lived way out in the boondocks was, "an estate" which she planned to will to me. Its value was next to nothing and barely inhabitable at best.

By the time my mother was in her 50's, she was a full-blown, bipolar, paranoid schizophrenic without any concept of reality. Her voluminous letters to me were mostly unreadable and filled with bizarre lists and scrawled numbers. The little pieces of her psyche that she'd used to fool others in her youth could no longer be hidden. She insisted on living in the streets instead of the apartments we rented for her because she wanted her freedom, and any kind of enclosure was meant to fence her in. She also didn't want, to be tracked by the government. By then, she not only didn't listen to reason, she was completely incapable of it.

Having grown up in a culture where mental health issues were always kept quiet, it is a shock for me to now see them regularly discussed in TV commercials. In today's world, my mother would be offered a multiplicity of drug choices, along with therapy. Who knows, if such things had been available to her then, she might not have ended up living in a baseball dugout and pushing a shopping cart in her later years. Perhaps I might even have had a relationship with her. As it happened, though, neither was to be.

The idea that a mother could or would abuse her child in the 50's was simply not part of the normal equation. Despite my grandmother attempting to get custody of me, few intervened to help. One stands out: A neighbor who watched me walk by myself to kindergarten must have noticed how thin I was. Several times, she met me at the end of her driveway with a loaf of freshly, baked bread. "I've made too much," she said each time, "perhaps you'd like to take this home?" I was ecstatic the first time but had to eat as much as I could before returning home or mother might get furious. I hid what I couldn't finish in a palm tree but the next morning it was riddled with ants.

Grandmother eventually did gain custody of me, but it took her twelve long years and a lengthy court battle. Ten years later, in 1974, only sixty thousand cases of child abuse were even reported. By 1990, there were over two million. Now, of course, those numbers are staggering and people are more than ready to intervene.

Depending on which clinician you ask, I am either the child of a bipolar manic-depressive or a paranoid schizophrenic. No one could fathom the depth of illness in a woman so attractive, accomplished, and articulate in her early years. A crackpot with a genius IQ who couldn't balance a checkbook and stormed into the bank once a month to yell at any poor teller who happened to be in the way, "You have made a mistake again on my account!" A crazy who wore pajamas to church, then dressed in her best mink for an afternoon at the pool. A neurotic who encouraged me to be independent then beat me if I either talked back or remained silent. A lunatic who forced me to re-chew the oyster I had just vomited, "In case there is a pearl in it." A psychotic who was placed for observation at New York's Bellevue Hospital in 1968 and three days later literally talked her way out the front door. A seductress so desperate to have a man in her life she took almost anyone to her bed.

I am also the child of a woman who was beautiful, cultured, and uniquely original. A cover girl whose face was often described as "that of an angel." A linguist who could converse in several languages. A singer who knew the words of every song, from "My Funny Valentine" to the score of Tosca. A musician who played both piano and guitar. A dynamic yarn-spinner who could convince you that a lion was indeed a lamb. An unbiased idealist who treated the garbage man with no less deference than she did a doctor. A parent who felt that her daughter's seeing a Broadway show was just as important as her attending school. A bold woman who was not intimidated by anything or anyone and indelibly, if accidentally, instilled that quality in me.

In short, I am the child of my mother. Living with her made me adaptable to most people and situations. To this day, I consider it her greatest gift to me. When I was younger, people told me I should write a book about my life with her. But since we only lived together consistently for eight years of my life, when I was six to twelve, I couldn't understand why. How much of a story could a mere six years be?

Now that I am older, I realize how very different from ordinary my life has been. So unusual that at first my own husband found many of my life-experiences incredible. Who would believe that the five-year-old daughter of a Smith College graduate would be locked for days on end alone in an apartment with no food? How do you tell your fiancée you were first made to perform oral sex at the age of six, without making him question your sanity or his for wanting to marry you? Why would it take thirteen years of negligence and abuse, scores of police reports, and ultimately a court battle for a mother to finally lose custody of her child?

Beyond the pathos of a troubled childhood, I have not just survived but thrived in life. I graduated from Stanford at twenty. Taught high school English. Had a successful career as a songwriter, recording artist, and performer. Received a Master's degree from Vanderbilt. Worked as a clinical therapist. And now have a forty-year marriage that includes two grown daughters.

Mine is a story of inspiration and triumph. In a way, Mother's life was too. She lived a full and long life on her terms. She never really saw herself as the pathetic creature that others did, and that in itself was probably the greatest blessing of all.

GROWING UP WITH MARY
BY LISA LAX

Lisa Kenwyn Lax, EdD, LICSW, MSW, lives and works in Burlington, Vermont. She is a practicing psychotherapist and social worker, mom of two wonderful children, climate change activist, and amateur violinist. In addition to writing a dissertation for her doctorate in Educational Policy and Leadership, Lisa has written articles for the *Invest EAP Newsletter*.

   ❦   ❦   ❦

This is about my experience growing up with a mother who most likely had a version of what is called manic depression. I say "most likely" because the details about her prior diagnoses or treatment are not available to me. The inability to verify whether or not my mother had a formal psychiatric diagnosis doesn't stop my speculation or the need to know. It's not surprising that I gravitated towards a career in mental health practice. Looking back through the lens developed in my professional training and experience, I see clear evidence of a mental health disorder, and specifically, the symptoms of a milder form of manic depression or Bipolar II.

Over time, I put the pieces together from my recollection of memories. One give-away was that my mother was hospitalized at least three times in psychiatric wards during my childhood, and at least one of these was an involuntary admission instigated by my father. The involuntary admission was later corroborated by mom in a rather crazy letter to me during one of her paranoid periods. I also remember her having appointments with private psychiatrists during an era when this was uncommon among the people in our middle-class circles in the 1960's and '70s. And according to my younger siblings, after I left home there were times when she was actively suicidal.

During much of my mother's life, there was limited public discourse about mental health and mental illness, and much of what existed was hyperbole. Given this context, my siblings and I had few reference points for what our family experienced. I am guessing too that my mother couldn't safely disclose her experience to others.

As a social work professional, I know full well the damage that stigma can cause and understand the discourse has tended to harm more than help. For this reason, I can easily appreciate perspectives that reject mental health diagnoses or other types of labels. Psychiatric diagnoses in particular tend to reduce a person to a category. Historically these have been misused for social control and have led to great harm. At the least, such labels are dismissive of a person's complex humanity.

Despite knowing this intellectually, there was still a part of me that resisted believing that my mother was someone who suffered from a diagnosable mental illness. Even now, I prefer to remember her as the eccentric, often difficult, remarkable human being that she was. However, a diagnosis would have offered some comfort, an explanation for disturbed behavior, as well as validation that there was a problem. For her children, a diagnosis might have provided some reassurance that what we experienced just wasn't right.

Who was my mother? She was the middle child and only daughter born to a white, Midwestern storekeeping and farm family at the beginning of the Great Depression. While raised as a devout Catholic in a conservative community, it didn't take long after leaving home for her to reject Catholicism and embrace such belief systems as tarot and astrology. After high school she wanted more than anything to become a classical musician, but instead yielded to her practical-minded father and trained for a career in nursing. Given her own mental health proclivities, it is hardly surprising that she was attracted to psychiatry. She worked for a number of years on the hospital psych ward and eventually worked as an unlicensed psychotherapist during a time when that was still acceptable.

In many ways she was quite extraordinary and gifted. She was self-taught and proficient in areas such as photography, fine art reproduction, upholstery, astrology, writing, and sewing. She mastered the use of computers and other digital technologies without formal instruction, well ahead of the curve. She also had a compelling personality that drew people of all kinds into her orbit. Many of her friends were colorful characters, fellow artists, and iconoclastic thinkers. This included questionable relationships with past and present clients. Her work roles in nursing, bartending, counseling, and art reproduction, in addition to her habit of writing impassioned articles and letters to the editor of local newspapers, led her to become a mini-celebrity in each of the communities she occupied.

When my mother was doing well, she seemed capable of anything. She could fix a radio or a toaster on the fritz, steer a car safely through a nasty storm, create architectural designs for two of her homes, and rig a water line from a river to her home located in the north woods of Minnesota. She rescued birds with broken wings and runaway teenagers.

Seemingly fearless, she navigated a number of dramatic and abrupt changes in her life circumstances, including the death of my father when he was thirty-seven years old and she was thirty-two, and when the oldest child (me) was ten and the youngest barely one year old. Adults in her circle would justifiably declare her to be an amazing person, as she seemed to manage a life that most other people would find either extremely challenging or impossible.

However, essential parts of her were hidden from most people in the community who rubbed shoulders with her, such as our teachers who saw her neatly dressed in her home-tailored outfits, her admiring mental health clients or art reproduction customers, or a neighbor who was charmed by her piano playing and conversation at a cocktail party. Looking back, I wonder if some of these adults actually did have some sense of her darker side and were just trying to reassure her family, and possibly themselves, that she really was the amazingly competent person she seemed to be.

For her children, the reality of living with her was often at odds with her social presentation. The thing was, others didn't witness the times when she sat for hours and weeks on end on a stool at our kitchen counter staring blankly into space with the flattest of expressions, her primary companions being an ashtray containing a mound of cigarette butts and a cup of cooled coffee. Others didn't see the red-rimmed eyes caused by daily episodes of weeping.

On those days, the mother we knew didn't get out of bed until long after she had been delivered her a cup of instant coffee and all of her children had managed to dress and breakfast themselves before running outside to catch the school bus. When our school day ended and we returned home by the same school bus, we would find her in her usual position sitting in the kitchen and were barely acknowledged as we grabbed a snack and went off to another room or a friend's house. During these times, the house was a disorganized mess and dinner might be frozen fish sticks and corn prepared spontaneously by one of her older children when Mom didn't come out her room.

Nor did others see her erupt into a rage over something like her missing hair curlers or a suspicion of stolen change from the money jar. Or see that the laundry, bathroom cleaning, dinners, vacuuming, and childcare were mostly taken care of by the older children. Nor would they guess that this was a woman oblivious to evidence that her second husband, and before him a medical student boarder, was engaged in sexual abuse of several of her children.

Then there were the other times, when my mother seemed to break out of the hard chrysalis of her melancholy to emerge as an effervescent being who whipped up parties, made gourmet Christmas cookies for all the neighbors and my dad's clients, sewed complete wardrobes for her family at Christmas, and worked into the wee hours on such projects as stripping paint off a stone fireplace or reupholstering a piece of furniture. During these times, no project was too much or done half way.

Of course, her sparkling energy during these times might not have been focused on the care of her children. In fact, she could be downright neglectful. One memory is the time she left most of her underage children at home alone and unsupervised for several days to attend a training program to learn how to be an insurance adjuster, a scheme that failed to pan out.

Another set of memories involve coming to my mother with a question or a need of some sort, when she was busy with perhaps a few sewing pins stuck in her mouth or hovered over a notepad working on correspondence course for how to become a great writer. The response was usually an irritated, "Can't you see I'm busy right now?" The problem was that she was often either too busy with some grand project or too severely depressed to respond to the mundane needs of her many children. When there was a crisis however, such as a potentially fatal health problem or an accident, her deep empathy and experience as a nurse would propel her to take appropriate action.

It took most of my adulthood to reckon with and make sense of this complicated mess of experiences. Did my mother love us? Had I been an abused child? Had I experienced emotional neglect? Did my mother, in fact, have a mental illness?

I could see that the sexual abuse by the men was clearly abusive and her lack of response was neglectful. However, for a long time the rest seemed pretty ambiguous. After all, we were all painfully aware of the rough hand she had been dealt by the universe. In spite of everything, she still managed to keep us together, housed, and fed. Other mothers we knew also yelled at their children and didn't always tend to their every need. In many large families, the older kids look after the younger ones. What woman doesn't have the right to depression after losing a husband and being left alone with the overwhelming responsibility of raising so many young children?

Another source of confusion was that my mother's hypomanic episodes weren't flamboyant or cause for social disgrace. She didn't run off to parts unknown, spend all of the family funds on exotic purchases, or engage in serial sex. If she had, others might have noticed her mental health problems and then perhaps her children would have had more validation and support. Perhaps I wouldn't have spent half of my life questioning what I experienced. Instead, people frequently told us how remarkable and wonderful she was to carry on as the single parent of eight children. This mythology had a way of reproducing itself so that even now we might question the memories that contradict such an image.

As a mature woman with a thirty-five-year career in social work, I now understand that many parents today are reported to child protection hotlines for much less than what I am describing here. The 1960s and '70s though were a different era in this regard. The average person didn't know much about child abuse or neglect, and public child welfare wasn't the same institution it is today.

When I was young, we were told that children were supposed to be seen and not heard. My siblings and friends played outside in the neighborhood, unsupervised for hours, and turned up at each other's homes unannounced for lunch or dinner. Helicopter parenting had not yet come into vogue. The children in our family walked to school, to the public library, music lessons, and the candy store by themselves. The older siblings' help was needed to run the household so we assisted with cooking, cleaning, childcare, and laundry. At times, our mother might not know where we had been until we showed up for dinner. We went unchaperoned to catechism classes and sporting events. We went to the doctor only for vaccinations and emergencies as opposed to regular well-child checkups. This was all perfectly normal at the time.

Given this context, it's hardly surprising that I can't recall any adult asking my siblings or me how we were faring after one of my mother's hospitalizations. We were generally well-behaved, high-achieving children, and so perhaps the alarms just didn't get triggered. Or maybe the adults thought these episodes were best left unmentioned. I also remembered the warning from my mother for revealing too much about our family business when my indiscriminate sharing as a child had come to light.

Someplace deep within, I understood early on that my mother was not the same as the other moms in our suburban St. Louis neighborhood. Even before I was in elementary school and invited over to other children's homes, I had the sense that something was off. I felt a reserve and caution around her rather than deep affection and trust. I tended to rely more on my father for emotional connection, despite that he was rarely at home. Her eruptions of anger for no apparent reason caused fear, confusion, and guilt. Over time I grew to believe I had done something wrong to deserve these rages, even if I actually hadn't. When Mom was in her severely depressed state, I felt the desperate urge to cheer her up or do some wonderful deed to snap her out of it.

But I had nothing else to compare with my experience and I didn't have the language to explain it. As far as I knew, this could have been what my peers experienced in the privacy of their family lives. I didn't dwell on it because that wouldn't have helped to do so. Like most people when faced with difficult circumstances, I focused on what was immediately in front of me and worked hard to keep my fragile sense of self-worth, anxiety, and sadness under wraps.

I am considered by others to be strong and resilient. It wasn't by chance that I had been given the ironic and unexplained award for most mature student at high school graduation. My experience as the oldest daughter of a woman who suffered as she did helped me become strong. It fueled my drive towards a career as a social worker and a therapist.

But my experience with my mother also left many scars, one of which is difficulty recognizing and accepting the need to lean on others, to open up and ask for help. Some others are the inability to validate my own good sense when someone in my personal life isn't treating me as they should and the knee-jerk feeling that I am somehow responsible when communication goes south. I tolerate a lot of oddities and unusual behavior, possibly too much in some situations. I've learned to soldier on through many difficult scenarios and have done so when it might have been better to acknowledge craziness and respond accordingly. It's also been a struggle for me to feel competent and worthy when comparing myself to a mother who seemed to excel at everything and lacked capacity to provide consistent praise and support.

Every human being has challenges, hurts, and wounds that shape our life journeys. None of us gets through a life unscathed. My mother couldn't help that she had mental health problems that affected her parenting. Unless a different kind of help had been available to her, she couldn't have done any better. I have certainly felt angry for how she affected my younger siblings and me. Fortunately, in recent years much of this anger has dissipated and what I feel mostly is sadness, loss, as well as compassion and forgiveness. I can now admire and appreciate her too.

Regarding our fate, our family is still fractured and wounded to this day as a result of our experiences growing up with our mother. However, I am sincerely grateful that no one ever filed a report with child welfare, and that my siblings and I avoided the potential for being split up and placed in foster care. As life evolved, each of us children found surrogate families on our own, which might not have met every need but did provide some added attention and sense of belonging somewhere.

A different kind of help for my mother, other than forced hospitalization and medications, probably would have made a positive difference for my siblings and me. But her paranoid tendencies made it hard for her to trust, and she generally wasn't a willing customer for service, so in reality this is quite uncertain. More so, I firmly believe having caring adults within and outside the family to talk with us about what was going on and to ask how we were doing, could have helped us children a lot. Then we could have known it wasn't us imagining or causing mom's mood shifts and crazy ways. Also, my mother could have been supported to consider the impact of her behavior and moods upon her children, so that there could have been some acknowledgement or dialogue with her instead of the proverbial elephant in the room of which no one dared speak.

I can't recall anyone in our family talking openly about my mother's mental health problems. I was well into middle age before this was discussed among my siblings and, even then, it spurred a sense of extreme disloyalty. We certainly wouldn't have talked about mental health when my mother was present. She never referred to these problems herself and wouldn't have tolerated any overt reference to her mental health by others. Her absolute adherence to this stance persisted even as our culture shifted to one of more openness and less shame for those who experience mental health problems.

At the crux, what stood in the way of acknowledging her frailty and the need for support was shame, hers and ours. Shame still is something that our society needs to confront if we are to deal with mental health problems in a truly compassionate way. I look forward to the day when a mother's mental health problems can be discussed with others in the community in the same way as when a child's mother has a serious medical issue and needs support. Unfortunately, we are not there yet.

In 2018, my mother Mary died at age eighty-six after being diagnosed with stage four lung cancer, three weeks before her death. Her long-held distrust of and paranoia towards the medical system not only kept her from getting treatment for her mental health problems for much of her life, but also enabled her to avoid any type of health care for decades. As a result, her death and dying process were needlessly painful and traumatic.

One of Mom's flaws was that she rarely acknowledged her shortcomings or expressed apology for any hurt she may have caused. I now understand this as a form of self-protection against vulnerability, but it left a wake of harm nonetheless. Her mental illness affected her life in many ways, especially the relationships with those close to her. As a result, my love for her was reserved and quite complicated. Yet, in some ways, her death provided a release both to her and her children from these complications. I know, for example, that I couldn't have written this account with complete honesty while she was still alive. In the end, in spite of her failings, I mourned Mom's death. I loved her.

LIFE LINES:
BRIGHT LIGHTS AT THE END OF DARK TUNNELS
BY ANN B. LIST

Ann B. List, PhD, MSW, lives in Albuquerque, NM, and is currently a free-lance editor of academic manuscripts. Her latest interests focus upon the lived experiences of adults with Asperger's disorder. annlist@comcast.net

The First Part of My Story

The day Mom went crazy is forever etched in my brain and body. I was barely eleven years old at the time.

The night before I had slept at the home of a hard-of-hearing neighbor, because she always hired either my sister or me to stay with her whenever her husband was out of town on business. We both liked the job because she always left treats on her kitchen counter, provided space to complete our homework, and had us sleep in her beautifully decorated guest room across the hall from the master bedroom. It was easy money for both my sister and me, enabling us to buy a coke or ice cream whenever friends suggested meeting after school at the local drugstore.

In the cafeteria on that day at school, a friend said, "I stopped by your house this morning to walk to school together. Your dad answered the door reminding me you'd spent the night at your neighbor's, and that your mom was saying strange things."

I asked, "What kind of strange things?"

My friend replied, "Your dad said she thought your house was burning down because of burnt bread in the toaster." It was a hurried conversation, because the cafeteria bell signaled time to leave for afternoon classes.

I dismissed my friend's comments for the rest of the afternoon because they seemed so bizarre. But because my friend had after-school activities, I walked home alone with increasing fears of seeing my home burnt to the ground, with fire trucks in the driveway, and firemen watering down the smoldering remains.

Instead, as I approached my home and opened the back door, I heard one of our neighbors say loudly, "Oh good, the children are coming home. Maybe they can talk some sense into Vida!"

What? I thought. *There's nothing wrong with my mom.*

But there obviously was.

Mom was on the front lawn yelling, screaming, and trying to tear off her clothing. A neighbor (I don't remember which one) held my arm to help me down the front steps toward Mom, saying, "Here, Vida, is your daughter Ann who just came home from school."

I quickly approached Mom and tried to embrace and comfort her. But she so forcefully pushed me away that I lost balance and fell to the ground. She screamed, "You're not my daughter. I don't have any children!"

When I was able to pick myself up off the ground, I noticed our family doctor among the neighbors gathered on our front lawn. I saw him pull a large syringe out of his little black bag and approach my mom. She saw the syringe as well and screamed even more loudly than before, "Get away from me. Get away – you're the enemy!"

At the same time, the ambulance (or paddy wagon, as it was often called back then) arrived and two big strong men jumped out and quickly wrestled Mom to the ground, wrapping her in a white straight jacket, and loading her into their van.

It all happened very quickly, but I heard sighs of relief from the neighbors. I burst into tears as the ambulance left. I blew Mom a kiss and watched as the vehicle drove slowly down our long dirt and gravel driveway.

But my tears wouldn't stop, and I needed to escape from the puzzled yet concerned looks of neighbors still lingering on our front lawn. I knew they wanted to comfort me, but nothing at that moment made sense to me. So, I smiled and backed away saying, "Excuse me, but I need to use the bathroom in the house right now."

I don't recall actually going inside my house right then. Instead, out of sight of the neighbors, I remember jumping up onto the large boulder next to the two-foot stone wall behind our house and making another small jump onto the wall that retained the small piece of wooded property my parents had purchased many years earlier.

On one end of this strip of property, Mom had planted a vegetable garden she tended on a regular basis. On the other end was a small pine tree shaped like a large beach umbrella. I often sat under that tree to either read, think about stuff going on in my life, or simply daydream about a happier future.

It was such a place of comfort that I named it "My Little Tree." No one in my family seemed to pay any attention to this small tree 'midst all the other trees, bushes, and overgrown weeds on that strip of land. And I never invited anyone to join me there, as I wanted it to remain my private secret place.

So, on that day after the paddy wagon left with Mom strapped inside, I sat under my special tree for hours all hunched up, crying. I let the tears flow freely, wiping them away on my sleeves and skirt, and eventually on the fallen leaves of other trees on the ground. All the while I kept praying, *Please, dear God, take care of Mom.*

I recently asked my sister if she was there watching our mom's first psychotic episode, because I couldn't remember. She replied that yes, she was there. She has also told me in the past that she's tried to forget those days, which is the main reason she dropped out of college with a full scholarship after her first year to marry a man who promised great wealth and a prosperous future.

I don't recall seeing my brother there either, even though I've recently asked him, with no response. After all, he was only four years old at the time and might either have been at a neighbor's house or repressed any memory of that day.

After that day, I went into a pretend mode that everything was okay with my family, even though Mom eventually went into a state hospital for the mentally insane for about two and a half years. We were not given a diagnosis at the time, although my dad regularly visited Mom and reported on her treatment and state of mind.

We knew she was receiving electroshock treatment for a period of time, with no positive results. One day our dad reported at dinner, "We nearly lost your mother this week. They gave her a course of insulin shock therapy, and she didn't respond well. The doctors worried she wouldn't come out of the insulin-induced coma, but she eventually did."

I completed my undergraduate degree at Cornell University majoring in the hard sciences (zoology, chemistry, and physics). After all, Mom had graduated from Radcliffe/Harvard with a master's degree in similar studies with a dream of obtaining either a PhD or MD.

But I continued to have the nagging question of, *Why did my mom go crazy?*

After Cornell, I decided to go for a master's degree at the Smith College School of Social Work, thinking I might find something in its library system to help me understand Mom's weird behavior on that day. At Smith, we visited a local state mental hospital. I teared up, remembering the shadow-like figure of my zombie Mom whenever she came home from the hospital for a few hours to visit. The doctors had thought these brief home visits might help Mom regain her memory and enable her to function better during her treatment.

There was one visit at home when I tried to hug and comfort her. But in her drugged state, she didn't acknowledge me as her daughter. She sat still as stiff as a board, and with a slight move of her elbow pushed me away. Once again, I retreated to my little tree, crying tears all over my body and the ground. It was like a repeat of the day I had spent a few years earlier.

When I returned home from my first "real job" as a school social worker in Rochester, New York, there was an incident that prompted me to engage in intensive psychotherapy. I was sitting in a long line of traffic waiting for a red light to change to green, and suddenly a wave of panic came over me. I slowly edged my way into the right-hand lane of traffic and finally found a spot to park my car against the curb. I felt totally immobilized, fearing I would faint and not be able to get to the safety of the small apartment my husband and I shared across the street from the medical school he attended.

My immediate fear was, *Am I going crazy like Mom?*

Since those days, I spent many years in intensive psychotherapy. Yes, it was pricey, but I truly believe all those years enabled me to shed my fears of going crazy like Mom. An important issue I dealt with in my first six years of psychoanalysis was my fear of having children. I married at the age of twenty-two in 1961, and the expectation in our social circle at that time was that young couples would raise children. The problem was that I worried I'd someday erupt like Mom and all the pain and anger inside would turn me into a battering abusive mother.

Then there were always the dreaded anniversaries, especially my forty-seventh birthday, the same age as Mom when she had her first psychotic break. And I dreaded every year when any one of my three children turned eleven years of age. In the back of my mind was the fear that her psychosis would finally erupt in my own life and that my children would become as bewildered as I had been at that age.

In my final year of my first course of psychoanalysis, I gave birth to my first child. I remember saying to my psychiatrist Dr. L., "I can't believe I can love another little soul so much." Of course, I did what Mom had done with my siblings and me: I breast-fed my first child until he was ready to drink from a cup. No baby bottles in my house, please! It was the same with my second and third child.

The early years of raising my children were among the happiest years of my life. I had the luxury of being a full-time mom, without having to split my time between motherhood and my career. After all, I had worked to support my husband and myself during his medical training, paying many of his medical school bills. So, I felt entitled to devote full time to raising our children until they were ready for morning pre-school sessions and eventually all-day public school. I had no guilt about the arrangement.

Also, during that time I improved my sewing skills and made most of my young children's clothing. I became a voracious recipe-reader and learned how to make the best use of leftovers from supermarket sales of protein and fresh produce in nearby stores. I think it was in my genes to live frugally the way my parents did during the Great Depression of the 1930's.

✧

A few words about my youngest child at almost four years of age. One day she said she wanted to go play with her friend next door. I replied, "Okay, let me call her mother to see if it's okay, and then I'll walk you on the street over the arroyo." When I called my neighbor Marla, she said, "Of course they can play today, but Malia is already in our driveway. She apparently walked across the arroyo by herself."

"What?!" I screamed. But then the thunderbolt hit me. *Oh, no, oh my… my little girl doesn't need me so much anymore.*

It was on that day that I realized my children were on their way to independence, and it was time for me to return to my career as a school social worker.

✧

But there was still something I needed to deal with. I called it my "face-cracking phobia." No, it's not a diagnosis, just my own little name for it. It went like this: Whenever I was in an intense, serious conversation with a friend, colleague, or supervisor, I felt the need to place a hand on my face. It didn't matter where on my face. At first it was on one of my cheeks, then later on my forehead, chin, or an ear. I knew it was a self-soothing tactic, but I couldn't help it.

If I couldn't in some way place my hand on my face, I feared it would crack wide open and all kinds of ugly pus and blood would spew out. It was as if I were trying to corral my ongoing fear of "going crazy" just like Mom.

✧

There came a time when I realized my marriage was falling apart. Yes, it had once been one of those white picket fence dream marriages, but something was missing. Even though we had spent seven years together camping and backpacking all up and down the Rocky Mountains during summer vacations prior to beginning a family, there was definitely something wrong. It was as if I had married my adventurous brother or a handsome successful best friend. But sadly, there was little chemistry in our relationship as far as I was concerned.

That's when I returned for a second course of psychoanalysis. "What's wrong with me?" I asked. Here I had three thriving kids, an active social life in my community, and a job I enjoyed because of the challenges it presented. This second series of psychoanalytic sessions lasted five years. I appreciated that I could once again lie down on a couch and not have to look face-to-face with my psychiatrist. I could be "me, myself, and I" without feeling any need to touch my face for fear it might crack wide open and explode with all the ugly feelings I'd spent decades trying to conceal.

By the fourth year of this series of therapy sessions, and after my husband and I had engaged in several weeks of couple's therapy, I came to a huge realization. It was during our final session with our couples therapy psychiatrist when Dr. G. announced, "This marriage is going nowhere. It's neither going forward nor backward; it's just stuck. Any more effort you put into it will be like pouring water into a bucket with a hole in the bottom."

That was it for me. Time to move on and proceed with a divorce.

I subsequently met with an attorney one of my friends had recommended to initiate the divorce and sign the necessary paperwork, but my larger concern was the impact of divorce on our children, who were by now eight, ten, and twelve years old. In my work as a school social worker, I knew it would hugely impact them. So, I lined up a psychiatrist for them to see as needed. The most important credential of this particular psychiatrist was that she was interested in meeting with family members of her patients without violating the confidentiality of her clients. I said to her on our first visit together, "I don't want to know what you and my kids discuss. All I want to know is how I can support them at this time – and also what I shouldn't do that might impede your work with them."

Continuing my quest to understand Mom's behavior, I became involved with my local National Alliance for Mental Illness (NAMI) chapter.

Most members were parents of mentally ill children. Even though I couldn't really relate to their concerns as parents, I knew I had finally found a community where I felt comfortable. It was like, *Thank God, I can finally remove my mask of pretense that all is well, and be able to talk with and learn from other family members with mentally ill children, siblings, and/or parents.* I sensed that we had all lived with shame and guilt for many years and finally needed to get out of the closet and begin taking action.

I was energized by the vibrant determination of the members of this local group to make changes in the ways the medical community, police and sheriff detectives, and political figures viewed our family members I subsequently facilitated many educational courses and support groups for people and their families dealing with mental illness.

In one of my support groups, a young male participant stated, "I'd rather my sister live on the streets as a homeless person, because that's when her real personality comes through. For me, it's so much better than when she's in a medical setting all drugged up like a zombie. Yes, I do get calls from the police now and then alerting me she's in jail. And that's okay. I do my best to help with the situation, because after all, she is my sister. I've been fortunate with my own family and career, but she has not. And so, it might be guilt on my part that life has gone well for me, but not for her. That's why I do what I can, and that's why I'm here…to find some support from this group."

I was eventually recruited to take the lead in introducing a packaged educational and support program into our state (initially called Journey of Hope, but later named Family-to-Family Support and Education Program). I was scared to death of assuming such a role, as I had always been hugely anxious about talking to large groups of people, always looking over my shoulder for a rest room or back door I could use to escape from my terror. But I didn't want to turn down the invitation, so I enrolled in a local Toastmaster's Club to overcome my immobilizing fear of public speaking. It took four years of regular weekly attendance at my Toastmaster's Midday Madness club for me to finally conquer my terror. (It was called Midday Madness because we met every Thursday at a downtown facility throughout the year from noon until 1:00 pm, no matter the weather.)

Joining Toastmasters and working hard to prepare presentations to fellow club members was truly a life-changing experience for me. It enabled me to take on the role of the New Mexico Coordinator of the Family-to-Family program, sponsored by NAMI, during which time I traveled around the state to assist several communities in setting up the program. It also enabled me to organize workshops in Albuquerque twice a year to train others to facilitate Family-to-Family programs around the state.

It was so wonderful joining with others who had family members with mental illness. Of course, we had boxes of Kleenex always handy. And the real joy was seeing family members shift frustration into action to raise awareness about the need for improved services in our communities.

Because of my own experience with mental illness and interest in supporting families dealing with similar issues, I positioned myself as a school social worker to obtain assignments working with some of these most challenging students and families in my school district. It was often heartbreaking when community systems failed to work together to provide services for these young students and their families. But we kept trying and did manage to make some small but important improvements. As far as I was concerned, it was with much joy on the day of my retirement from the school system that I had made a difference in the lives of my students and their families. It was similar to the joy and satisfaction I had felt during my many years of volunteer work with NAMI.

Thus, in spite of several rough patches over the course of my life, I feel incredibly blessed in so many ways. There have been numerous people I regard as my lifelines, who have helped keep me afloat during choppy times. They have buoyed me with their faith that I'll find a way to make things better, and they have opened doors to opportunities I never would have found on my own.

The Second Part of My Story

It was only two years ago that I realized my dad fit the profile of someone with Asperger's disorder. This realization turned my world upside down in the sense that I shifted from a daughter who had despised my father all my life to a more compassionate adult daughter.

After a considerable amount of reading on the topic of Asperger's, it became clear to me he fit the profile: extremely intelligent and successful in academic environments but totally lacking in social skills, along with outbursts of uncontrollable anger. (That was my dad, when he'd belt me severely and relentlessly for reasons I didn't understand.) Nevertheless, he had completed college in three years with nothing less than all A grades and was inducted into the academic honorary society of Phi Beta Kappa.

His main interest focused on English words and their origins and derivations. He taught most of his career as an English professor at a prominent Boston university, specializing in linguistics and semantics. After retiring, he spent his remaining years driving up and down the East coast helping colleges and universities establish and maintain Phi Kappa Phi academic societies.

There was a story he often repeated about his childhood, when his eyes would light up with pride and he would glance at anyone listening. In it, he recalled guiding a mule and plow up and down numerous rows of cotton on the family farm. At the end of each row as the mule and plow were turning around, he would pull a little dictionary out of his shirt pocket to learn a new word. He always emphasized he had ordered the dictionary from a Sears catalogue, because that's how his family shopped for anything they didn't grow or raise on their farm.

His other major interest was anything related to machines. During World War II, when educators were not in high demand, he managed to obtain a night job working on jet airplane engines at the General Electric plant in Lynn, Massachusetts. He and Mom worked out an arrangement to drop off my sister and me at day-care or kindergarten, so they could both maintain their jobs. It was a fine arrangement with Dottie and me, because we met new friends and engaged in fun activities with them.

But my dad's interest in machines often became obsessive. For example, sometimes our annual trips to visit his family in Georgia were delayed for many hours and even a day or two, because he needed to work on the family car to insure it was safe enough to travel. It really didn't matter to Mom and my sister, as even though the refrigerator had been emptied, we got through the delays by eating peanut butter, jelly, and crackers from the kitchen cupboard. Plus, there was still water and electricity in the house so we could use the toilet and drink water from the bathroom and kitchen faucets, and there were lots of books in the house to read while waiting to embark.

∽

Thankfully, I did have one small connection with my father through my interest in playing the violin. He didn't play any musical instruments, nor did I ever hear him sing anything in tune. But once when my violin bow became nearly hairless, he agreed to take it to a specialty shop in Boston to get it re-haired. I was grateful, because my music teacher had said she'd stop taking me on as a scholarship student unless I did something to fix my bow. He also did drive me to a few musical events whenever I performed and it was too dark for me to walk there and back. Those were mainly times when Mom was either in the hospital or too sick to drive, so I very much appreciated my dad supporting me, even though he usually complained about the cost of gas for his car.

He was one really weird guy. But now that I realize he was very likely a person with Asperger's, I'm much more content and able to write something about him without a slew of curse words flowing from my mouth onto the written page.

He actually lived to be four hours short of one hundred and one years of age. My sister, who lives in Massachusetts, called to let me know me know our dad was actively dying and hoped I could catch a flight to be with him before he died. I checked the schedules of all the major airlines and told my sister I couldn't possibly get there in time because of the many different connections I'd have to make between Albuquerque and Cape Cod. She said she understood and would call me soon after our dad took his last breath.

And so, she did. I asked her to please put her cell phone next to Dad's ear so I could say something to him. I told him, "I know you and I have had many tough times with each other, but I want you to know I love you in spite of it all."

Somehow, those words were very easy to say, knowing he was now dead and could no longer belt me nor push me away whenever I tried to hug him.

This realization about my dad as an "Aspie" (as they're often called these days), has also helped answer the main question my sister, brother, and I have had for decades: Did our dad cause Mom to become mentally ill?

Possibly, but who knows? My dad often remarked that mental illness seemed to run in Mom's family, and he would cite examples of my maternal grandmother's weird behaviors. I barely knew her, so I couldn't respond to his remarks. By contrast, he would often launch into memories of his own mother as a very loving woman. I don't recall ever being with her. But I'm sure she must have been proud of her very bright son's success in the academic world. After all, he was her only son among several daughters, and he had helped the family by working in the fields and assisting his own dad with various tasks required to run a farm.

I'll probably never find answers to my questions, but it really doesn't matter anymore. I'm just happy to have good-enough genes to still be alive and able to write this essay.

JUST PASSING THROUGH
BY RENA MAAS

Rena Maas is s part-time writer and a full-time mom. She
lives in Tempe, Arizona with her wife Melissa, two kids,
two cats, and a dog named Booker. Go Suns!

Kids don't have to pass
They are just kids doing kid things
They are present to themselves and others

But soon I learned that passing was all about race
Once we were old enough to be cruel
once alliances were drawn and the boys made the rules
I was cast as "other," - no longer Mexican-enough to be part of the group
They laid it out: skin too light wrong last name can't hang in Spanish

Passing as White was a consolation prize for a devastating dismissal
I found myself in a whole new world
with a gift I didn't want and couldn't use
a "pass" that only served to make me an outsider in two cultures

Eventually reverence for family and culture were restored
I was allowed into the group again but the sting remained

Later passing was all about sexuality
Being labeled as gay
was a disorienting blow to my already-confused mind
My first defense was just a gentle push-off
"you don't know what you think you know"
I wasn't sure of anything myself

Passing meant safe harbor from the ire of friends and family
And sometimes physical protection from perfect strangers
It got better as I got older, but the nastiness lingered
both in my head and all around me when I least expected it

I wasn't trying to pass I just wanted to be left alone
Maybe that was the same thing
And then one day all the difficulties fell away
Without my noticing my sexuality morphed into something new

I had a baby never knowing it was the ultimate pass

Overnight people's faces softened and their tone changed
I had joined a protected class – women and children
The nastiness from when I was younger lived on in my head
but outwardly everything changed

Motherhood flung open windows and doors
and invited me into places I never could have anticipated -
Parent groups, play dates, and gymboree classes
even restaurants treated me different
Kids were a force so strong that even when people knew I was passing
they waved it off
I was dismissed before I could confess

But for as long as I can remember I've never passed as sane
Not as a kid not in the halls of adolescence
Not as a parent in the mainstream middle class
And not with my own children

Despite all the normalcy I was handed
I talked too much or too little
Too loud or too quickly
then sometimes pressured speech and no speaking at all

I pushed the idea of normalcy
and sometimes I felt like I was managing pretty well
Each of my behaviors felt excusable on its own
but my pile of symptoms was a mile high

Generalized anxiety sometimes raced to low level panic
The buzz and glare of commercial lighting
sometimes led to disorganized thinking and jumbled speech

Most debilitating was the isolation brought by failure
the dissolution of work and friendships
I'm not a liar
and there were way too many gaps to explain away

Times are changing of course (however slowly)
Like diabetes, depression and anxiety are sometimes now
"just one of those things"
But I know I mustn't stray far from there
Schizoeffective is more like terminal cancer (or leprosy or the plague)
Bipolar is a short hop in either direction

I'm somewhere down the line making the most of my situation
I wasn't passing and I was facing that fact
but I never had to pass as anything with my kids

With tremendous support both personal and professional
I am able to be fully present to them
never demanding perfection but always demanding their presence

My goal is not just normalcy but some kind of ordinariness
I am the real me and we connect in a very real way

Somewhere along the line my kids came to realize
Not only that I needed them but that they were already helping me
and that I relied on them
My kids and I reached a type of equilibrium
and fortunately this brought us closer

Just like when I was a kid
my kids weren't thinking about passing (mine or theirs)
They were just kids doing kid things
present to themselves and others

And I return to where I started never an interloper to myself
My passing was never about being surreptitious
trespassing and traveling where I don't belong
Instead it was about allowing people their own assumptions

Passing might not be an easy way to get through life
But sometimes it is the only way

Gleaning the Gifts from Inner Darkness
By Myra McKenzie

Myra McKenzie holds a Bachelor of Fine Arts in Sculpture from The University of Tennessee at Chattanooga. She has an intuitive interest in symbolic studies explored through world religions, Jungian psychology, spirituality, myth, and dream work. Her mixed media art assemblages are a reflection of these explorations. Myra lives in a wooded sanctuary in Santa Fe, NM with her amazing husband and their extraordinary cat.

"If you bring forth what is within you, what you bring forth will save you.

If you do not bring forth what is within you, what you do not bring forth will destroy you."

– Gospel of Thomas, verse 70

I like to say that what some might call "pathological" could also be a path through another kind of logic. Learning to swim in the undercurrents of depression and navigating the shatterings of mania can bring forth some unexpected treasures. Jean Houston, the brain/mind researcher, talks about looking into what we may see as pathology and finding an emerging mythology, a cosmology, and a deeper psychology at work in the psyche. She calls this process "pathos to mythos." (Houston, 1987, p. 108)

To look for the mythological dimension of mental illness is not to dismiss the reality of mental illness. This can invite a deeper look into the mythological dimensions of our minds and lives. The Arthurian legend of the Fisher King is a good illustration of how ancient myth can and does work through the modern psyche. In the myth of the Fisher King, the King's wound cannot heal and therefore the land and the people of his kingdom are also suffering. For the King to heal, the right question must be asked, and that question is: "What ails thee?"

This seems to be an essential question to ask in regard to mental illness. It is a question to ask on many levels, as it is a living question. There is another essential question to consider when discussing mental illness. We need to ask, "For what purpose does this serve?" Being a person who inherited some configuration of my father's bipolar chemistry, working with these questions helps me to navigate my path through what is called pathology. The journey has been a fierce gift and a mythological voyage for me, in its own right.

Pathos is the Greek word for suffering. Buddha said that life is suffering and that the root of suffering is attachment. Attachment, aversion, pushing and pulling, are all forms of resistance. To resist is to suffer. By resisting my own pathology, namely depression, I created even more suffering. In retrospect, I see that one of the purposes that depression served in my life has been to slow down. This has cultivated a rhythm in me that goes counter to the cultural norm, but it is something I have come to appreciate.

It seems that I inherited the flip side of my father's chemistry. While he was definitely more manic, I have tended to be the "daughter of darkness," my tongue-in-cheek nickname for myself. Yet when I am able to not resist or judge what ails me, I can see how depression contributes a deeper purpose to my life.

My father died at forty-five, when I was six years old. I am the youngest of five children. Even though he was never diagnosed as bipolar, I know that he was. Like I know that I had learning disabilities, even though I was never diagnosed. I went to kindergarten and first grade twice, had a nightmarish relationship with school, and barely attended five different high schools before dropping out in tenth grade.

My first full-blown anxiety attack may have been in first grade, triggered by the dreaded arrows: The greater-than and less-than signs. Those arrows still hold a charge for me. I just didn't get it. It is still confusing to me. I scarcely read any books until I was twenty-one years old. At sixty-four, I am still trying to tease out the tangled web of layers of what's what.

Did the trauma of my dad dying cause me to have learning disabilities or was it the trauma of growing up in an alcoholic household in a conservative Christian environment? There was an impressive saturation level of alcoholism in our home and in the extended community. Both parents were committed drinkers, and then two stepfathers came on the scene to keep the party going. My mom loved to play bridge, as it was a good way for her to drink all day.

I was diagnosed multiple times with bipolar as a young adult. It took going through four manic episodes and three "shatterings" (profound disintegrations) before I got that Lithium might be a good friend to have. Breaking the denial and moving through the layers of stigma around being manic depressive was a process. Over the years, I have drawn heavily on Marion Woodman's words: "Shattering into wholeness." (Woodman, 2001, p. ix)

Lithium may not be a fit for everyone with this diagnosis, but for me it has been a synergistic key to the mythic question, "What ails thee?" After fourteen years on a prescription of Lithium Carbonate, last year I made a supervised shift to the over-the-counter supplement, Lithium Orotate. Lithium is a good friend for me, maybe even a lifesaver. It has provided an essential container. It sure helps to take the edge off.

In contrast, I see the ways my father tried to take the edge off. He was an alcoholic, a compulsive gambler, and he smoked himself to death, ultimately dying of lung cancer. I smoked for thirty years. Maybe that was another way to have a relationship with the mythological creature that was my dad.

Smoking, Smoking
A lifeline ritual of carrying my father's compulsion.
Needing the fix of elemental support - the ritual
of earth and fire and spirit and breath.
For thirty years I was loyal to the tobacco sticks
- a love affair of sorts. Sending smoke signals
as a way to stop and see my breath.
The intimate obsession that would take me outside,
into my protective alcove,
with early light and starry night,
my galactic womb time.

I quit smoking about nine months after I got on Lithium. Burning Palo Santo, known as the "holy stick" (kin to Frankincense and known as the sage of South America) is such a fragrant friend. This and making art in tobacco boxes continue to be a huge support for weaning off my smoking obsession.

I will confess that food and shopping are still addictive outlets for me, as I continue trying to get those primal connection needs met. Untangling this web is a life's work. In our own way, it seems we are all trying to make friends with the howling void.

The addictive impulse runs deep. Thrift stores may always carry an irresistible urge for the treasure hunt they hold. And how compelling is that "Buy Now" button! Hunting and gathering. Food and weight and stuff all seem to provide an added buffer for my hypersensitive nervous system. As I have been immersed in this writing, the food thing has been rearing its head. As I unpack this family trunk, I feel the urge to numb down. I remembered a tin of those cream-filled cookies that I stashed in the surplus refrigerator. Can't eat just one.

My relationship with the fast-food world took on a life of its own when I got my driver's license. This was around the time that I went through a violent rape, in my sixteenth year. I am still under the spell of those fast-food forays. Will this spell of compulsion ever be broken? How to be with this yearning, seeking, hiding, cloistered in my car, feeding the fury. I am hooked on this toxic communion and then wash it down with Coke!

What is it I really want? Catch the Wave, break the spell ... give me the Real thing. And I don't mean soda pop ... give me the Ultimate effervescence . . .

My Invocation
Give me the Bread of Life
Wash me in the Living Waters
Ignite my Heart with Holy Fire
Blow the Breath of Life into me
May I Be Still and Know
May I shed old skins
May I rest in the Peace that passeth
May I allow space for Grace!

I love this insight from Joseph Campbell that says, "It would not be too much to say that myth is the secret opening through which the inexhaustible energies of the cosmos pour into human cultural manifestation." (Campbell, 1968, p. 3) Perhaps aspects of what we might call mental illness could also be secret openings, invitations into the portals of the psyche yet to be explored or understood.

My dad was a live wire for mythic energy, sadly lacking the tools to harness that energy in a sustainable way. An outrageous fellow, he was an honorary assistant coach for the Detroit Lions because he was such a huge fan. To make it official, he was sent a company check for a dollar. My brother still has this framed and on display. During football games, Dad would buy racks of Cokes, top them off with bourbon, and hand them out to the crowd. He was probably roaring like a lion as he fueled the spectators into a frenzy!

When he was traveling, Dad would parade the aisle on his airplane trips (back in the day when that was allowed) and engage the passengers in card tricks. He was extroverted out the wazoo, an entertainer, and a wild man. He never went anywhere without a prop, some sort of a gimmick.

 He was a dazzling salesman, and a key player in our family business. He never met a stranger. He had a gift for remembering people's names and was the life of the party. The Joker is wild! It was all in the cards for him, gambling and card tricks. The Trickster, the Fool - he was burning on both ends and casting himself off cliffs. He lost the mortgage on two different houses in gambling debts when our two oldest sisters were little. He was a gambling fool.

Speaking of cards, the Fool is the first card in the Tarot deck. The Tarot is like a pictorial dictionary for myth and symbol and covers a comprehensive swath of archetypes. The Fool can be seen as the alpha and the omega of the Tarot deck because the major arcana begins and comes full circle with the Fool card. The Fool's quantum leap holds the possibility for an integration into an ultimate stability. I find my way along the continuum between mania and depression, always aiming for that mystical middle.

"'Tis better to light one candle than to curse the darkness." (Attributed to William L. Watkinson) I would add that it is better to keep one candle lit than to try to burn it on both ends like my dad clearly did. A tragic story line in our family revolves around my father having a psychotic break in 1945. He broke a Coke bottle and cut his wrists and his throat. When my mom got to him at Walter Reid Hospital, on a Fourth of July weekend, he was in a strait jacket hearing voices. Strangely, two of my manic episodes also peaked on the Fourth of July.

This bipolar trip through manic depression holds an ongoing opportunity for the practice Carl Jung offers when he says "to hold the tension of the opposites." (Sharp, 2001, p. 39) This union of opposites is a gestalt, the synergistic goal of alchemy, the gold of consciousness. I have heard it said, "It is not the yin or the yang, but the silver thread that connects the two."

My alchemical integration of support includes Lithium and an arsenal of tools to help keep me on track. My inner work includes lots of counseling, therapy, much study, art, and meditation, as well as close friendships. These are my essential touchstones that have given me access to more of a sustainable stability than my father was able to find in his forty-five years.

As a mixed media artist, most of my artwork has been born from an all-consuming need and desire for containership. Even before I had the first shattering that came with the second full-blown manic episode, I was making baskets, coiling and weaving. I pulled grape vines, honey suckle and wisteria, even kudzu from the trees. I dyed reeds. I worked as a full-time basket maker for a good dozen or so years. I sold my baskets at art shows, and had gallery and museum representation. I taught basket making. I was a professional basket case.

Basketry was the first phase of physically creating an artistic expression out of the need for containership. This morphed into creating bags from men's neckties (I called this venture MetamorphaTies) and making books and art altars. I continue to work with assembling medicine bundles, many in cigar boxes.

All these art forms are containers in their own right. After spending five years in art therapy, this pattern really revealed itself. I still have lots of these box assemblages, fifty-seven at last count. They are like little anchors, links to my inner world. Each has a theme, a collection of objects that represent some essential symbol. They represent a core paradoxical theme in my life around how to contain the uncontainable.

The term "creative illness" has been defined by Henri Ellenberger as "struggles at self-healing" and he suggests that both Freud's and Jung's systems of analysis were very much the result of their respective "creative illnesses." (Aziz, 1990, p. 13) Jung spoke of this as a "confrontation with the unconscious." (Jung, Memories, Dreams, Reflections, 1989, p. 170) Creative illness navigates through the unconscious. The wounded healer is born from these struggles with self-healing. This is worthy encouragement for those willing to make the soulful decent into the introverted realms of the psyche, where gifts and gold are gleaned in unexpected places.

Creative illness has a decidedly different ring than mental illness. Creative illness suggests the tracking of trauma and the excavation of treasures, with the wound being the portal. Speaking from personal experience, I see that our wounds are sacred. As the now famous words from Leonard Cohen say, "There is a crack, a crack in everything. That's how the light gets in." (Cohen, 1992)

A salient question for Jung was, "What is the myth you are living?" Mental illness, myth, and the unconscious are immense subjects. As the ultimate treasure is the gold of consciousness, the insights and synergistic connections make this adventure a worthwhile quest. How do we align with the individual myth that can help us on our unique journeys to be more conscious, to get to the heart of the questions, "What ails thee?" and "For what purpose does this serve?"

I resonate with a personal myth of being a pearl diver. Making the descents into the oceanic underworld inevitably reveals unexpected gifts. Glimpses into the scintillating web of interconnectedness often will deliver a tangible manifestation.

I Want to Dive In

She says: You are a pearl diver
I say: Pearls come from such profound irritation

She says: Trust that profundity
I say: The strands of pearls I have given birth to…

She says: Do you see the gifts in this excruciating sensitivity?
I say: Yes, like a raku pot

She says: Follow the patterns of your own shattering
I say: Since I can never be lost in my own constellation

She says: Yes, rip up the map
I say: And make art from the remnants

She says: And offer it all to the fire

Jung said, "People will do anything, no matter how absurd, in order to avoid facing their own souls. One does not become enlightened by imagining figures of light, but by making the darkness conscious." (Jung, Psychology and Alchemy, 1980, p. 99) Following the imagistic threads from the interior worlds can bring insights and support for unplugging from limiting viewpoints, whether they be from familial or cultural conditioning or our self-imposed conditioned patterns of limitation.

I have gained a new appreciation from having spent so much time in the underworld (i.e. the inner world). After spending so many years thinking, Why can't I function like other people?, I now have a deeper appreciation for the gifts of abnormality. The upside-down place teaches me a soulful, symbolic, imagistic language that is not as available in the topside world.

Those dips into outer darkness have been catalysts for some valuable personal work. Years of depression taught me a way to be in the world, a way to see the world through an alternative lens. It took a long time to get this, but it can be like a meditation. When things slow down to a snail's pace and there is no energy available but for the bare essentials, there is another way of seeing that starts to emerge. It is more about being than doing.

Fragmentation can become a shimmering tapestry when we engage the salient questions:

"What ails thee?" and "For what purpose does this serve?" Pain can be the fuel for transformation. The humiliation that came from not being able to function (like other people) continues to cultivate compassion in me, for myself and for others.

When we can see that there is ultimately one mind, that we are each a facet in the Infinite Field of life expression, then perhaps all manifestations of this one mind can have a place at the table without discrimination. I like to think of it as the Unified Field, which reflects the words from Rumi, who said, "Out beyond ideas of wrongdoing and right doing, there is a field. I'll meet you there." (Jalal al-Din Rumi, 1989, p. 59) I am still working on taking up full-time residency in this elusive Field

Many years ago, I was enrolled in a master's class called Counseling Theory and Practice. The final paper assignment was to pick three theoreticians, pick an issue, and have an encounter with each one using active imagination. This was a powerful exercise. Of course, the issue I chose was my relationship with the bipolar dynamic, working with Carl Jung (Psychoanalytic), Gregory Bateson (Systems Theory), and Bonnie Badenoch (Integrative-Interpersonal Neuroscience).

As my father had the propensity to throw himself into life in some wild ways, I have had some similar inclinations in the interior dimension, including deep journeys into the underworld. The following is an excerpt of this class assignment, an exercise in active imagination and the remarkable fruits it bore. Since anything is possible in the imaginal world, I am pleased with my great good fortune to be able to create my first appointment with Dr. Carl Jung:

Stepping through the veil of time into Jung's office feels like déjà vu. He welcomes me into his office. I tell him about my history of depression, that there is much fluctuation in mood throughout my life. I tell him some about my family history and about some early trauma, and that in 1985 I had the first of four manic episodes. There seems to be a mythological theme to my episodes, and I am hoping that he can shed some light onto this for me.

I share the crescendo of my first manic episode, when I was twenty-seven years old. It happened during a session with a healer, a woman I had been doing some work with. After an in-depth period of studying ancient Egyptian mysteries, during one of the healing sessions, I landed in the Great Pyramid, in the Queens chamber. I tell Jung that thirty-seven years later, I am still processing this experience.

There are many layers to this Egypt experience. Leading up to and following this unexpected excursion were many mind-blowing synchronicities that would be the familiar signature for these manic episodes. This first full-blown manic experience blew my psyche open in a big way, and it felt like I broke through some sort of a time/space barrier into another dimension. But it did not have the same kind of fragmenting, shattering effect that the following ones had. I explain to Dr. Jung that true to form, after my manic episodes, I would spiral down into a deep depression that would last for months and even years.

Jung says that dreams and visions are ways that we access the collective unconscious and that interpreting life as if it is a dream is another way to gain access into this domain. He speaks of the archetypal energies in this dimension that can bring tremendous support, insight, and guidance. He encourages me to continue to draw on the energy of this revelatory breakthrough, that an experience with this much amplitude would be something that most likely would continue to unfold. This is true for me.

In this exchange with Jung, the Queen's chamber takes on a numinous quality, and I become aware of the power and the importance of preserving the feminine mysteries. Jung reminds me that the journey of the feminine involves a decent into darkness. He sheds insight into my history of depression by offering it to me as a journey of the soul.

Jung tells me that his life work came from an extended period of time when he thought he may have been losing his mind. This is so reassuring to me. I ask him about the rock tower he built in his later life. The glint in his eyes is palpable as he relays how playing with the stones by the river brought integration to his life work. He says he always encourages his patients to remember what it was they loved to do as a child and to set about to do it. Jung alludes to a therapeutic modality that would emerge after he is gone that would use art as a way to heal the psyche. I am excited to talk about this with him, but I can see he is fading. As I step back through the veil into another time and place, I hear him tell me that I might want to talk with a man named Dr. Gregory Bateson.

Crossing the mysterious threshold from Jung's office, I find myself in a most unusual tea parlor. This is the setting where Bateson appears for a brief but potent interlude. He is interested to hear about the "shattering" that I had mentioned to Jung.

I tell him that in my manic episodes, I experience an activation through the exploration of ideas that accelerate something within me, pushing the envelope of my psyche's capacity. The rev up of hyper overdrive tended to last for several months, with so much synchronicity pouring in, it would have a staggering effect. These periods of mania would culminate in a span of about eight days with very little food or sleep.

I tell Bateson that going through this process several times has taken its toll on my nervous system. I tell him about the very strange sense of suspended animation that would happen before the shattering. There would be a period of such deep stillness, it was as if my psyche were a raku pot and all the pieces would float out into space (now I know where the term "crack pot" comes from!) This is very disconcerting, to say the least. Bateson's response to this description continues to act like a scaffolding of support. I hear him say, within myself, "Radical disintegration is often necessary for the reconfiguration of profound reintegration, for the emergence of a more evolved pattern of possibility." This feels like the most potent feedback I could have hoped for.

Dr. Bonnie Badenoch, who teaches and counsels from a neurological perspective, seems to know that I have been diagnosed with bipolar disorder and that I want to understand this from a neurological point of view. She says that there is a lot she can share with me about this, and that it is good news.

Badenoch acknowledges that I have had a lot of therapy to deal with early trauma and goes on to talk to me about ways to regulate the nervous system. She explains that there are many ways to implement mindfulness practice. I ask her how therapy plays into the neurodynamic. She says that when old trauma is activated, the rapport with the therapist counts for so much. She makes the point that neurobiology, and how it translates into neuropsychology, is helping us to understand and cultivate the practice of compassion and empathy. These are the qualities that generate deep healing, for each other and for ourselves.

Another exciting thing in this field is the neuroplasticity factor. This offers us the knowledge that we are much more malleable than previously thought, bringing greater hope for the possibility of change. Badenoch, like Jung and Bateson, offers some exciting breakthroughs, not just because of the information they imparted, but also in the possibilities for future practice. It is surprising to get feedback from myself that brings insight, encouragement, and possibilities that are outside of my conscious awareness but clearly tapping into what I have studied.

There is so much written these days about the new research into neuroplasticity, the malleability of the brain. "Energy flows where attention goes," and what we pay attention to is what fires and wires new neural pathways. What an amazing thing! This taps into the power of inner work and brings to mind what Jesus said, "For where your treasure is, there will your heart be also." (New Revised Standard Version Bible, 1989, Matt. 6:21)

I like to say, "Where our attention is, there will our heart be also." Joseph Chilton Pierce, another brain/mind researcher, spoke of the Intelligence of the heart. So much research has gone into this. I love the way Pierce says that the brain has limited resources, where the heart has infinite resources. (Pierce, 2002) The heart is more than a metaphor and has the capacity to tap into the Unified Field. Dropping from the head into the heart is some powerful inner work in and of itself.

Manic depression is a full spectrum dance, and learning to hold this tension in the world of opposites is the work of a lifetime. I've heard it said that the truth is what opposites have in common. Maybe the shift into pure radiant spaciousness happens in the twinkling of an eye when we can follow the simple instructions to "resist nothing." (Tolle, 1999, p. 2)

Being bipolar is like having a built-in hard drive that programs the nervous system to dissolve boundaries. Having gone through several devastating shatterings, I yearn for boundaries. After quitting high school and those early years of acting out, wanting to be seen, flailing about and yearning for connection, it is a relief to find my true feeding ground in solitude. And yet I do desire and require meaningful connections with people. It has taken me a long time to trust my soul's inclination as a contemplative: Reveling in alone time, I follow my wander flow in the studio, on the land, or just doing the laundry. Another lesson in living my truth in the dynamic tension of opposites!

Depression for me relates to earth and water. Both embody the dark depths. Like the chthonic mysteries of mother earth and the vast primordial realm of oceanic feelings. Like Persephone abducted into the underworld or Jonah swallowed by the whale. Mania, on the other hand, is about fire and wind for me. Like being swept up in wild consumptive currents. Like Icarus flying too close to the sun. I know something about both ends of this continuum.

My sense of being in the world has been largely dominated by learning to navigate exaggerated wave patterns of hypersensitivity. My reality has been a complex mixture of highs and lows, emphasized and exaggerated by being bipolar. My father was more on the hyper overdrive end of the scale. The contrast of our lives is poignant to me as my overall signature has been more underscored by radical descents.

Learning to ride these elemental waves in a gentler way, with the help of Lithium, holds gift beyond measure. This is a spiral journey. I'm learning to breathe under water. I'm learning to excavate the treasure from the bottom of the sea and relish the alchemical mystery of the oyster in its shell and the way irritation can produce luminosity. I find reassurance and a mirroring support in the phases of the moon, in the shifting seasons, in circadian rhythms. I find that I can celebrate and appreciate lunacy as part of a soulful life as I continue to work to unplug from the false feeding grounds. My friend Jesus reminds us that the kingdom of heaven is within. (New Revised Standard Version Bible, 1989, Luke 17:21) It's an inside job!

Lithium has given me a parachute and it acts as a landing pad that I am deeply grateful for. I have spent much of my adult life doing inner work, learning to see in the dark and weaving the fragmented pieces back together again. Years ago, I had a dream about baskets and a message came through that said, "Find that which can never be known but is woven throughout all of life." This reminds me of some endearing words from Nisargadatta, "Love says 'I am everything'. Wisdom says 'I am nothing'. Between the two my life flows." (Maharaj, 2012)

I have to say that my dad's iconic presence continues to reverberate, not just through our family, but also through the community where he made such an impact during his forty-five years. He knew how to capture an audience. He would burst on the scene, embodying the roar of the lion! He left a legacy of tragedy and comedy in his wake, in a delightfully unhinged and grievous sort of way.

I really wouldn't trade anything for my journeys into the "other" world. Being pulled into the undertow, disassociating, being blown open, and having profound disintegrations have all contributed to a holographic, holistic, symbolic way of seeing and experiencing the world that may not have come about otherwise.

Being a "Bipolar Bear," as my stepson says, has its challenges. Even so it has given me a full spectrum to draw upon and has been a surreal way to have a connection with my father.

What we call pathological can be a path through another kind of logic. This chemistry I carry from my father I claim as a hard-won badge of honor.

Bipolar Bear

Black Bear - White Bear traversing wobbly rope
How to find the tension in this dance of opposition
Earth Bear - Spirit Bear dancing circuitous slope

Hi Bear Nation - going down deep, only way to cope
Suckling wounds aching to balance bad nutrition
Black Bear - White Bear traversing wobbly rope

Slow motion flat line burrowing in like dope
Emerging from dead zone yearning for transition
Earth Bear - Spirit Bear dancing circuitous slope

Boundaries blurring, filters fading, outside of envelope
What a challenge to metabolize an overload of intuition
Black Bear - White Bear traversing wobbly rope

Following primal cord connection, sizzling with hope
Timelines shattering, spinning hot ice transmission
Black Bear - White Bear traversing wobbly rope

Blazing sun refractions yearn to buffer down the scope
Finding common ground is the work of a magician
Black Bear - White Bear traversing wobbly rope
Earth Bear - Spirit Bear dancing circuitous slope

Works Cited

Aziz, R. (1990). C. G. Jung's Psychology of Religion and Synchronicity. Albany: State University of New York Press.

Bateson, G. (2002). Mind and Nature: A Necessary Unity. New York: Hampton Press.

Blake, W. (1950). Auguries of Innocence. Poets of the English Language. Viking Press. Retrieved from https://www.poetryfoundation.org/poems/43650/auguries-of-innocence

Boyle, G. J. (2010). Tattoos on the Heart: The Power of Boundless Compassion. New York: Free Press.

Campbell, J. (1968). The Hero with a Thousand Faces (2nd ed.). Princeton, New Jersey: Princeton University Press.

Campbell, J. (1988). The Power of Myth. New York: Doubleday.

Cohen, L. (Composer). (1992). Anthem. [L. Cohen, Performer] On The Future. Columbia Records.

Houston, J. (1987). The Search for the Beloved. Los Angeles: Tarcher/Putnam.

Jalal al-Din Rumi, M. (1989). The Enlightened Heart. (S. Mitchell, Ed.) New York: HarperCollins Publishers.

Jung, C. G. (1989). Memories, Dreams, Reflections (Rev. ed.). New York: Vintage Books.

Jung, C. G. (1980). Psychology and Alchemy. Princeton, NJ: Princeton University Press.

Jung, C. G. (1981). The Archetypes and The Collective Unconscious. Princeton, NJ: Princeton University Press.

Maharaj, N. (2012). I Am That. Durham: The Acorn Press.

New Revised Standard Version Bible. (1989). National Council of the Churches of Christ.

Pierce, J. C. (2002). The Crack in the Cosmic Egg (2002 Edition ed.). Rochester: Park Street Press.

Sharp, D. (2001). Digesting Jung: Food for the Journey. Toronto: Inner City Books.

Tolle, E. (1999). The Power of Now. Novato: New World Library.

Woodman, M. (2001). Bone: Dying into Life. New York: Penguin Compass.

THE ACCIDENTAL DAUGHTER
BY VERUSCHKA NORMANDEAU

Veruschka Normandeau is a healing arts coach, Master EFT practitioner, photographer, writer, yogi and inspiritress of Rose Yoga, a hub for the inquisitive soul to be empowered via psycho-spiritual programs, offering energy medicine tools to assist with heart courage to uncover your unique embodiment of your true nature. She is a self-love activist and intuitive magic dealer and has been guiding people and upgrading lives since 2007. Serving your inner beauty and embracing the paradox of life. roseyoga.weebly.com

My German Scorpio mother worshipped Mick Jagger, a triple Leo. Of course you attract that which you glamorize. My mother unexpectedly became pregnant and produced a triple Leo in Southern California, while partnering with a hippie California surfer dude she met in London in the late 60's. After getting married, they separated a year later and I spent summers with my father in Malibu.

My mother's toxic behavior towards me prevented my little lionheart from truly shining. I never knew my light was precious. However, my mother did create one major spark in this accidental daughter: I rejected her for most of our lives.

As a single mother, she lost me when I was four-years-old, framed by a narc thinking my mother would give up the main drug dealer. She had German integrity and was sentenced to ten years on Terminal Island in San Pedro, CA. My father was so uncomfortable taking me to a prison environment that it took him fifteen months to reunite my mother and I for a visit. We ended up arriving fifteen minutes before visiting hours were over and everyone, including the guards, cried witnessing our reunion.

My mother was released two and a half years into her sentence and was deported to Germany. I was put on a plane with a now strange-to-me woman, flying into the cold of winter of Northern Germany. There we were greeted by her parents who helped raise me.

My mother felt exiled back in Germany, and took waitressing and bartending jobs to jump right back into the drinking culture. Since running away from home at seventeen to London after an influential encounter with Jimmy Hendrix, who she smoked her first joint with, she entered into the world of escapism via psychedelics, pills, and heroin. As long as I can remember, she was an escapist and an addict.

Not until my late thirties, after a visit to Germany where she suddenly became her own version of Martha Stewart, and I returned home with absolute rage and anger, did I pull up the Alanon website and answer the twenty intake questions, saying "Yes" to nineteen of the questions. Until that point, I had no idea that I identified as the model of a child of alcoholics. Buttoning down this anger, I got the insight and realized I was the neglected child without a voice that, at the end of the day, was always afraid to hurt my mother and always the helper.

Although I escaped her at sixteen and moved across the globe to gain my sovereignty, as an only child I did not know I had permission to make boundaries. It would be four more decades before I realized that every time I got off of the phone with her, I would feel agitated, provoked, low self-esteem, and powerless. Despite the fact that she was healed from alcoholism by a Native American when I was nineteen, which gave me great relief, she never worked on herself. She didn't change.

To me, everything about her were qualities in a woman I never wanted to become. Even though she was an attractive, fashionable, popular, loud, fun, progressive woman, her mere image in my mind's eye was pure toxicity to my system. The way she held her glass, standing naked in front of the fridge each morning to hydrate her hangover from the night before, when I was getting up to go to school. The tone of voice that she only used with me. Witnessing her in constant pain from either severe migraines, hangovers, or heavy periods.

All I could feel was her pain and continuous discontent. We even had a huge letter "E" carved out on our living room shelf for the word Elend, meaning "misery" in German. She and her friends proclaimed the meaning of life was this literal reminder and altar dedicated to misery. She struggled with addiction into her early sixties, in and out of rehab, lastly overmedicated with a cocktail of high doses of prescription methadone, sleeping pills, and antidepressants.

I despised and detested her pain and vowed to never be like her.

I had no respect for her, nor the way she spoke to me. From the time I was a teenager until into my forties, her two ways of communicating with me were throwing commands at me or criticizing me. Zero curiosity around my opinion or how I felt. Conversations did not exist. Most of the statements she made to me, the style of her delivery, and the sound of her voice, were tattooed into my flesh. Her voice became my inner critic, and although I attempted to run away from her, she was part of my inner landscape. My only revenge was silence, because I knew no response would drive her crazy.

Although I never spoke this to anyone, I felt depressed my entire life. Not good enough, not having a voice, feeling alienated wherever I went. It was the vibration I absorbed in my upbringing. I could not fathom how a woman from such loving, stable parents could turn out like that, so I could only perceive her as the wicked witch with no morals. I rebelled by following a spiritual life, since my parents showed me a counter-culture to a conservative world and I knew that I did not want a part of either.

No matter how much ego-eradicating work I did, my mother's pathways in my body and psyche remained in tact. After fifteen years of hypnotherapy and psycho-spiritual work, finally EFT (emotional freedom technique) resolved some major traumas and I was able to start releasing some of these energy signatures from my nervous system.

When I was about forty-three, my mother found a good addiction therapist who I got to meet. Sharing my pain with him, he agreed to help me take some distance from her, which I really needed. He explained to my mother that I was going to take needed time away from communicating with her. This included unfriending her on social media and limiting necessary communication to emails. I chose a six-month time period and she took it hard. But for me, at last, I tasted freedom. Slowly, I opened to my personal power on my terms, not the helper, the peace keeper, or the good girl that always listened but didn't have a voice.

Then I hit my own road blocks in relationship, community, and work. I felt unseen, unheard, and disrespected in my environments where I lived very remotely. I experienced health problems and turned to wine to offer me support and relief while I cooked every evening, just like my grandparents and parents. I was now walking in her shoes, although to a much lesser degree.

At the same time, I felt more love inside of me, more spirited and joyful during that time. More me. I started relating to my mother. I learned that she was raped on her sixteenth birthday by a stranger the first time she got drunk, and ran away from home the following year. She wanted to escape the small town hellhole she felt she grew up in, and live a more glamorous, psychedelic hippie life. She lived in guilt for hijacking her life so young, losing custody of me and going to jail at twenty-five, so she worked forty-five-hour weeks as a single mom. Alcohol was her only comfort and reward. I finally got it. My mother was only trying to escape her unresolved pain. I was able to forgive her wanting to evade her pain from a place of understanding and knowing.

A few years ago, my mother connected me to a German journalist who was writing an article for a famous magazine on "wild mothers" after she was featured in a talk show as a party woman who led a life of addiction. I felt it was a huge risk and she assured me that this was for me, to say whatever I needed to say to heal. I weighed out the options and felt that even if one daughter or even mother could identify with me, they could have more understanding and maybe could make a shift. I shared fully about my lifelong chronic pain, fibromyalgia, and debilitating lower back problems that I believed my mother contributed to. I talked about how I healed myself from all physical pain in my early forties, with hot yoga and EFT, literally changing my mind in my body by talking to them and releasing the emotionally toxic past that lodged the pain there.

The journalist got a book deal out of it because of my story. I read it and to me, it was an interpretation of my story but got the job done in what I wanted to relay and inspire for others: that healing was possible. I knew my mother would read it. Come to find out, everyone and their dog read it in Germany and my mother had people leave her life as a result and cancel their friendship. My mother called me crying and bitter, "I wish I never told you to do the interview."

I felt bad, for a moment. This was not my time to feel bad. After all, she encouraged me and promised me I would be safe to have a voice. She wanted to be in the spotlight so badly and now it bit her in the derriere.

And at the same time, I felt bad, I also felt seen and heard. As if there was justice in the universe. Finally justice served.

Nobody knew how she spoke to me or treated me, it was hidden. I felt sad for her, and I felt so much empathy. And then, I became angry, as the silent, accidental daughter in me erupted. I shouted at my mother, "This is not fair! YOU told me this was for me, and now you want to take it back because there were consequences? Now I have to help and console you, and feel at fault? Do you not see that YOU created this? You pursued it, you assured me, and now it is another unhappy ending that you want me to fix? I am the child of addicts and I am refusing to take this position. I did not need to do the interview, YOU encouraged me. Now I have to pay with guilt? This is on you."

It was a wake up call for my mother, and she agreed. She got to feel what it was like to not have approval. How she made me feel, how she squashed her personal Jagger. She never felt that from her parents, she was always proud of her persona.

I was glad I spoke up and reminded her why this backlash was happening in the first place. I realized that sometimes it takes patience to stand up for ourselves and it is not on our timeline. Self-advocacy required temperance and taking responsibility for my responses. Sometimes it was a revelation to realize the emotional immaturity of my parents.

During this time, I starting making art. I leaned into it as healing art, as I had no skills or experience and was laden with self-judgment. I sat down every Friday with a group of renowned artists. It was dedicated time to allow the inside to come out on paper, tempering my inner critic. I kept at it, although it felt difficult. The very act uncovered my lack of confidence and shame around my noviceness and revealed to me that I had never felt invested in, that my parents chose substances over connecting with me.

The time I spent giving voice to the quiet, magical child inside of me squeezed out the parts of me that felt neglected, abandoned, and rejected. I grew more courageous and bolder in my expression, and these expressions informed my passion and gifts of photography. New worlds emerged in my graphic work with imagery that made me feel proud of myself. Art gave the voice silenced by my mother an outlet to roar onto paper and through digital photography.

This commitment to myself revealed to me that I was worth investing my time in. I improved my art and shared it, despite the old, critical maternal voice that echoed in my self talk. Creating art was an act of expression and transmutation, communicating without words all that was withheld in my perceived submissive relationship with my mother.

Although my mother's depression filtered through to me, I realized that I also garnered her love of beauty, fashion, and the thrill of traveling to sunny places and reveling in glorious environments. We traveled a lot and basked in the sun every chance we got, always accompanied by rock and roll, a delight we continue to share. Because of summers with my father in Malibu, I shared his love of nature, the oceans and mountains, and his passion for music and good food. I adopted all of these values and channeled them into my art. By living the values my parents shared with me, I found appreciation for them.

Today I bless all of my hard experiences, for without them, I would not have turned to creative outlets and discovered the benefit and reward of all of the healing solutions and beauty I found to transform myself. I have a whole body of photographic artwork and it continues to grow. Finding approval for myself in my creative visions gives me more confidence to inform my mother of my needs for respect. I have been able to request she learn about nonviolent communication, which was a game changer for us and her second marriage.

For me, the war is finally over. The toxicity has transmuted into unconditional love and understanding. The pain in my body, along with my hate for her and myself, has dissolved. I respect the woman she has become. I am proud of the woman I am becoming. It is sobering to realize that the depression came from unresolved pain and that there is nothing left to numb. She still doesn't ask me anything about what I am doing and only talks about herself. I still feel her love and the seeming disapproval has waned.

My mother has since written her autobiography, and recently, she asked me to write a chapter in her book on how I experienced being her daughter. I am honored to participate. We have turned from enemies into allies. Our saying is, "Everything will be okay in the end. If it's not okay, it's not the end."

At last, I have found my footing to welcome this lioness magical child to roar her inner sunlight. I have even received my mother's applause and admiration, and finally feel like her personal Mick Jagger. It is a relief to feel like we are truly in this together.

THE TWO SIDES OF DAD
BY MARK PARKER

Mark Parker works in sales and marketing in the recreational vehicle industry. He has a passion for helping families get out and explore the many beautiful places our country has to offer while creating lifelong memories together. Mark also enjoys being close to nature and listening to music. He continues to better understand his bipolar disorder through reading and behavioral health lecture series.

My daughter shared this story with me, and gave me permission to share it with others.

Picture these two men:

A man who attends every single soccer game his daughter plays, starting when she was just five-years-old. He is on the sideline, wearing a soccer jersey with his last name written on the back, cheering at every recreational game, every select game, at every high school and competitive tournament.

Now picture a man, stumbling and mumbling random words to his wife while trying to fight his way down the stairs. He is in a drunken, mentally-unaware state, almost pushing his daughter down the stairs as she tries to hold him up from falling. Then he stops fighting and seems to almost pass out at the top of the stairs. This description is more recent than the first.

These two men sound like complete opposites. However, in reality, these two men both represent my father and the two significant ways he has impacted my life over the past eighteen years.

The first thing I learned is how these hardships taught me a key lesson about life. There are many recent memories over the past two years that I would like to forget. But, when I remember the great memories that I have shared with my father over the entire eighteen years of my life, I know that there is a reason I endured such hardships with my dad.

My father's support, not only through soccer, but throughout my entire life, proved how much he truly loves me and wants me to succeed in life. Through thick and thin, my dad has always been there. He has driven countless hours just to see me play in one soccer game. When I didn't even know he was going through his depression and alcoholism, he still came to every game he could, and would buy me any soccer equipment I needed. The fact that he still supported me in such an unimportant thing, compared to his diseases, showed me what an amazing and loving person my father is. He knew that soccer was very important to me, and encouraged me every day to do my best. I think, deep down, my dad just wanted me to live a better and happier life than he had at the time.

∽

The second big way my dad impacted my life was learning that there is no such thing as a perfect family, and that everyone is fighting a secret battle of their own. The description above of the man struggling on the stairs recalls the night that my dad tried committing suicide. My mom and I learned this news after we followed the ambulance to the hospital. As he was strapped down on the gurney, he told the doctor what his plans were for that night.

I cried when I heard my dad speak those words to the doctor, and at the same time, I was in shock with the news. I never thought something like this would happen to me. Not my dad, not my family. Slowly my family was starting to break apart and become like a movie.

That night, we had to put my dad in an inpatient rehab, and he stayed there for five days. Those were easily the hardest days of my life. I had to visit my dad and listen to him beg me to get him out.

But what I learned from this life experience will stay with me forever. So now, I try not to judge as quickly, because I never know what someone else might be going through, just like people don't know what I am going through.

If I could only thank my father for these two things, it would be the life lessons that he taught me through all of our hard times together, and how loved and cared for he made me feel through his support.

Following the manic episode described in the essay, I returned to school and became certified as a Registered Addiction Specialist focused on reality-based behavioral health. Over the years following my suicide attempt, I learned to manage my bipolar symptoms without the need of medication. I worked as a prison re-entry specialist during this time, and assisted many inmates who were also diagnosed with co-occurring mental health disorders. Because of my own experiences, I was able to understand these people in crucially important ways, and helped them overcome some of the obstacles that led to their incarceration.

I recently walked my daughter down the aisle. We continue to work on our relationship, and have made great progress.

THE COST
BY SARAH POBUDA

Sarah Pobuda, MFA, MEd, is a current MFA student at DePaul University. She is a poet and writer primarily, but she also obtained an M.Ed from University of Florida in 2020. A Michigan native, Pobuda now lives in Chicago. She plans to complete a PhD in English as the next step of her academic career.

∽ ∽ ∽

My grandfather's mind was like a penny in a perpetual coin toss. My mother, after a lifetime of dealing with his volatility and a degree in clinical psychology, diagnosed it as a mixture of metals, ADHD, a shiny copper that coated the bitter zinc of his bipolar disorder. Often I watched as his brain flung itself up into the cloudless sky of a mania.

It always started with his latest idea scribbled in chicken-scratch cursive on napkins, tissues, receipts, even business cards. Sometimes those ideas would become poems or stories for my sister and me. He was brilliant as an author, though unpublished, as his distractibility and lack of organization prevented him from finishing anything. In these times, my grandfather was so funny and crude that my parents had to warn me not to repeat the things he taught me, like how to give someone the bird in Italian, or what exactly a proctologist did. He moonlighted as an inventor during his highs, sleeping rarely, as he always seemed to dream better and bigger when he was awake.

Once, he developed a new sport called Bravo, loosely based on soccer. My sister and I spent the summer helping him create the rules and guidelines. Most of our ideas were rejected with a wave of his hand, in order to make space for others he had decided on, as recently as in the middle of us speaking.

This game, like the rest of his ideas, was cast aside near the end of the summer, never to be discussed again, when his brain made the inevitable flip and began to plummet back down into a depressive episode. He never bothered to watch his mind on the ascension, so he couldn't ever predict when or where the fall might occur. Perhaps he wouldn't have been able to guess anyways, as I imagine it would've been like looking into the sun.

Unfortunately, the result was a hard landing every time. Although I loved him unconditionally, it was nearly impossible to be around him when he was on a downswing. During our visits, he hardly left the couch, only doing so to refill his coffee cup. The blooming and well-adorned prose written just days before bled with the slashes of his harshly corrective pen. The television remained on all day and night at a near-blaring level of volume. My mother said it was because he was losing his hearing. I think he really just wanted to drown out his worst and loudest thoughts.

My conflicted feelings about him became slightly bitter, like the metallic taste of coins, as my mother came home crying after every visit. In his mid-eighties, he rebelled against her attempts to help him while also revolting against the dwindling life that he found himself facing, a fact that brought him into an unending low.

Often, I was asked to accompany my mother on her weekly trips to his house, if only to keep my grandfather preoccupied while she attempted to remove gnat-infested foods from his refrigerator or refill his pill box. I could usually improve his grouchiness to near complacency by prodding him for stories of his adventures and the variety of curious characters involved in them, enough to distract him from berating her.

On one of these visiting days, my mother decided to take him to the grocery store since there were two of us to corral him. He was in so foul of a mood when we arrived to pick him up that I knew within minutes this expedition would end in catastrophe.

This was the first time I experienced his venom spat out in my direction. It started with a thundering "ungrateful" in the produce section, aimed at me as I discarded a half-molded plum, he had chucked into the wire basket of his motorized cart. Whether a lasting impact of being raised during the depression or just the first insult he thought of in response to my newfound guardianship, I'm not sure. My stomach curdled with shock at his words. As my mother darted around the store, collecting the food and supplies he would actually need for the week, I was charged with following his haphazard journey through random aisles, keeping him distracted while she shopped.

Half an hour later, I caught her eye at the end of an aisle. She nodded towards the door, a silent cue that she had finished and would meet us at the car. On our way towards the checkout, he picked random things off shelves without glancing at the packages, deluging insults upon me as I tried to urge him towards the exit. Then, he sprinkled "deceitful" and "liar" into his diatribe after I informed him that the pharmacist was not available to answer his questions because she was on a lunch break. In truth, he was right about that, it was a lie, but I desperately wanted to get back to my mother who was loading the car with bags of groceries. By the time we made it back to the car, his ranting was so vile that I didn't dare to even look in his direction.

In retrospect, by that point of his life, his brain was so corroded, rusted green from oxidization, that even during his best attempts to toss himself back up again, there was no way of telling up from down or heads from tails. But in the moment, it didn't ease the bite of betrayal as my favorite grandparent slandered me, only to offer a box of stale brownies in place of the substantial apology I felt I was owed. I declined them and went to the car to wait to go home as my mother said goodbye to him. I glowered in the front seat, arms crossed as my mother got in beside me. He hobbled to the window, tentatively waving through the blue iron-worked door. I knew it was a second attempt at reconciliation, and before my mother could prod me to, I waved back sharply.

Once we left, traveling down the small street lined with ugly, one story homes with chipped paint and abandoned yards, my mother told me that was as good of an apology as I was going to get, so I should take it and know that he loved me more than he loved anyone. I knew she was right, but the imbalance left my chest hollow.

I cried and asked her why I had to accept that, why she and I and everyone close to him had to be part of his darkness, why he couldn't find his own way out. She told me that was the cost of loving someone with a penny mind.

A Year with No Moon
By Mardi Storm Clewett Von Ronne

Mardi Storm Clewett Von Ronne, MA, is a psychotherapist and doctoral candidate working in western Colorado. She previously worked two and a half years in a community mental health clinic and fifteen years in private practice as a breathwork healer and coach in Sonoma County, California. She is an artist, raises animals, and gardens with her partner of eighteen years, and is passionate about the outdoors and our beautiful natural world.

Sometimes, when surrendering to the wind, it blows us right where we need to be.

I didn't sign up for this.

I used to have an allergy to the word ancestors. It seemed to be tossed about freely, like popcorn, or salt. Sprinkle some on and it instantly sounds deeper, richer, or more supportive. I would feel my hackles go up when instructed by well-meaning facilitators to call in our ancestors. I'm certainly *not* calling in *my* ancestors. I don't want them here. They're a hot mess. I fantasized instead about imaginal support from much more enlightened beings or more helpful guides.

As if we can decide *not* to work with our ancestors. A better reframe would be how do we want to work with our ancestors? Do we want their unconscious patterns and choices to have power over us, or do we wish to help them by being true to ourselves in a way they were never able to be?

If it weren't for the Sonoma County housing crisis of 2017 it might have taken me another decade or two before I'd be ready to deal with family. I preferred to keep the visits short, sweet, and infrequent. Once or twice a year was plenty. I'd personally grown, so I no longer wished to put myself in the mix of the rough and abrasive energy that stung old wounds with cynical and oppressive opinions.

I might have waited until my parents passed away, and for my siblings and I to become grey-haired and lonely. I probably would have remained living indefinitely in the little rental house in Occidental with pasture for our livestock and gardens. It was only twenty minutes from my mother's house. I'd followed her to Sonoma County after her bout with cancer, out of concern in case she needed help, but there was not much connection other than a monthly phone call at most.

I'm not proud of that, but you don't know my family.

I'd always wished I'd had the kind of mother I wanted to call every week. The kind of mother that was supportive and openly cared. The kind that asked how my day was, my week, I'd even take a question about my year. The kind of mother to call when there was trouble, or upset, or a difficult decision to make. You know, the kind of mother other people had, the kind that expressed an interest, and paused to listen.

I avoided the inevitable disappointment, chronic emptiness, and dissatisfaction from lack of connection. What I learned is that I had to go deep into the darkness itself to face what was there, and to understand the ancient rhythms of my family.

I can't say my mother had the look of excitement when I pulled a U-Haul truck in front of her house. Can't say I did either. What an unlikely pairing after thirty years of successful and peaceable distancing. The idea of pulling up a moving truck stretches reality to new limitations. This was strange. This was unprecedented. My mother didn't want to help us out, she didn't believe in helping anyone out since she had to struggle and fight for everything she had, as she put it, but she couldn't say no to us parking our camper on her land for just a couple months.

Or could she?

She wanted to.

The beauty of mothers is that sometimes when you show up with a moving truck they let you park, for a little while. Because I sure as hell wasn't going to stay here.

Baba Yaga invited us in. Don't make yourself at home in Baba Yaga's house. She didn't tell you to. But in little ways, you can throw scraps to the dogs and crumbs to the rats, and keep the peace while you dust cobwebs off the bats. Just don't provoke them. Leave her be, stirring her pot, one glowering eye on her soup, one on us.

Even this moment, this unexpected opening would not have been possible only a year earlier. That Fall, prior to showing up at her doorstep with livestock and a pack of cats in tow, incidentally the very same month I accepted admissions to graduate school, my mother almost died. Misdiagnosed as a heart attack due to her weight, she had a blood clot larger than the doctors have ever seen a person recover from, and complications developed from the false start towards open-heart surgery.

My mother ended up in the ICU, and I visited her every day for a month. I advocated for her with her doctors, halted unnecessary and risky procedures, googled medication side effects, bonded with some nurses and got baleful looks from others. I knew, and my mother knew, she was still alive in part because of my obstinate and vocal interventions. It was the first time I ever saw my mother vulnerable. It was the crack in the veneer of her persona I had waited a lifetime to see. It was the first time I ever saw an opening for a possible healing between us. The first time she ever got quiet, listened, expressed tender feelings, and trusted me.

The pain of returning to an insufficient mother was immense, larger than the stretch of sky over the expansive landscape of western Colorado, equal in magnitude, but opposite in feeling. From one side to the other, no end in sight. You can see a hundred miles; just like my pain, it went on forever and ever. The mother who could not be there, the mother who could not tend, the mother who didn't express caring. The mother who fell silent when it came to moments when a mother's words were needed. The mother who only talked when she needed to listen. The mother who ignored me. The mother who was there in name, the mother who sometimes fed me, the mother who gave me shelter when I was too young and foolish to run away.

*Why did I always come back? I wondered. If I could do it
all again, I most certainly would have run away, knowing
what I know now, knowing all the years of damage caused
by staying in the field of an emotionally absent parent.*

Of course, that's what I said for those past thirty years. I gave myself a hard time, that I was chicken, that I lacked courage. I ran away but always came back. I never went far enough.

Here I was, nearly fifty years old, and looking back I wondered, why was I so upset all the time? Where was the rampant abuse to justify my feelings? Why is our family so split up and cast to the winds? Why couldn't I emotionally handle life with my family? Was it just me, was I too sensitive? Living with my mom again shed light on all those places that time and distance overgrew and cast into shadow.

My family, like all families, had its own version of what was normal. The undermining, insidious energy was almost invisible. This was far from a beneficial family system. Invoking each other into states of rage, pain, panic, and sorrow was not healthy. I discovered I could go zero to a hundred in one second, and apparently that wasn't normal. Time and personal work can heal a goodly amount of wounds, and can hide those buttons of activation. However, my mother knew how to push those buttons so very well, effortlessly. The pain of familial connection, the wound, the reflex, and the button pushing all fit like a hand in glove.

I remember telling a grade-school friend that my mother was *manic-depressive*, a grown-up term that was an attempt to grapple with the reasons our house was a mess and the weeds grew up to my chest; explained the six broken cars in front of an otherwise tidy subdivision neighborhood; and why my mother hadn't been seen in days or weeks. The inside of our house was just as bad. The negligence was pretty high while my mother focused on her second chance at youthfulness and the career she wanted, alternated with long bouts in bed. Recently divorced, she went back to college and was working in a small town where women didn't get divorced. This was the 1970's when an unmarried woman couldn't even have a bank account or credit card in her name.

Being a single mother divorcee was scandalous, and there was little by way of support in our agricultural community for these choices. She left her four kids at home to pursue her dreams, the dreams she had prior to getting married and having a family, which she claimed to have done only to escape an abusive home life growing up. She wanted it all but had little to back her up, from lack of child support payments to her own mother who withdrew her emotional, financial, and childcare support after the divorce. She was determined to find her own way. She might have been able to pull it off if it weren't for the troubles to come, the mood swings, the emotional and mental roller coaster that had just embarked as she started to shake off the anesthesia of depression from years of unhappy marriage.

There was a lot of shame within me growing up, as children often internalize and make wrong their perceived differences from others. We lacked what others in our neighborhood took for granted, from a running vehicle to electricity and food. Our house was dark for weeks, sometimes months when the power was cut off. In those days, we warmed food on the wood stove and bathed from stove-heated water or took a cold shower. Our ceilings were blackened with soot from the kerosene lanterns, from reading and writing homework until the late hours.

When I was a teen and my insecurity started its uphill climb, I took those cold showers. Later, when we moved to a rural location and no power meant the pump didn't work for the well, I would get up before dawn to wash my hair in the neighbor's irrigation ditch before anyone could see me, even in mid-winter with the pasture grasses coated in frost. As my mother's depression and alcoholism ramped up, the habitableness of our home declined. These secrets were not to be shared, making it hard to bring any school friends home.

Between work and school, my mother was gone all day and sometimes nights too. I'm not really sure where, but later I'd hear stories about an adventure or a party in San Francisco, a two-hour drive away. The raucous laughter and non-stop boisterous conversation, likened to a shouting match in volume, would carry through the whole house while she relayed her stories, full of embellishment, seemingly to impress some young college friend on mysterious and intriguing subject matter above my age to understand. My mother sounded so powerful, so able, so important, so on top of her game, and so intelligent. Her goals seemed oriented towards outwitting everyone else with her sharp mind and quick repartee. She turned down a few offers from men whom she felt would want to own her, having so recently overthrown indentured slavery as a housewife.

It was when she invited a young college student, who had a dubious line of work and was living out of a converted bus, to come live with us that our lives really began to shift in a different direction. This young man seemed to ignite something very different in my mother. Her mental health appeared to destabilize before our eyes. Initially she seemed elated, but it wasn't long before I witnessed her in strange fugue states where her eyes were dark, and she appeared unable to see me, her face red and puffy. She would have emotional outrages and throw the family's gold-rimmed china against the wall across the room, or smash out the windows of our only running vehicle, slicing open her arms with the broken glass. On one occasion she had to be wrestled to the floor by my older brothers to subdue her attempts at self-destruction.

That same VW van, with the windows now made of plastic and duct tape, was the one she'd later take us on a whim, bound for Mexico. I did not want to go with her, that time or on any of her trips. The whole world felt so unstable, so scary, with the sense of needing to manage the shame in part by remaining hidden. Being out in the world with my mother meant there was no place to safe place to retreat, subjected to her changing moods and mysteriously darkening emotional rampages.

On these adventures out, I'd feel embarrassed to get back in the vehicle with the plastic over the windows. We'd sometimes run out of gas, and if we couldn't find enough quarters and dimes in the seats of the car, my brother and I would beg strangers for money at the gas station. On a few trips to San Francisco, my mother and her boyfriend would be so intoxicated in the backseat of the car, my brother and I would tour a museum by ourselves. Sometimes we'd return to find them laying in the bushes of a park and have to round them up, incoherent, for the trip home.

On one occasion, as a pre-teen I stomped off in a fit of anger and disappeared for half a day in San Francisco, alone. I was secretly glad to see her relief when I showed up at the car that evening, because that meant she had worried, which meant she must care about me after all. My disappearances were never talked about. In fact, there was no communication about anything.

Most teenagers experience embarrassment over their parents. However, there was little to counterbalance that perception, as my mother seldom struck the semblance of a responsible parent in the second half of my childhood. She just wasn't able to be emotionally present. She occasionally could clean up and attend a school function, but I received little of what I needed from her in terms of actual emotional support or healthy modeling. I know she tried and had no skills or tools, or even a smidgen of emotional intelligence to understand the mess of her own life, much less the impact she had on her children. That reflection wouldn't come until decades later, after she had a brush with mortality from serious illness and countless conversations during the time I lived on her property as an adult. I had so little emotional engagement with her that the holes in my development were something I had to work hard to overcome, as well as my early depression and urges to self-harm.

My mother had that indomitable spirit that led her to chase oversized ideas, with a sense of self that was a bit larger than life. Bragging about herself to others, along with her superiority complex, became a familiar and exhausted meme. She would have at least graduated from UC Davis, but one-quarter short of her graduation, my eldest brother, in his impulsivity and rage, shot and killed a man.

While my brother was diagnosed as a child with attention deficit disorder, his cluster of traits would become more appropriate to bipolar, which included antisocial behaviors of harming animals and people. Once my father left, he filled the role of tyrant in the household by being oppressive and controlling. Without strong parental input, I had no protection from his emotional and physical outbursts. When his mood swung the other way, he was a likeable fellow who could express caring and remorse for the damage he had inflicted.

My brother spent the last half of his teen years in juvenile hall and prison, where my mother hauled us on every available visiting day. Like clockwork, those years of our lives revolved around his court case and visiting him twice a week. My eldest brother was her precious firstborn, and she gave him everything she could. She scrambled to help him feel part of the family while he missed out knowing about our actual family experience, including his dog's untimely death and the reality of the hardships that were unfolding at home. She led him in a world of fantasy, keeping him hoping and dreaming for the day he would rejoin us, and that day, when it came, would be a shock. That shock was enough that he broke away from the family emotionally, the first to split off from the dysfunction those of us not old enough to leave home were still ensnared by.

I wonder if our family might have pulled out of the approaching nosedive if the homicide hadn't happened. My brother, despite his weak impulse control, also had the eldest sibling sense of responsibility; maybe he would have told my mother what he thought and pushed back when she was out of control. We would still have had a home, at the very least. My mother chose to sell our house to pay for my brother's lawyer, leaving us with absolutely nothing while putting all three of her other children into peril. A single mother launching out into the world with three kids plus one in prison, and consumed by a court case that prohibited her from focusing on finishing her degree, didn't have much to lean on.

Her own mother turned her back, based on moral objections to divorce, despite the abuse present in my parents' marriage. In my grandmother's generation, a woman often turned the other way when there was abuse of herself or her children, for survival. I was too young to know what it was like for my brothers and my mother when my father lived at home, I only saw the after effects. Only as an adult could I gain perspective about my brothers' potentially learned behaviors.

After he left, my father did not pay a day of child support and took everything he wanted in divorce court, having a better lawyer. Being a California Highway Patrolman may have influenced how authorities looked the other way while he neglected his children and started a new family. My mother was either too proud to apply for welfare, or didn't qualify as a student, and was determined to find her own way anyhow. After her nervous breakdown, she latched onto a man who was mentally broken and an alcoholic, and she sank into what would become even darker years of her life, and my life. The fights, the rages, and the smashed furniture and doors were hallmarks of that period, along with an increased absence of food, attention, or care.

As a teen, I finally let one teacher know about my nearly nightly suffering. How I sometimes blocked my door with furniture and tried to sleep through the raised voices and loud thumps as bodies slammed into walls or on the floor, sometimes knocked unconscious, while lamps broke and heaters were torn off the wall. It wasn't that unusual to get up in the morning for school and have to step over adults that lay slumbering where they fell on the floor. It was often tough to sleep at all, and I regularly caught unwanted naps face down on my school desk.

When my teacher braced to meet these monster parents at an awards ceremony, she was met by an attractive, severely obese woman who could charm just about anybody, and her boyfriend who, when sober, was equally intelligent and witty, though unfortunately that was rare. Afterwards, I lost the trust and belief of my one confidante and supporter at school. From that day forward, I decided to not talk to anybody about anything that happened at home again. I'd have to find my own way through this, and I tried for another fifteen years while struggling and suffering through my own interpersonal issues and chronic depression.

The premise of this writing was to share about our emotional experiences growing up with a bipolar parent. The moment I consider the emotions of my childhood is the moment I draw a blank. I consulted my therapist to help jostle a reflection of what my emotional experience was growing up. I couldn't think of anything beyond the prevalent anger, the one emotion that I expressed daily, and the one that I know the best.

She kindly reminded me of my dissociated experiences, my rich inner world where I went in order to feel. In the outer world, there was no safety to have other emotions besides anger, rage, and humor. There was no space to be sad, to cry, or to be happy. All emotions were punished with condemnation and ridicule by my brothers, or simply went unnoticed and unmet by my mother. Sarcasm and anger were the only currency one could barter with at my home during those dark years.

I don't remember much of my emotional experience growing up because that felt dangerous to keep conscious with the intense amount of shame that was present, but I do remember ongoing feelings of inexpressible pain and sadness. The range of emotions I remember more clearly were connected with the experiences occurring in my dissociated realm, where there was space to feel, especially the pain and loss. There were tears there, and I'd come back to this world to find my pillow damp from the crying. There was no crying here on this side, where I had to be tough, ready to fight back with my anger, express my grief and longing through anger, or even attempt to instigate change in the family with it. This more tender expression was only in the middle of the night, when I would be in a dreamy twilight consciousness, caught up in the distraction of feelings and events happening in the other world.

Even at school, I would dissociate frequently and sometimes for long periods of time. I went from being an engaged, attentive kid in school to a very distracted one, as it became hard to focus. Sometimes I wouldn't remember what took place that day, or recollection was foggy, with a detachment to the experiences of that period, as if it happened to somebody else. I didn't have language for how I was feeling then, but I can look back with my adult words to see the oppressive shame, insecurity, hyper-vigilance, fear, and anxiety.

It was easier, even perhaps necessary, to check out for survival. The nights I did sleep were filled with nightmares, and the repetitive theme was that of being chased by demons or monsters. My suicidal thoughts started around the age of ten or eleven amid a strong desire to not be here due to the intensity of anger, rage, and confusion. I began praying each night to God to be killed by angels with their fiery swords while I slept, even writing a suicide note to explain what happened, so strong was my belief that the angels would save me from this intolerable nightmare. Each morning, I'd wake up enormously disappointed.

Perhaps what made it more difficult was that I knew what it was like to have a family and a safe home for the first eight years of my life, something by which to compare current circumstances. Now that stability was gone, and even if my mother was not available emotionally, her former presence as a housewife still grounded the house, along with her motions of tending her children with it. It's easy to look back and see that she was unhappy with her station in life, but she kept up appearances. With the divorce came freedom, and my mother became a different kind of person, too busy for her children, or cooking and cleaning, or holding us accountable for our chores and actions, or modeling any type of self-regulation.

I remember few emotionally bonding experiences, but instead recall a general emptiness around what to do with my inside feelings, along with an inability to express how I felt. This continued well into my adult life.

There was such a lack of attunement and empathy. For instance, when I didn't clean my room to her liking, she took an arm and swept all the ceramic dinosaurs and dragons I'd made onto the floor, leaving me with only a pile of broken clay. My artistic creations were simply clutter to her, while art was one of the only things I found joy in as a kid.

One summer I returned from a stay with my grandmother to find the room I shared with my sister completely re-decorated in hideous pastels and pinks, with matching water pitchers and collector plates, along with images of frilly girls. She'd given away my stuffed animals and removed all my dragons and art that I'd made. The sadness of no longer feeling at home in my own room was unbearable

There were many strange instances that occurred with my mother, and with family, that I found hard to understand in my child's mind. Many times I was scared, but did not have anyone to turn to, who would understand, or even with whom to find comfort. I only had my dog and my other, dissociated, world. The closest person to me was my father, and one day he abruptly left, with minimal contact except an approximately twice a year visit that eventually faded away.

The next closest attachment I had was with my dog Missy, and one day I came home from school to find she was just gone too. There was no consideration of my feelings, there was no reflection or mirroring for anything I was going through, simply a screaming match about how Missy had to go because our house sold.

In such a rough household, hate became turned inward, along with shame and humiliation, so that I struggled to get close to anyone. My original bonds were gone, and I was left experiencing loss after loss with no reprieve, as we proceeded to move five more times.

To this day it sometimes is hard for me to access my emotions, not because they are not there, but the language gets lost in a state of deep feeling, which can pull up the proverbial drawbridge to shut out the connection between the intellectual and the emotional mind. This is the defense I learned, to shut out, to go away somewhere else, in order to tolerate what was happening in my environment. My childhood created superb skills in tolerating dysfunction. Yet, like most early coping adaptations, these skills were also detrimental.

A few years ago, I was living in my mother's backyard out of a vintage Fireball trailer with my partner of thirteen years. I started writing about my experiences and the small degree of healing that had begun to occur between my mother and I on this topic of family and ancestors. The title of the book for these writings came to me while pausing at the trailer's threshold late one night. I looked straight up at the small patch of dark sky that could be seen through the thick of enormous redwood trees. In that forest, the trees were so tall they blocked out the sun, the stars, and light. I sighed, thinking of the moon, knowing she was out there beyond my sight. I thought about living here in this darkened place, a year without a moon.

I have always tried to live where I can track the moon across the sky, relying on a clear view of her phases to know whether I'm rising in energy or falling, attuning to the monthly cycles. When I was a teen, I'd slip out at night and sit in a dark field in my favorite ring of stones, and find comfort gazing upon her cold, pale face. This was my secret go-to place and I could be lost for hours under the night sky. The moon was the epitome of feminine power to me, even though she was distant and removed. She became a source of inspiration, guidance, and visionary conversations for many years. That year in the vintage Fireball, there was no moon to guide me, deep in the underworld of the redwood forest with my mother, whom I likened to the Baba Yaga in her harsh and unpredictable ways.

In my years growing up, that feminine reflection was likewise absent. My mother, whom I could not track with reliability, and who could not track me, couldn't offer support, couldn't be present for any of my emotional needs. My mother, detached and confounded by her own complex feelings and revolving moods, couldn't reflect me, empathize with me, or even get to know me. I felt abandoned from the day my father walked out of our lives, but the abandoning happened long before then, from my mother's absence. She was present only as a blurry figure in the first half of my childhood, moving into focus after the divorce in a way that was impossible to feel safe and secure.

As we re-acquainted in her elder years, my mother spoke about her depression that began after the birth of her first child. She told me she was a mother who did not want to be a mother, who then birthed three more children. The depression lasted many years, overlapping the time when I was born, and blanketed my early childhood with her disengaged presence.

I had so little sense of her during those years, even though we lived in the same home. As a youngster I vied for her attention, and couldn't seem to get enough, only fleeting moments. I took to catching snakes because I knew she hated them the most, and proffered them when she'd "mm-hmm" me, a response she gave when she didn't want to look up from her magazine. As I became more insistent that she must look up, much to my delight, I would get a shrill scream. This level of satisfaction encouraged repeat behavior, and many other types of insects and reptiles were then enlisted in attempting to procure any kind of attention from her. These became some of my fond moments of connection.

It appeared the depression lifted for a while after the departure of my father. As my mother moved back into life as a force to be reckoned with, for me details of my home life faded in a form of dissociated, imaginative, and inwardly turned self-protection. Life became a lot to deal with.

My brothers were often left in charge of us younger girls, and they were mean. At times, they got up to horrible and scarring things like cutting the heads off newborn kittens. My brother thought it the best solution since my mother was angry about his pregnant cat. My sister and I screamed and cried, begging for their lives, and managed to rescue only one. On another occasion, my pet rabbit Thumper was skinned and served for dinner. To add insult to injury, my brothers cruelly teased me at the dinner table when I asked about the peculiar looking dish. Needless to say, I didn't eat dinner that night. As an adult, in an extreme circumstance I might understand a hungry family needing to eat. As a child, I struggled to reconcile the cruelty and absence of compassion in my household, and how that choice and countless other situations were handled.

This lack of reflection became a source of self-condemnation, and self-blame. I loathed myself such that I intermittently suffered from suicidal thoughts, like my mother, until my early thirties, when I began receiving support from breath work healers, and later, therapists. The impacts of such emotional scars fade slowly, and I struggled with identity and abandonment issues, acute sensitivities, and the push-pull patterns of emotionally unavailable relationships. I learned to disconnect from others at a young age to protect myself, to lessen the emotional blows. I struggled internally with pervasive feelings of disconnection and not belonging.

Pleasure and happiness were often hard to access. Misery, rage, depression, elation, impulsivity, and grandiosity were modeled to me instead. Calm and peace have always sounded boring, not goals of mine until I understood the roller-coaster I was raised to believe was just life. When one grows up immersed in excitement and drama, the nervous system is geared towards over-stimulation, to its own detriment. I found myself ensnared in the web of being drawn to drama to try to help fix it as an unconscious urge to heal my family patterns, over and over.

The sense of *anything is possible* was either a gift or a curse from my mother, where there was no sense of limits, rising and falling with emotional crashes that come from overextension. Creativity can blossom in that limitlessness then dry up in the depressed periods. Growing up with scarcity sets up an unconscious belief there is never enough. This fuels a drive to always want or do more. It took a long time to develop a more independent sense of self, to recognize what I need, separately and differently from all those around me, and not only respond to others' needs. That is part of the legacy of this unsteady upbringing. Balance has to be found in order to get off the roller coaster. With that growing awareness, what comes is a deeper language for feeling states that were once forbidden and are now allowed to be felt and expressed in the light of day.

I'll leave you with the healing thought that sometimes, *anything is possible*, maybe just in small ways, if we adjust our expectations and see what may happen. I now call my mother every week, reaping the fruits of hard work and having passed through the fires during that dark year. She will never be the mother I wish she was, but she is the mother I received, with all the gifts and curses, and curses that become gifts, as I claim the benefits of understanding and compassion. I now track the clear phases of the moon across the broad Colorado skies and revel in the support of all the shimmering stars and planets above.

This essay is excerpted from Ms. Storm's forthcoming book *A Year With No Moon.*

I INHERIT MY MOTHER'S KALEIDOSCOPE
BY CASSANDRA SAGAN

Cassandra Sagan is an ordained Maggid (Jewish storyteller/educator/instigator) artist, poet, singer/songwriter, mystic, and all around cultural creative. Through InterPlay (international arts and social justice organization) she leads trainings and classes where spiritual leaders and others learn to "play with challenges instead of working on them." Cassandra is a mom, stepmom, grandmother of seven, wife, devoted friend, and over-the-moon dog lover.

∽ ∽ ∽

My mother, *Pesa Brahna bat Shaindl v'Mordcha*, had a beautiful death. Drug and pain free, she hovered between the worlds with a mystical smile on her face. And she was lovely, as if she was being played by Meryl Streep. The hospice nurses gazed from the foot of her bed and said, "Your Mommy is so sweet. Was she always this sweet?"

Well...no. In life, my mother had been a wretchedly miserable person who suffered loudly and long in body, mind, and heart. She had gone to bed thirty years earlier, waiting for a miracle. She was writing her masterpiece, "Love Is An Inside Job." She got as far as the title. Her untreated mental illness became increasingly toxic, alienating everyone who loved and cared for and tried to help her.

Her deepest longing was to be totally spiritual, at one with God, free of the burden of her body and the insults of this world. Both of her parents had taken their lives and she was determined not to follow. The only thing that got her out of bed was the Florida Lottery.

In the last years of her life, I'd receive calls from the office manager at Mom's low-income senior community. She's at it again! "It" was Mom racing down the center of Linton Boulevard in her electric wheelchair, barefoot, a ratty brown poncho thrown over her nightgown, hair flying out from her head like a cartoon witch.

The same witch who snuck around dream corners to curse my childhood with a *ha cha de cha* like Jimmy Durante. "It's the witch," laughed the other children as Mom leaned out our fifth story window screaming sharp, distorted versions of our names.

Turning her wheelchair off Linton, screeching into the convenience store, Mom swung her leather pack from beneath her poncho, scratching off her tickets right at the counter. If she won anything, whether two dollars or two hundred dollars, she'd immediately turn it into more lottery tickets.

Mom put all of her creative energy into the lottery because she had squandered everything Dad had given her when he finally left. She went from frugal housewife, budgeting every dollar in labeled envelopes that she kept in a burgundy, leather clutch, to spending indiscriminately. She began to follow Ramtha, an alleged ancient master channeled by a real estate agent in Yelm, Washington. The realtor encouraged Ramtha's followers to gamble because the master would help them win. The realtor said that a time of great change was coming, and everyone should move up to Washington State, which would not be destroyed. She also said that money would soon be worthless, so Mom saw no need to invest, to plan, to budget. Or to share. My sister cried and begged for help buying a piece of land; I reasoned with Mom, laying out my case for helping me finish college. Our little brother had already given up.

When I was growing up, any time she wasn't fiercely and effectively cooking and cleaning, Mom hung out on the bed, chain smoking, soap operas droning in the background. Sometimes she'd come down to the kitchen to have coffee with friends; sometimes her friends hung out with her watching TV upstairs.

When we were lucky, she lounged in housecoats, lightweight snap front smocks. Other times she wore a one-piece tan-colored undergarment, her pale flesh quivering when she got up to kick or scream at us. Sometimes she'd sneak a frozen Sara Lee cake up from the basement freezer and lock herself in her room. My sister and I would pound on the door, Debi begging and weeping, me reasoning, "Let us have just one slice, we'll share it."

When Mom got angry, she slammed the kitchen cabinet doors, screamed, wept, and kicked us with her bare feet. When we practiced our instruments, she'd *kvetch*, whine, "Do you have to play the same song over and over again?" I was the oldest, the peacemaker, the caretaker. I would tell her she was beautiful, while glaring daggers at my sister for provoking her.

In her 50s Mom moved to Washington State to follow Ramtha, where she became convinced that her parents had ritually abused her and that this was the source of all her tsuris, troubles. Recovered memory "therapy" had led to "satanic panic," with a surge of victims, quite prevalent in Washington in the mid-80s, suddenly recalling details of satanic abuse in childhood. Outraged, and protocol be damned, I called her therapist.

I said, "My Jewish grandparents on Long Island were not angels, but they did not ritually abuse my mother. They did not dance with devil worshippers around a fire."

The therapist responded, "Her body doesn't lie."

I said, "She isn't even IN her body!"

Eventually, recovered memories of ritual abuse became associated with dissociative identity disorder, as well as anti-government conspiracy theories that are still widespread today.

Things got crazier. She backed into a car in a parking lot and drove away. The security cams caught her and her license was revoked.

She decided to leave Washington for Florida, without a plan about what would happen after she got off the plane. At the last minute she was taken in by a friend of a friend. She stayed with her for almost two months, verbally abusing the woman so relentlessly that her hostess moved in with her daughter until Mom finally got an apartment in a low-income senior community.

Near the end of her life, Mom had a "friend," a man about my age who was crashing on his mother's sofa in the next building. I would set Mom up with home help, drivers, social workers, doctor's appointments, but Mike told her not to trust them and promised that he would take care of her. Mom employed a combination of foul language and a can of Raid to force the prospective helpers from her doorstep.

Mike would disappear for weeks at a time, and Mom would call me, desperate. I would hire new helpers and set up new appointments. Then Mike would return, and the cycle would continue. When I visited, I would find her fridge empty, her apartment filthy, and Mike nowhere to be seen.

After she hit bottom and ended up in the hospital, withdrawals disappeared from her bank account daily, and the twenty thousand some odd dollars she had hidden in videocassette cases and a safe deposit box had vanished.

Mom asked, "Why isn't Mike calling?"

Gently, I said, "Mike has been stealing from you."

She said, "Oh he's not stealing, I gave him the money." Mom told me that she was doing a mitzvah, a good deed, by "helping Mike with his program."

I asked, "What kind of program is that, Mom?"

She furrowed her brow in concentration. "They give him, I don't know what it's called, it's like fake whiskey for alcoholics but it's not whiskey."

My historically selfish mother had given all her money to a junkie. She unwittingly shot thousands of dollars' worth of heroin into the arm of a human being suffering from a devastating addiction.

Her well-intentioned, ill-fated act of generosity broke my heart open.

Once she began to get some care and treatment, Mom was adorable, in a mercurial, time-space confused kind of way. She'd try to get sardines out of the TV remote because I looked hungry. She kept asking me how the babies were, although she couldn't specify which babies she was referring to. She'd give me her chicken soup recipe and then perk up and ask what time the seder was starting. She looked at me suspiciously as I fluffed up her pillow, assuming I was only being nice to get something from her.

She narrowed her eyes. "Did I win the lottery?"

I said, "Yeah Mom, you did."

She rested back on her pillows and smiled.

I decided that when she got out of the hospital, I would bring her back with me to Portland. Together we would retell her life story as a dot to dot of joy, so that by the time she died she would think she had lived a good life.

But that was not to be.

On the day I placed my mother in hospice, her doctor leaned close and revealed to me that she, too, was a Jewish mystic. She said, "I should be studying medicine in my free time, but all I want to do is study Torah."

The doctor told me that when she met Mom, she felt a special connection, beyond the caring she generally feels for her patients. She said that my mother was a profoundly spiritual being, but whose vessel was so broken, so completely shattered, that she could not hold anything in this world. The doctor looked me in the eyes and said, "Never underestimate the power of the work your mother is doing for you and for your children and your grandchildren in the world to come."

Dying was the miracle my mother had waited for her whole life: To be totally spiritual while in this world. She floated in primordial light. In a rare, lucid moment, the day before she passed, Mom looked at me and mouthed, Thank you.

When my mother died, I lost something that I never knew I could lose – the visceral, physical disgust and loathing which overcame me whenever I even thought about her or glimpsed her face in my mirror. I began to think of my neuroses as spiritual gifts my mother had passed down to me, using the only crunchy, messed up, sharp-edged packaging she had access to.

My mother, *Pesa Brahna bat Shaindl v'Mordcha*, was a priestess, albeit a broken one. I inherited her kaleidoscope, the way the shattered world rushes towards us in brilliant sparks and slivers of light, multiplied by mirrors and multi-dimensional moments of exquisite beauty that shift, gather speed, and spill into the next, and the next, into now.

I inherited my mother's kaleidoscope completely disassembled. It broke her, and I create art from the beautiful fragments.

To transform the past in the present, and repair the world, *tikkun olam,* we must gather the broken pieces, the shattered light, and rebuild this world in love.

May we all be blessed to gather the broken shards of light from our past to reveal our beauty and strength.

LIFE ON A ROLLER COASTER WITH DAD
BY BARBARA SCHWARTZ

Barbara Schwartz, MSS, LCSW, has recently retired after practicing social work and psychotherapy for over thirty years. She received a BS degree in Pharmacy from Temple University in Philadelphia, PA. She earned her MSS degree from Bryn Mawr College School of Social Work and Social Research in Bryn Mawr, PA. Barbara's professional expertise focused on guiding her clients to access their natural talents and problem-solving skills, in order for them to lead more satisfying lives.

❦   ❦   ❦

The thought of writing about my deceased manic-depressive father at this particular juncture of my life jostles my already shaken sensibilities. Some background information is essential to explain my present state of mind. Three months ago, on September 27, 2021, Allan, my dearly beloved husband of sixty years, departed from this earth, as we know it. Tragically Carl, my much-loved brother, died in November. I am slowly recovering emotionally from these terrible losses.

Recently I retired from my thirty-year career as a social worker/psychotherapist. I have explored in-depth the impact of growing up with a father who suffered from manic-depressive symptoms. He was born in 1907. When he became ill, around 1933, his condition was not yet properly understood.

My earliest memories are mostly visual. When I was about four, we moved into a house in Philadelphia. I can picture standing in the entryway, staring at some furniture, a sofa, a couple of chairs, and empty walls in the living room. Nobody was present except me. It's a strange recollection, because no feelings or other people are attached to it. We lived there for only a few weeks. Our frequent moves all take place in Philadelphia.

When I was five, Dad followed his dream of moving to Miami Beach. His brother Tom and sister-in-law Fran, both pharmacists and a few years older than Dad, had moved there years earlier. They had no children. I learned many years later that Fran protected Tom, because of concern that he showed signs of depression. Mental health issues were never discussed in our extended family.

After we packed up our worldly possessions, Mom, Dad, Carl (nine), Harriet (seven) and I (five) traveled by train to Miami Beach. I don't recall much about that trip. Harriet remembers that the train was filled with soldiers coming home from Europe and we had some fun mingling with them. When we arrived, we initially had nowhere to live. Mom and Dad left us on the hot, sunny Miami Beach for the day while they went house hunting. Carl remembered that experience quite vividly because he wound up covered with blisters, sick from sun poisoning. Harriet and I simply had nasty sunburns. Most places would not rent to families with children, Jews, or dogs. We fit two of those categories, and we didn't have a dog. Our parents found a tiny cottage, or shack, with huge creepy insects inside and outside our living quarters. We had to contend with extreme heat. Air conditioning didn't exist.

Shortly after our arrival, Mom developed an ear infection and Dad became depressed. Our problems piled up. We returned to Philadelphia at the end of the summer. I have vague visual memories, but no particular thoughts or feelings, about that brief time in my life. Mom and Dad felt like failures. They had to start over and asked Dad's parents, who ran a chicken farm in Vineland, New Jersey, to house us while they reestablished a home for us in Philadelphia. It was, without a doubt, one of the worst years of my life. Grandmom and Grandpop were not very warm toward us. I felt frightened and abandoned, and missed Mom and Dad terribly. No more hugs and comfort from Mom. They visited us every other weekend.

Grandmom and Grandpop, both in their sixties, were busy tending to the chickens. Grandpop arose every day about 6 am to the sound of a rooster crowing "Cock-a-doodle-doo!" He fed the chickens and collected their eggs. Grandmom washed the eggs in their cold and damp basement and packaged them to be sold to local dealers.

Our dinners consisted of eating boiled old layers (chickens too old to lay more eggs). Ugh! Tough and tasteless! I didn't eat chicken again until many years later. When our one-year stay came to an end, we three were skinny. While there, we slept in cots in the attic without heat or air conditioning, Carl at one end and Harriet and I at the other end.

My strategy was to perform well in school, which I did. I was obedient and avoided any wrath from my grandmother. We three walked to and from a small country schoolhouse. My teacher required the class members to bring a handkerchief with them every day, so they could be a 'fairy'. If a student forgot, the punishment was to put his or her head down on the desk in folded arms, for a certain amount of time.

One day I forgot my handkerchief. The principal, who was my teacher, knew my grandmother and apparently called her. My grandmother must have gone to school to bring my handkerchief, saving me from shame that I surely would have felt. Did I underestimate my grandmother's capacity to care about us?

Carl was feistier than I. He planned to run away by bus to my parents in Philadelphia. He asked Harriet and me if we wanted to join him. At that moment, we were in our beds in the attic, shivering under the blankets. We told him, "No." I was too scared to join him. He asked if we had any money to donate to his cause. We gave him the few coins that we possessed. We were worried about him. He sneaked out and traveled by foot to a nearby store where there was a bus stop. He told the proprietor that he was waiting to catch the bus that was going to Philadelphia, to visit his parents. Within a short time, the police brought him back. He was visibly furious. I picture him angrily throwing his coins into the sand in front of the porch. I worried, what would be his punishment? I have no memory of the outcome or if my parents were told.

One Saturday morning, I was anxiously waiting for Mom and Dad to visit and didn't see them. While we were in the kitchen, I asked my grandmother if they were coming and she said, "No." I ran upstairs and burst into tears. I then looked out the attic window at the backyard, and saw Mom hanging clothes on the clothesline. I dashed downstairs, ran outside crying and grabbed and hugged Mom, who hugged and reassured me that everything was okay. For me, the year was a disaster, indelibly etched into my brain.

When I was an adult, Mom informed me years later that Grandmom blamed her for Dad's depression. Mom tolerated so much negative treatment from my grandmother, yet she never appeared bitter. I felt anger and resentment toward my grandmother. Grandpop never displayed hostile behavior toward Mom or us children. He appeared tired and was a quiet man. Grandmom treated him dismissively. I wonder now if Dad ever felt loved by her. Grandmom clearly favored her youngest son, Herman, who was twelve years younger than Dad. Was Herman a replacement for her first-born child, Herman, who died from the flu epidemic in 1918?

At the end of our school year in Vineland, Mom and Dad moved us back to Philadelphia. They saved up enough money and bought an end house on a street of row houses. The basement was a candy store that Mom successfully ran by herself for a year, while Dad worked at a nearby pharmacy. The customers immediately liked mom. My parents decided to incorporate a pharmacy into the store. Our family was reinvigorated. The year was 1945. We lived above our pharmacy for fifteen years, giving all of us some stability at last.

We referred to our pharmacy as a "mama-papa" business. This was a fortunate circumstance, because Mom was Dad's rescuer when he was deeply depressed and unable to function. I can still picture Dad sitting in our comfortable wing chair in the living room, in front of the staircase leading to the bedrooms, his hands covering his face while he quietly expressed guilt about not being able to work. I would kneel in front of him and offer encouraging words to hopefully bring him out of this stuporous state. It was to no avail while he was that depressed.

Dad liked to gamble on the horses and secretly had a bookie. When he was depressed, he expressed his remorse about this habit. However, he always returned to those gambling behaviors when he miraculously came out of his paralyzing state of depression. We were not aware of how much money he lost. During those phases, we children tiptoed around the house, so we wouldn't make him worse. Our family had zero knowledge about mental illness during those years.

When Dad wasn't severely depressed, he sometimes exhibited manic behavior. This usually was displayed as angry outbursts. I remember feeling frightened, wanting to hide somewhere to avoid his outbursts. Throughout our childhood, conflicts arose between Dad and Mom. I do not recall what triggers lit the match for Dad's anger. Mom was always our defender if the subject of conflict involved one of us. Mom never raised her voice and hated conflict, so the end product was silence for a few days. We just cringed and felt tense. I hated the silence.

I learned to take on the role of family mediator at the tender age of ten or eleven. I recall sitting halfway down the flight of stairs that led from the kitchen down to the store. I pled with Dad, "Please talk to us!" I could see Dad behind his counter, out of view of the customers, filling prescriptions. He tightened his brow and I felt sad and frustrated. I desperately wanted a happy family. After my plea to talk to us, Dad responded by saying, "You're all against me!"

Sometimes, I heard Dad yell at a salesperson that annoyed him and tell him to leave. I felt embarrassed, and wanted to hide. I taught myself to be the good little girl to avoid being the recipient of his anger. That good little girl behavior ruled my life for many years.

We were able to relax when Dad was calmer and more like a normal person, often exhibiting another side. On bad weather days, he drove us and neighborhood friends to school while Mom minded the store. He also took us to all of our necessary appointments. Mom didn't like driving and Dad did. I needed braces. That required monthly appointments to the orthodontist's office. Dad was my driver and these were very pleasant memories. Memories of my father are not all dark. Dad showed his love by doing things for us, but was not good at showing affection or saying, "I love you."

Six days a week, my parents worked from 9 am to 10 pm. Throughout those earlier family years, Dad closed the store on Sundays. Almost every Sunday, we happily scrambled into our car on excursions to visit our relatives. My aunts, uncles, and cousins lived in various cities in New Jersey. I was allowed to sit in the front, between Dad and Carl. Harriet and Mom sat in the back seat. I claimed carsickness when in the back, therefore, I was granted the delight of the front seat. Dad was always in a good mood on these days. I don't remember any family quarrels. I was truly happy.

I especially loved visiting family in Margate, New Jersey. My favorite cousin, Barry, was my age. We had fun being on the beach and running in and out of the salty Atlantic Ocean, while Mom and Dad had a chance to relax as they kept an eye on us. They worked such long hours, and never took a vacation, only a few hours on Sundays. I wonder if this demanding schedule contributed to his frequent bouts of depression and mania.

As I contemplate this tale, my mind wanders to a story revealed to me by my dear, sweet mother. I was probably about twelve or slightly older. Mom and I sat alone on our soft cushioned, red velvet living room sofa, and she confessed, "Barbara, I tried to end my pregnancy with you. Dad gave me some medication that would have aborted you. But it made me sick, so I stopped taking it."

Mom filled up with tears. I just stared and listened intently, not yet feeling the impact of her words. There was a chance I wouldn't have been born. Mom continued, "I was so overwhelmed at that time with taking care of Carl who was four and Harriet, who was only two, I didn't think I could manage a third child. I was already dealing with Dad's unstable moods, especially when he got depressed. I'm so sorry, I love you so much. You bring me so much joy."

We hugged each other tightly. I loved Mom and wanted to soothe her so she wouldn't worry or feel guilty. Perhaps that was the earliest hint that I would become a therapist. She and I revisited this story throughout her life. Her love and devotion to my siblings and me conquered any hostile feelings I might have felt. To us children, our mom was a gem, full of hugs and kisses, and a naturally empathic person. She always made the time to listen to us, and was never judgmental. She balanced our father's instability. Dad's unpredictable cycle of behaviors existed throughout my young life.

My brother Carl initially followed in Dad's footsteps and attended pharmacy school. He then changed directions in his career path and went to medical school. Lo and behold! My brother put the pieces of this puzzle together, and realized that Dad was displaying clear symptoms of manic-depressive disorder.

I also began to follow Dad's path and attended Temple University School of Pharmacy. I was a commuter because Carl told me that our parents couldn't afford the cost of dormitory living. During my junior year, Dad sold our Philadelphia store and opened up a pharmacy in Pennsauken, New Jersey. Small, mama-papa stores were being overtaken by large, corporate-owned stores. Our larger New Jersey pharmacy rapidly started to do well. Dad and Mom ran it during the week. My brother, now a Registered Pharmacist, and I ran it on weekends. The hours were exhausting.

In my senior year, my sister and brother-in-law who resided in Philadelphia invited me to live with them. I had learned to drive by then and asked to join a carpool. This way, I no longer had to commute alone to school. I also had the opportunity to sit beside Allan, my classmate in pharmacy school and a member of the carpool. That was the beginning of our budding relationship. By this time, Carl was married and in medical school. He and I continued to work on weekends at the family pharmacy.

The busier and more successful was the store, the sicker Dad became. His depression stretched into longer periods, with his deterioration escalating into a psychotic breakdown. He thought fire engines were coming to our store.

It was an emergency situation. My brother contacted Dad's neurologist, who admitted him into a private psychiatric hospital in Philadelphia. Dad received shock treatments, which were brutal. Mom and I visited Dad frequently, and those visits were emotionally draining. Dad was initially in a locked unit. I was horrified and extremely tense. Dad looked despondent. I wanted to see him, and yet couldn't wait to leave.

I was living with Mom and Dad at that time. Mom and I ate ice cream at night. I gained a lot of weight and didn't like myself. This dreaded period remained a secret we kept from everybody, outside our nuclear family. Mom hired pharmacists to help us run the store. She was amazing, clear-headed, and competent!

I concentrated at school the best I could, under the circumstances. In that era, mental health issues were not revealed. I felt shame and embarrassment. I had to cancel going to our senior class trip, and shed many tears. In recent years, Allan told me he had been looking forward to seeing me on that trip and was very disappointed by my absence. During this family crisis, I fell in love with Allan. Apparently, it was reciprocal. I guess I was able to compartmentalize family from my social life, a strength I was not yet aware I possessed.

Dad recovered. Though horrendous, the treatment was successful. At that time in history, around 1960, some medication became available and it was helpful. Dad didn't discuss his hospitalization with me until many years later, when he shared his reaction to the intrusive electroshock treatment. The two of us were sitting on a park bench. He described the humiliation he felt when the hospital took away his belt during his hospital stay, and how painful the shock treatments were. It was a rare heart-to-heart conversation, which I cherish. I felt a true and deep love for him at that moment.

In between traumatic events, I pursued Allan until he caught up with me. We passionately connected as we were preparing to graduate from college. We married in 1961, less than a year after graduation. Around the same time, Mom and Dad sold their store, and chose to move to Miami Beach. Many years earlier, he had passed the Florida state boards and obtained licensure to practice pharmacy there.

After they moved to Miami Beach, Dad was always able to get work in a pharmacy. In his role as a pharmacist he worked as an employee, not the proprietor. His responsibilities were significantly reduced. He never again experienced such a debilitating state of mind. We all recognized that stress exacerbated his depression and the potential to decompensate into a psychotic state. Antidepressant oral medications helped to stabilize Dad's fluctuating mood swings as well. Dad's improved mental state was a great relief to my siblings and to me.

Mom and Dad lived in Florida for the rest of their lives. Warm weather, friendships, and fewer work hours gave them an extended lease on a more satisfying life. Allan and I remained in the Philadelphia area, where he practiced medicine and we raised our two daughters.

A few years after they moved, I asked Mom, on one of our frequent phone conversations, "Do you miss working?"

She responded, "No, not at all. I'm enjoying the chance to relax and have female friends."

Wow! I was shocked! I didn't recognize how much she had sacrificed her life to take care of Dad. She finally was having some fun. Dad still exhibited some similar but much less serious behaviors. We siblings also could relax a bit. Mom and I discussed the Pennsauken chapter of our lives during one of our many chats while she lived in Florida. She revealed that she decided to live in Florida, away from us, to protect us from the risk of in-person conflicts between Dad and us adult kids.

Mom and I remained very connected via phone all the years my parents resided in Florida. They visited us every few months. Dad always loved to drive, so he enjoyed the automobile trips. When they stayed with us, visits were very pleasant. Sometimes, he annoyed me with his joke telling. I never was certain if that was his mania or simply his personality trait. He was never good at social cues. I did feel surges of annoyance and impatience with him. Old reactions and memories don't fade easily.

When I was in my forties, I followed my heart, returned to school and earned a much-desired master's degree in social work. I finally confronted my family history, attended therapy sessions, and began the work of unscrambling all those memories. Mom and Dad were in the latter years of their lives. Dad was retired, still ornery and annoying at times, but never again seriously depressed! The nightmares of those years are mostly tucked away, but never completely gone.

HER HIDDEN STRUGGLE
BY GABBY SPATT

Gabby Leon Spatt spends her time at the intersection of business and social good as a creator of movements around important topics – leadership, diplomacy, film, mental health, women's empowerment and the Jewish community. A personal tragedy led Gabby to work with the Blue Dove Foundation, an Atlanta-based non-profit focusing on mental health and substance abuse education, outreach, and awareness through a Jewish lens.
www.thebluedovefoundation.org
www.gabbyleonspatt.com

My younger sister, Sari, and I grew up in the affluent, tightly knit Jewish community of Coral Springs, Florida. We were raised with strong family values and were lucky to spend a lot of time with our grandparents, cousins, and a large group of very close family friends. Overall, even with our parents' divorce when we were in elementary school, we had a very normal American upbringing.

But as Sari got older, coping with the day to day was difficult for her. In high school, she finally was diagnosed with bipolar disorder, and like many others who suffer with this disease, she cycled through medications, treatments, and therapists. Treatments would help for a few months and then suddenly wouldn't. Different triggers would set her off. Little issues became big ones, and she met them with screaming, insults, and sadness. Faced with constant frustration at herself, she started looking for other ways to be happy, including occasional drug use.

Unable to help herself, Sari responded outwardly by devoting her life to helping others. In college, she volunteered with children who had autism and eventually earned a master's degree in sign language education. She taught third grade, and both the students and their parents talked about how much she cared for them. She even made YouTube videos translating popular music into sign language. When things were good, she was good. Really good.

At thirty years old, Sari had touched many lives for the better and seemed to have kicked her bad habits. To others, she presented a warm, nurturing young woman. But when things got bad in her mind, coping without drugs must have seemed an impossible task.

It was our grandmother who found her. Hurricane Irma was battering Florida, and Sari had lost power, so she went to stay with our grandparents. After spending a wonderful day together cooking and grading school papers, she was set to spend the night. Later that evening, Grandma heard her on the phone having a tough conversation and then heard the front door close. This call obviously had been a trigger for Sari. Looking in the hall, Grandma realized she was gone.

When Grandma called her cell, Sari said she just had to run an errand and would be right back. She returned about midnight and immediately went into the bathroom. After about ten minutes of silence, Grandma knocked. No answer. She opened the door and found Sari hunched over, barely breathing. She called 911. Can you imagine a ninety-year-old woman doing CPR on her granddaughter? The ambulance came, and the EMS team administered Narcan before rushing her to the hospital. (If you don't know, Narcan is a medication used to block the effects of opioids, especially in an overdose.)

When my mom called me early that morning, I knew something was wrong. But I expected it to be about my grandparents, who were ninety and ninety-nine. I never thought it would be the news she shared: "We're in the hospital. Sari overdosed."

I immediately booked a ticket and flew home, and for the next several days, I don't know how we survived it. Why did this happen? We had so many questions. How did we not know what she was doing?

We do not believe Sari intentionally took her life. After losing a dear friend years ago, she said, "I won't kill myself. I don't want people to experience how I feel now." And there was no way she would do it at our grandparents' house. She loved them so much. But likely unknown to her, the drugs she took were laced with fentanyl, a powerful and dangerous additive, and the drug became a game of Russian roulette.

She never regained consciousness. After several days and yet another brain scan, there was minimal brain activity and no improvement. She was living only because of a machine, and my family had a tough decision to make, one I don't wish on my worst enemy. Eleven minutes after she was removed from the ventilator, she was gone. It was crazy to experience. You never think this could happen, but it did. Things can change very quickly.

Sari died on September 14, 2017 from a heroin overdose. Even worse, she wasn't the only one. Within two days of Sari's death, twenty-one other people in South Florida of various ages died from fentanyl-based overdoses.

So here we are two years later. Sari is buried with our other grandparents and a dear friend who also struggled with mental health. Her headstone is simple yet descriptive: Daughter, sister, granddaughter, friend. A menorah and a playing card. She was buried in the dress she was going to wear to my wedding, which was four months after she passed away.

At Sari's funeral we talked about how she struggled at different times in her life. We did not say she died from an overdose at the funeral, but most people knew. It took me six months to tell people outside of my inner circle how she died and to share my story. How do you talk about it? There is a stigma attached. Today, I feel comfortable saying it. I think it just took time. At the time of her death, I couldn't even focus on what happened.

Mom wasn't ashamed. Our community knew she had a daughter who struggled with mental health. She talks about it today, and she's OK. She's stronger than we all imagined. My father, who lives far away, connected with other parents on Facebook and locally who have suffered through the same thing. My stepfather suffered a stroke shortly after Sari died and is talking about it too. We couldn't have gotten to where we are today without that same wonderful community of family and friends who supported us so much growing up and supports us just as much today. They never cease to amaze me by showing up with food, stories, and big smiles.

I'm less of a talker and more of a doer. I have taken every opportunity I could to make a difference in an area that needs so much work. I immediately started volunteering. It helped me with my grieving process. Being involved and trying to make change happen is the only way I know. Today, I am the executive director of the Blue Dove Foundation. I see daily how much connecting with people means and how many people are looking for light when dealing across the spectrum of mental illness.

I have learned a lot over the past few years. I learned that in this national endeavor to fight opioid use, recreational users often get overlooked. I learned how tightly mental health is connected to drug abuse. And I learned it can happen to anyone, even when you come from a nice Jewish family.

We as a society have made a lot of progress, but there still is so much room to grow. I learned help is out there through various organizations and a wealth of people, you just have to ask. And we need to talk more. We as a community need to quiet the silence that surrounds the issues of substance abuse and mental health overall.

This story first appeared in the Blue Dove Foundation's book, Quieting the Silence: Personal Stories.

RED CARDINAL
BY JULIE STRONG

Julie Strong, BA, MB, ChB, is a semi-retired family physician and shamanic practitioner in Halifax, Nova Scotia, Canada. She holds a medical degree from Trinity College, Dublin, Ireland and a BA in Classics from Dalhousie University, Halifax. Julie gives talks at the local library on insanity in Ancient Greek Literature and on shamanic healing. She plays viola in a string orchestra and can't get enough of pickleball.

Introduction

Cheryl Strayed, an author I admire, exhorts us to write like motherfuckers. I try, except the mother and father and one-eyed dingo dog I wanted to fuck have been dead now for a long time.

I think Sigmund Freud was the first to realise that children are a bundle of libidinal impulses and that these impulses are directed towards both parents and towards any other love object. If all goes well for children and they are loved and respected by their caregiver(s), they develop into an adult who can develop a loving, sexual relationship with another adult. If things go badly, children are left with a vacuum and they may spend their life trying to fill this void with whatever they can find, including thoughts of self-criticism, suicide, murder, and self-torture. They may eventually find themselves resorting to drugs, alcohol, sex, and more to deaden the pain.

Things going badly include being the victim of war, accidents, famine, or pestilence. On a smaller scale, things going badly is parental illness, including mental illness, and in my case, a deranged father.

I have been struggling with writing my memoir for over twenty years now. What has held me back is, first, fear that revealing the depth of my own self-loathing would encourage another to commit suicide. I fear someone wavering would see only the adamantine cruelty I exerted on my own psyche to encapsulate the pain, but not possess the strength and gifts with which I was blessed to contain it. They might think, hell, if such horrible things could happen to someone who did not experience war, accident, famine or pestilence, the world must be a really bad place, better just quit it.

Second, fear that the Inquisition would run me down and rape and burn me if they knew what desperate murderous, incestuous, and bestial images exist in my mind.

I would advise young people that if they have no one to talk to about their grief, and have no positive container for it, such as art, or writing, or sports, then they need to create a torture chamber to do the job. If you can imagine sharp instruments ripping at yourself, you will gain a sense, albeit false, of being control. You keep these instruments locked away in your imagination and this way you appear normal and survive. You hold the concept of suicide very close; never let it go, just in case, but never act on it.

I would also advise young people to smile and attend school. You will likely get excellent grades, because you will shunt the vacuum that lives inside your core, created from lack of nurturing, and instead fill this vacuum with information and facts to pass exams that will get you into college. After school, pursue a career in health care or teaching, so you will learn about compassion and helping others. This will help you to marry and have children, if possible, and when the cracks begin to appear in your psyche, enter therapy. With therapy, you can look after your own needs, as well as those of your children. In doing so, you can start to reclaim joy in your life.

My sister lives with a diagnosis of bipolar I and I am fairly sure I have cyclothymic mood disorder. For ten minutes each day my mind races so fast I cannot write down my thoughts. It is a pleasurable experience. I surfboarded a little in Tasmania, Australia and when I am "up", it feels like surfing in my mind, only the waves keep coming; there is no need to pause to wait for the next wave. Then the slump sets in, yet I can still go to work or yoga class and I can practise music and write my historical novel.

Once a week I visit and read to my grandchildren and this gives me a lot of pleasure. However, sometimes by the end of the day I feel like a heap of shit and hate myself. The only difference now from years ago is that when I feel this way, I can, if I try very hard, convince myself that I won't feel this way forever. And at this present time I am thankful that mostly I love my life.

Four Reasons Why I Am Writing This Essay

1. Two adopted Chinese girls from different families in my province committed suicide a month before Christmas. I do not think their parents suffered from bipolar, but their daughters must have felt horribly cut off and felt dreadful self-loathing to kill themselves. My story is about being cut off and self-loathing. Perhaps it will help others.

2. The isolation of the pandemic prompts me to write. I have few close friends but I have a number of friendly acquaintances, such as people I play music and pickleball with and people I hang out with after church on a Sunday. All of these social activities have mostly stopped. I am lonely and this writing is an opportunity to connect with others who may struggle with similar issues to mine. I think I can teach a few things and I expect I can learn much from others.

3. My ex-husband, who is a good friend, was diagnosed two months ago with relatively advanced prostate cancer. He is sixty-six, a year younger than me. For years when we were married, Brian exhorted me to write. He would ask, "How many doctors know Ancient Greek? You survived a bizarre and horrible childhood. Tell others how it can be done." At the time I refused, but his illness has brought home to me that I do not have many years left on this planet. If I am to write, it is now.

4. My youngest daughter's husband recently started transitioning to female, just before the birth of their first daughter. Thankfully, she is good with this, but I have found this hard. It has made me realise we have to live our true lives, and part of that, for me, is telling my story.

Growing Up With My Bipolar Father, Trevor Stronge

This is an account from the first suggestions of my father's bipolar in his mid-thirties until he burned out and took to his bed around age forty.

My father, Trevor Stronge, was born in Toronto, Canada in 1926. His parents, originally from the seaside town of Colwyn Bay in North Wales, had immigrated first to California then settled in Toronto in the 1920's. Jesse, his father, built their house in Toronto single-handed. Daisy, his mother, was the eldest girl of fifteen children. She won the award of Miss San Diego Banking 1919. When Trevor was eleven, my grandparents took him and his older brother back to Colwyn Bay to live. My father was a small, clever child who wore glasses and loved the snowy Canadian winters. He never forgave his parents for the move.

My grandparents Daisy and Jesse did not get along and eventually divorced. My dad left school at fifteen to work in an accounting firm in Colwyn Bay. At age seventeen he enlisted in the navy and after the war he studied accountancy at Manchester University. There he met and married my mother, Trudy, a nursing assistant. Seven years later I was born, named Julie by Dad because I was born by C-section (after Julius Caesar). Dad had a good job and we lived in a pretty little house in the suburbs of Manchester.

Four and a half years later my baby sister was born, likewise by C-section, after which our mother developed deep vein thrombosis and died from a pulmonary embolism. Dad threw out all of my mom's possessions and made it clear no one was ever to mention her name around him. He mentioned Mom to me only three times in the remaining forty years he survived her. One of those times was to say how glad he was Mom was dead and not able to see what "rat-bags" her daughters had become. He also said she baked an excellent apple pie and once had tried to kill herself. Essentially it was as if my mother had never existed.

My dad disliked his own mother but took my sister and I to live with her in her boarding house in Colwyn Bay. I hated it there. There were three whiskery old ladies of whom I was terrified who lived in rooms off the landing. There was one toilet and the old ladies poured their slops down the toilet, including old fish skins and cabbage water, and never flushed. The house was damp and wallpaper peeled off the walls. I hated the school where everyone spoke Welsh and resented the English.

Despite this, Dad was the center of my world. Even as a toddler I worshipped him and used to tell him how I wanted to marry him when I was grown up. Of course, Mummy and he just used to laugh about it, but I knew if he gave me a baby I would not eat it like Mummy did so she had to go away. Not for another thirty-four years would I admit to myself she had actually died.

I loved it when Dad took me down to the promenade late at night. We would lie side by side on the benches and he would hold me warm in his arms and point out the constellations: Orion, Cassiopeia, Ursa Major and Ursa Minor. Big bear and little bear, like Dad and me.

When Dad was "up" he would take us to the fun fair down by the beach. We rode the bumper cars, went on the Ferris wheel, and played the slot machines. We went up and down holding onto the pink wooden manes of the ponies on the carousel. I loved the loud music of the calliope. He bought us all the candyfloss we could eat. I loved candyfloss. It was like magic. A little sugar in the big steel whirring machine and out came masses of floss.

When Dad was "down" he would not speak to us for days. I could not bear that. It was the worst feeling in the world to be ignored by him. I felt if I could stretch myself really long and thin until there was barely anything at all left of me, I could maybe reach him and he would see me. But nothing I did could bring him up. I rolled his cigarettes for him and brought him his tea that he liked very strong, with two teaspoons of sugar and a lot of milk. I felt very important taking care of him.

Dad gave me a dictionary of classical mythology when I was nine. At night I used to imagine myself in the Greek myths. I loved that Perseus slew Medusa using his shield as a mirror so he did not have to look at her petrifying face. I also absorbed the tortures the gods inflicted on those who offended them. Like Zeus sending an eagle to peck out Prometheus' liver, which grew back the next day, so his torment lasted for eternity.

My favourite was Apollo's punishment of Marsayas. I would fantasise at night about being flogged where the skin would be ripped off my body. It was a way of feeling touched, any kind of touch would do and it was pain I could control. I knew it was bad to do this, and I didn't care. To imagine pleasant things felt like a mockery of my life. That I could not and would not bear. I imagined having a poison capsule hidden behind my back tooth, so even if my hands were lopped off I could swallow it and end it all. All these painful fantasies became eroticised as I grew older.

Dad bought a hamster and I loved having a warm soft creature to hold. It was almost as if Hammie held me. Because Dad was angry with his mother, we were forbidden to even speak to her, even though we lived in her house. I had a couple of friends at school but never invited them home, and it never occurred to me hug my baby sister of whom I was jealous because she had blond hair where I only had brown. Also, I knew that before she came I had a mother, and after she came, I hadn't.

When Dad was up he glowed. To me he was god, like the Sanskrit meaning of the Greek god Zeus, meaning "He shines." He was the world and I was a bug in it. But a radiant bug so long as he was up and I reflected his glory back to him. When he was down he was a miasma, a dark malevolent cloud and I was an abject slug for him to despise and step upon. Either way, I adored him.

When I was ten I stole, then replaced, three pennies from his mother's purse. When I confessed this to him, he would not look at me and did not speak to me. It seemed to last forever but it was probably only a few days. My sister had a birthday party when she turned six. A little friend grabbed her favourite present, a doll, and my sister slapped the little girl. Dad spanked my sister hard and made her apologise to the little girl and her mother.

In our Dad's eyes, these two lapses were criminal. He sent off for information on orphanages in Australia. He got very excited about the idea of emigration. Convinced that we were evil in nature and to curb the rot, we moved to Tasmania where he had arranged for my sister and I to live in a children's home. We flew there. It took three days. We landed for re-fuelling in Cairo, Karachi, Singapore, Darwin, and Sydney. I memorised the names so I would know how to get home later, when I was grown.

I don't believe the house-parents abused us as they did some of the other kids. We were well behaved and did our chores and homework. What was bad was seeing another child being beaten and feeling glad it wasn't me. But I felt safe for the first time since leaving Manchester. There was a routine, and daily life was predictable. I could be a kid. It wasn't my job to keep Dad from falling into one of his terrible downs.

But Dad soon regretted his decision. He realised he could not live without us so he took us out after six weeks. We stayed with him at his digs where the landlady made us pretty sandwiches in rainbow-coloured wax paper.

My father would get excited about random thoughts that came to him. I remember when he announced over breakfast, "Today we are going to Moriarty." Moriarty was a tiny place with a dozen houses and a gas station in a remote part of northern Tasmania, but because it bore the name of Professor Moriarty, Sherlock Holmes' nemesis, we had to visit. My sister and I did not know who Sherlock Holmes was. We had no car and there were no buses, so we hitchhiked there. He was all happy about it, even when we had to walk for miles. My sister was seven and complained because it was hot and she was tired, but I wouldn't dream of complaining. I was with my dad and he was happy.

Dad bought us two rabbits. This was when Australia was waging war against rabbits. But again I was so glad to have something soft and warm to cuddle. Then Dad got a job in Hobart, the capital of Tasmania. We had to let the rabbits go. I think he cried. I expect I did too.

I thought the animals in Tasmania were wonderful. I loved the idea of the echidna, the spiny anteater. It is a monotreme, meaning it lays eggs but suckles its young. I could imagine I was a baby spiny anteater in its mothers pouch and safe from the rest of the world. And I loved wallabies and platypuses, and the noisy kookaburras and the bright red and yellow flowering trees. Tasmania was Technicolor compared with the slate grey drizzle of north Wales.

Dad's ups became more rare and his lows more frequent when he started drinking hard. He would stay in his bedroom drinking sherry and doing crossword puzzles. I watched a lot of TV. I specially liked Flipper the friendly dolphin because it was about a widower, like Dad, only he has two little boys and their life seemed normal and they were happy with each other.

In the TV room was the guinea pig cage where we had three guinea pigs. Mesh wiring covered the base and their pee dripped onto newspapers beneath and onto the rug, which made for a big stink in the room. We had three budgies too that perched on top of the venetian blinds and their poops dripped down the slats. Dad believed it was cruel to keep birds in cages.

We were lucky to escape a bush fire that ravaged the island. When the fire was only twenty yards from our house Dad had to choose which of his possessions to save. He saved the guinea pigs, the budgies, and the complete works of William Shakespeare. It did not matter that we had no mother or car or phone or fridge. So long as we had William Shakespeare, the world would know we were the Right Kind of People and princes would line up asking to marry my sister and me

When I was thirteen, Dad got us a dog. Rusty was a mutt, a half-dingo dog from the pound. I liked this dog and used to fantasize about having sex with him. I didn't know anything about sex. I thought grownups had sex standing up. I would spend hours poring over the Bible reading the parts where they sentence women to death for having sex with animals. I found the Old Testament much more comforting than the new. In the Old Testament, God didn't seem to care much for what people thought about, only what they did. We were a nominally Christian household, and my sister and I attended Sunday school, but I was terrified that Jesus could look inside my mind. I also thought Dad could look inside my mind.

When I reached puberty Dad became convinced I was a sexually depraved predator. He would interrogate me for hours as to what dreadful thing had I done that had changed me from the angel that had sustained him after his wife's death to the monster I was now. I was far too ashamed to tell him about the feelings I had for Rusty and I wasn't aware of the sexual feelings I had towards him. Now, looking back, I am aware I had them, at least as a child and quite possibly as an adolescent. But I would have killed myself before admitting that to him.

I did very well in school. I didn't play sports, as I was ashamed of my body, but I got great report cards. In one of his manic or drunken fits he threw all the photos he had kept of Mummy in the fire. Now I would never know what she looked like. How would I recognise my mother when I went home to Manchester to find her?

Around this time I decided to do medicine. Up until age thirteen I wanted to be a vet.

One day a hockey puck hit me on the head. The doctor who sewed my eyebrow up was so kind and gentle, and Dr. Kildare on TV was so handsome, I knew I had to become a doctor too. I also watched *M*A*S*H*. I felt I could be totally detached around sewing limbs back on or amputating them if they had to come off. I had no idea that when I did encounter a patient in pain, later on, in medical school, I would feel helpless and would have to fight my instinct to freeze.

I had to become a doctor and preferably a psychiatrist or neurosurgeon so when I started experiencing out of control episodes like Dad, I would know where the wiring had come unglued and be able to fix it.

Dad hated doctors, considering them the epitome of the petit bourgeois. Respectable, stodgy. He wanted us to be astronauts or croupiers in Monte Carlo and have Chinese triplets. Medicine seemed to offer me everything Dad could not: reasonability, compassion, and security. As a doctor I could sacrifice myself like Jesus and take care of the multitude. Even better, I would be able to pass for normal. But underlying all this was the hope that if I took care of everyone, then someone, surely, sometime would take care of me.

When I was fourteen and he was forty-two, Dad decided to take us back to Gran's in Wales. Later he told us he was going to kill himself and realised he had better not leave us alone in Tasmania where we didn't know anyone.

He arranged for us to return the opposite way to which we came. We traveled to Hawaii and then to California. He took us to see the Grand Canyon and Yosemite and the Golden Gate Bridge. My sister and I pretended to be enthusiastic, to please him, but I didn't care about those things. Yes, they were all big, the biggest in the world, but I had made friends at school and felt Tasmania was my home now. I didn't want to go back to that ugly old boarding house in Colwyn Bay.

And I think I knew he was contemplating suicide and I was terrified of him killing himself. I was never sure about out mother. Years later, one of her sisters said, "Well she didn't have much to live for, living with him."

Dad did at one point say how our mother had once put her head in the gas oven. I don't know when this was or why. It might have been before I was born. I don't know who found her. Sometimes I wonder if I did.

Back in Colwyn Bay, Dad had a few spurts of up-ness. He took to running barefoot for hours in the nearby woods. He could not understand why other people did not follow his example. He stopped drinking and became infatuated in turn with Mao Tse Tung, then Lenin, and finally Christianity. Dad decided there was too much badness in the world for Jesus to address on his own, so God had chosen him, Dad, to be Jesus' helper.

Of all the phases of his illness, Christianity was his worst. My sister and I were flawed and evil and needed exorcising. He would corner me for hours, again demanding to know what dreadful thing I had done to make me an evil slut. And I always felt I was an evil slut. That I had done something very wrong, like kill my mother, or at least want her dead. And on a very young level I did lust after my father. And I think also on a very young level I wanted Mummy to go away so I could have him all to myself, so it was my fault she died. But at sixteen, when he accused me of wanting to have sex with him I certainly didn't think I did. He was forty-four, and to me, at sixteen, he was an old man. I wanted a boyfriend to kiss and maybe cuddle with, but I had never so much as held hands with a boy.

He would interrogate me, demanding, "How many sailors did you have sex with last night?" I would eventually break down and give him some outrageous number that seemed to satisfy him for the moment. Then he could despise me for being a total, worthless slut and advise me to kill myself and to make sure to do it properly, as it would be best for world.

"Lie down on the train tracks," was his suggestion, "And wait." After discharging his venom, he seemed to relax. I would crawl off to my room, thinking, I have survived.

Once Dad made me kneel in front of a crucifix for hours. During one moment it occurred to me that Jesus had a penis. Maybe my eyes dilated. I don't know. Dad had been watching me for signs of evil thoughts and he pounced, asking, "What did you just think?"

I felt so ashamed and did not want to say. I was crying, but after another hour I confessed. He said I was disgusting and threw buckets of cold water over my head.

Eventually I slithered back to my room feeling like a trampled slug.

And I still loved him, which meant I had to believe that he was trying to save me from my dark, bestial, evil side. And this of course meant I had to believe myself to be dark and bestial and evil. Words from his lips were everything to me, and if he told me I was worthless, I would feast on that slime.

He did not pursue me when he was "down." I would seek him out as he lay huddled under the blankets in his bedroom. I went voluntarily for him to verbally abuse me. I had to have something from him. I hated him for abusing me in this way, but I hated myself more.

A few years later, I went away to medical school in Dublin, Ireland. I didn't like it. I kept to myself and had just a couple of friends: the Icelandic girl I shared digs with and a couple of boy friends. I hated having to see patients. I was great at memorising facts but when confronted with patients,

I was afraid of offending them by asking personal questions, and I didn't want to touch their body. I was not happy about touch. Any kind of touch.

Dad followed me to Ireland. He had no money so I found him somewhere to live and took a job waitressing so I could pay for it. I was terrified that if I got someone's order wrong I would be fired. I was always waiting to be discovered as a fraud and banished. I moved into a house with my Icelandic friend. Dad came and one night decided to wallpaper the living room at 3 am. He did a terrible job, which was sad because he used to be good at wallpapering.

Dad became obsessed with the idea that people in two hundred years would think we in the 20th century were criminals because most had two eyes and a few people were blind. It was criminally selfish for the sighted not to be a living donor and give an eye up. He did all kinds of research into this, which lasted a couple of months and then he took to his bed again.

A few years after I got married and immigrated to Canada, Dad came to live with Brian, my husband, and myself and our two children, ages four and two in Halifax. But Dad would get up in the middle of the night and cook onions. Brian said he had to leave. I thought it was mean of my husband, but we found Dad an apartment downtown.

Soon after this Dad took to bowing in front of people on the street to salute the kingdom of God inside them. Then he took to kneeling in front of buses to salute the kingdom of God in as many people in one place as he could.

Then he went to hospital. Though he was formally diagnosed with schizoaffective disorder, in hindsight it was evident that he suffered from bipolar depression. He was treated with mood stabilizers and anti-psychotics and electroconvulsive therapy, but nothing helped. He went to live in a halfway house and when he was sixty-five he got a bed in the veterans hospital. He died at seventy-two. In some ways I miss him, but I am thankful he died when he did. He suffered terrible nightmares that no medication could help. The day he died, I felt a huge burden lifted from me.

The Process of Writing This Essay

When I start to write this a month ago I realise how great my shame still is and that I have never acknowledged it. Dad claimed God had chosen him to be Jesus's "special helper," when he was "up," and I believed for years that he was at least a great prophet, which made me special by association. Even when I had to work waitressing during medical school to support him, I told myself that I was privileged to do this for him. I realise just recently that I have been lying to myself, to prevent feeling dreadful shame at having a lunatic for a father.

I still live with aftermath. A week ago it was very cold here in Nova Scotia where I live and my pipes froze. They burst when a warm spell hit. I was frightened as I wasn't able to turn off the main water supply and water just kept pumping out of the ceiling. The water level in my basement kept rising and I felt helpless and panicky. I tried to phone a plumber at ten-thirty at night when I thought to myself, "You don't deserve to have a house with unburst pipes." My son-in-law found a plumber for me, and the problem got fixed a few hours later, but to realise I could think something so negative about myself was a shock.

Whether my negative thoughts to myself were residue from my father telling me I didn't deserve to be alive, or if it was from my mother's death when I was four, I do not know.

But thanks to being involved in writing this essay, I am aware of these thoughts and, in my experience, awareness is the precursor to change.

Another thing that has happened since writing this piece is I have remembered good things along with dredging up the bad. Like how much I enjoyed the *Beverly Hillbillies* on TV. I loved that they were mad in their own way, but they had fun and loved each other. It made me think that madness might not be all bad.

Also, I feel addressing the pain and shame from my childhood is a bit like digging down for something that decomposed many years ago, like all those ancient organisms buried in mud that are now converted to black sticky stuff and a source of power.

Among the painful memories are the occasional ones when I remember someone who was kind to me. The pain of a memory of kindness hits me in the solar plexus; I double over and sob with anguish. It is as if I have inured myself to the painful memories, but the shock of an unexpected kindness destroys all my barriers and leaves me helpless with no defenses. This pain seems to occur halfway between my chest and lower abdomen.I almost convulse, and I think it is partly due to mother loss but definitely in part to the fact that Dad could not express love as kindness, only as control.

This writing process has forced me to face depths of loss to which I was previously unaware. The resulting grief has, at times, made me feel sexually aroused. The passion of this grief is erotic and I have no partner. I feel the grief only leaves my body after I masturbate and reach an orgasm. The fantasies I use to get there tend to be negative. Like Dracula or the near rape scene in West Side Story. I am sixty-seven now and I hope one day I will have a partner again, or at least be able to fashion up some positive erotic fantasies, like Rhett Butler in *Gone with the Wind* or Jane Austen's Mr. Darcy.

Things That Helped Me In My Childhood

In childhood, I enjoyed school and had a few teachers who seemed to understand me. These were lifesavers for me. I especially loved English, and my English teachers responded well to me. I smiled and got good grades. As I mentioned in the introduction, school helped shunt all the pain from lack of nurturing up into my mind.

I spent a lot of time outdoors. I loved nature, especially tiny parts of nature, like moss and tiny shells. My grandmother, or someone, taught me to knit. I enjoyed making something wearable from a long piece of thread that bore no resemblance to the finished thing. A mystery. And it was soft and cuddleable. On some level it gave me hope I could one day re-knit myself.

I loved Jesus, who tells people to be kind to children. Especially Baby Jesus, who is warmed by sheep and cows in the stable. Dad bought us guinea pigs and a dog as pets. I slept with a stuffed bear until I was fifteen.

I loved to read. I felt mothered by *Little Women* and *Little House on the Prairie*. I loved the Katy books and I felt a kinship with Jane Eyre. I learned to play the violin and joined an orchestra. I traveled a lot. I got the awareness that there was a lot of world out there and that some of it was magical.

What Helped Me Heal

This is the closest I have come to reconciling my father; he had an idea of justice.

Along with his idea that it is wrong for millions to have two eyes and thousands be blind, he thought it wrong that the poor should be denied health care. I am grateful to have practised in the Canadian medical system, which despite its myriad flaws, holds at base, that everyone has the right to health care.

I got a job in medicine where I was required, every day, to put my own problems aside and focus on healing another. I spent three years training to become a psychosynthesis psychotherapist. Psychosynthesis is a transpersonal therapy that posits the existence of a Higher Self that is the organising principle of a person's life. Psychosynthesis holds that the ego consists of "sub-personalities," each with its own characteristics, and that sub-personalities exist in pairs. For instance, a critic subpersonality is harsh and demands perfection. Its corresponding victim sub-personality believes what the critic tells it. Subpersonalities are often disowned "split-off" segments of the young psyche, the result of unacknowledged and unprocessed grief. The goal of therapy is to work through the unprocessed grief that feeds the subpersonality pair and reclaim its energy to fuel a unified ego.

Twelve years of intense depth therapy. I became miserable when my youngest daughter turned four. I was thirty-eight. I think subconsciously I was aware that my mother died when I was four, although I had not thought of her in over thirty years. Therapy helped me re-parent myself as well as be more present for my growing children.

Other therapies I found helpful were Jungian, Gestalt, and Cognitive Behavioral. In therapy I was able to access the rage and pain I felt for years but had never expressed. Because my eldest daughter was eleven when I started therapy, some of my feelings were influenced by what I would do to a man who treated her as my Dad had treated me.

I eviscerated a lot of cushions, and then wept over them.

Through Dad's introducing me at an early age to the stars, I found a path to healing self and others through shamanism. Shamanism also has been most helpful, for it gave me a conduit to a spirit world that made sense to me on a visceral level. A power animal is rather like an angel, only with fangs and claws. I feel held by my power animals. Sometimes I invite my power animals to feed on the slugs I feel are still inside me. They have no problem with this, they find them tasty. I journey with my power animal weekly. I visit my mother and father in the upper and lower worlds, respectively, and seek advice from my own helping spirits and others who may materialise to help me.

Because of the book of myths Dad gave me as a child, I returned to school at thirty-three, received a Classics degree, and now give talks at the local library on healing with Greek myth.

Learning to do Qigong and meditate have also been very helpful, as well as belonging to an Anglican church.

What I do On A Daily Basis To Stay Well
- Say my gratitudes out loud with my morning coffee.
- Smudge using sweetgrass, and pray for my own and for the world's wellbeing.
- Write for thirty to sixty minutes with a lit candle.
- Go for a thirty to forty minute walk by the water, calling in my power animals and spirit guides.
- Do five to seven minutes of Qigong.
- Meditate for around forty-five minutes.
- Read a children's book to myself before taking it to my grandchildren and reading it to them. Read funny books like Little Red Riding Sheep and The Cow Who Laid an Egg.
- Draw or paint something with colours.
- Scream in the car. When I occasionally do this I always take a particular lightly travelled road by the ocean. I prepare for the screaming by checking carefully for traffic in either direction. When the grief hits me afterwards, I know where to pull in to cry. Then I go to a local art gallery or café and write.
- Smash old, chipped pottery when the need arises, again being aware of the pain that underlies the rage.
- Read literature.

Dad's love of literature helped me come to a love of writing later in life. Literature also helped me accept my father was neither a prophet nor a demon, but an ill human being. *The Glass Castle* by Jeanette Walls tells how her narcissistic father and mother nearly made a shambles of her and her siblings' lives, but she forgave them. Better still, she did not seem to think they had done anything that needed forgiving. My sister, who I am thankful to consider my good friend, occasionally asks if I have forgiven Dad. I find this is a hard question. Since he was ill, he could not help what he did. But he did hold down a government job until I was fourteen, so he wasn't crippled by his illness, yet he never said he was sorry after one of his destructive outbursts. So I am not at forgiveness yet. But I do feel love towards my father, now. Jeanette Walls helped show me how you can love someone even if they have treated you horribly.

Another author who helped me is the late Richard Wagamese. He was a Canadian indigenous writer, the child of parents who were survivors of the residential school system. Wagamese grew up in foster homes and spent an angry youth, living hard, before he found healing with an Elder. In his book, *Indian Horse*, Wagamese's protagonist is a young boy in a residential school. A priest molests him, but also teaches him to play hockey, which becomes a great passion in his life. I was shocked that this could happen. That the person who destroys you on the one hand, reveals to you your gift and encourages you to pursue it on the other.

Conclusion

I have an image in my mind of an iced-over river with a fast moving current beneath. I have the sense that Dad created enough ice floes that I could leap over them, yes, get badly cut in the process, but eventually reach dry land and safety, while he himself fell between their cracks and drowned.

Finally I think he always thought he loved us, even though no witness would consider it such. But because he thought it was love, I had enough of the idea of love in myself so I was able to parent my own children. For this I am very grateful.

Writing this piece has been hard, but I now have a greater understanding of myself, and even a sense of clarity and well being that I think must constitute a state of grace. Blessed Be.

STRANGER DANGER
BY JOHN TAVARES

John Tavares' short fiction has been published in a variety
of magazines, alternative publications, literary journals,
quarterlies, chapbooks, and anthologies, online and in
print. Born and raised in Sioux Lookout, Ontario, John is
the son of Portuguese immigrants from the Azores.

Once upon a time ago there lived a young woman named Anastasia
who stayed with her mother Elena. Elena suffered from mood swings and
never recovered from a major disappointment of her mid-life: She never
received a hoped-for promotion to vice-president for human resources at
the cannabis company where she had worked for many years. Elena's
alcohol consumption also became an issue with the actual vice-president of
human resources, who berated Elena for her rants and temper. The duelling
duo both nurtured a crush for the vice-president of corporate
communications, and fought over this Prince Charming, so the human
resources VP terminated Elena's employment.

After Elena's loss of income, she moved with Anastasia to an apartment
building in a bustling inner-city Toronto neighborhood, filled with the
constant background of police, ambulance, and fire sirens. The din and buzz
of incessant crowds of city residents, shoppers, and pedestrians, along with
motor vehicle traffic, permeated their apartment. The noise alternately
allured and irritated Anastasia, who often felt compelled to leave their
apartment.

Partly because of her long, radiant scarlet hair, Anastasia acquired the
nickname Big Red in high school. When Anastasia studied business
administration at university, her beloved grandmother, her *nonna*, gifted
Anastasia with a red Canada Moose parka, short waisted to show of her
granddaughter's hips and feminine figure. Anastasia so loved the parka,
insulated with goose down, and with a hood lined with coyote fur, she wore
the coat year-round. Her friends, remembering her childhood nickname,
started calling her Big Red again, and use of the nearly forgotten nickname
returned with vigor.

Anastasia liked to smoke and drink and nurtured a predilection for the recreational use of pot. Most men who encountered Anastasia found her physically attractive, with a pleasant personality, until she started drinking alcoholic beverages, at which point she became hostile and belligerent. She tried to mellow her mood swings and the edgy effects of drinking by smoking pot.

Her family physician and a clinical psychologist agreed she was medicating herself. The family physician argued she, like her mother, suffered from bipolar disorder, while the clinical psychologist who interviewed her concluded she had borderline personality disorder. But Anastasia refused to visit the psychiatrist to confirm a diagnosis. She also stopped taking the medication her family doctor prescribed; she said the side effects made her feel like a zombie.

Elena told her daughter she needed to work, so Anastasia found a job at a lingerie boutique. Her alternating mellow and perky traits formed part of the personality that endeared her to customers of the lingerie boutique in the supersized shopping mall in downtown Toronto. Other staff wanted her fired because of her temper and anger, but the manager thought she was an attractive young woman, and liked her athletic build, fair features, freckles, and large green eyes.

One afternoon Anastasia's mother asked her to deliver pain reliever, diuretics, and high blood pressure medication to her grandmother, who once again started to suffer the ill effects of congestive heart failure after suffering a mild heart attack.

"Your *nonna* is seriously ill," Elena said, as she vaped from an e-cigarette infused with cannabinoids. "I think a visit from you will boost her morale. Go and don't stop along the way or your *nonna* could miss a dose of her medication, which she absolutely needs or she could get sick. She could even go into cardiac arrest again without them."

Anastasia didn't reply from the other room, so Elena shouted across the apartment, "Do you want your grandmother's heart to stop?"

"Why wasn't the medication delivered straight to her door?" Anastasia yelled from the washroom, where she used the blow-dryer to shape and style her glistening red hair and weave the strands into a French braid.

"The pharmacist said his delivery gal tried, but no one answered the door. Your *nonna* probably couldn't get her big ass off her Lazy-Boy chair to answer the door. Do you understand?"

Anastasia reassured her mother that she would deliver her grandmother's prescription medications in a timely fashion. Her mother, though, knew about her tendencies: She liked to loaf and linger at bars and cafes along whatever route she took, drinking and smoking pot while studying for her business courses. Elena responded by berating the Anastasia's pot smoking that she often indulged to relieve her stress and letdown jitters associated with the prodigious amounts of caffeine she consumed in coffee, lattes, and espresso, which she substituted for food when she was dieting.

Anastasia's grandmother lived in a house at the north edge of Greektown Park, beside a college campus and a landmark diner and café, down the street from what had been described by one urban planner and architecture critic as the ugliest strip mall in Toronto. After Anastasia got off at the wrong subway station, she started to stroll along a meandering trail through a shady and tree-lined park. The wind started to gust, clouds billowed and covered the sun, and soon torrential rain started to fall.

Wearing her red parka, Anastasia took shelter in the mysterious Cypriot Park Café, conspicuous in a residential neighbourhood. When she noticed the pelting rain showed no signs of abating or stopping soon, she ordered a hard seltzer alongside a coffee, took a window seat, and started to read a chapter in her *Microeconomics* textbook.

As she sat reading, a man named Olek, a habitué of this particular café, brought Anastasia another hard seltzer and introduced himself. He told her his name was Ukrainian, and that his parents were Ukrainian and Polish refugees who escaped war-torn Europe. Before she could say another word, from out of the blue, Olek then told her he had a condition called bipolar disorder and he was on disability. He had been fired from his job as a hospital cleaner for inappropriate conduct and being overly friendly with patients and nurses.

Thinking him more than a bit peculiar, Anastasia just stared at him. She tapped the ends of the joint she was rolling, put the cigarette down, and sipped her second seltzer. Anastasia didn't regard him with any fear or trepidation, though, since she had few filters herself. Stranger danger was a foreign concept to her. Anastasia regarded no strangers as posing a threat or danger, especially since they bought her drinks in bars and offered her free joints to smoke. Anastasia said her friends had given her the nickname Big Red.

"Big Red," Olek said in a cheerful voice. "I like that name. It fits because you have beautiful red hair and a nice red parka."

"It's a Canada Moose parka," Anastasia said proudly, showing him the moose silhouette logo on the sleeve and the moose antlers logo on the opposing shoulder.

"Those parkas are expensive. I heard they cost at least a few thousand bucks."

"My grandma gave the coat to me. She said she gave it to me so I'd stop flashing my tits when it's thirty below. She didn't want me to catch pneumonia." Her *nonna* lamented the fact that Anastasia dressed immodestly, and had bought her the coat to protect her granddaughter from the Canadian winter.

"Smart woman, your grandmother," Olek said, eyeing her cleavage behind the black lacy lingerie and open front of her parka. Anastasia could hear his heavy breathing and smell the coffee on his breath.

"Generous, too. Is that a Victoria Secrets bra?" Olek asked.

"Yes," Anastasia practically shouted in glee. "How did you know?"

"I get the catalogue in the mail each month, even though I never order anything."

Anastasia showed him her legs in their black form fitting pants and smallish feet in thick brown sheepskin boots. "Do you like my leggings?"

"Yes, they're very nice."

Laughing, Anastasia said it was so nice of him to buy her a hard seltzer.

Eschewing alcohol, Olek drank a third coffee and offered her half his oat bar. "Where are you headed in the rain?"

"I'm delivering heart medication for my grandmother in East York. She lives on Park Street all alone in her house, next door to the Athens Cafe."

"Yes, I know Athens Café well, I used to go there for coffee with my buddies when I was in college. My classmates drank plenty of beer there."

Then, without prompting, he repeated, "I'm on disability." Then he continued, "People say I'm too friendly. My aunt says I'm overly friendly. My mom says I'm restless, fidgety, meddlesome, and can't mind my own business. I still live with my mother. My psychiatrist says I suffer from bipolar disorder. Either way, I'm unemployable. I get fired from every job they hire me for. After they fired me from my job at the East York hospital, I crashed. I think I slept sixteen hours a day for months. I loved that job. I was a cleaner for fifteen years. I really liked working around the doctors and nurses, it was so enlightening talking with them. Cleaning for them and patients made me feel I was contributing to society." He finally stopped talking to take a breath.

Anastasia narrowed her eyes as she listened to his monologue, shook her head, and then said, "I hope you don't mind, but I'm going to smoke some pot."

"I don't mind, but I think smoking isn't permitted in this café."

"Don't worry about that rule."

"When I worked in the hospital, I sometimes reminded patients and visitors smoking wasn't allowed. Come to think of it, that was also how I got in trouble with my supervisors."

"Because you were out of place, out of order," Anastasia said curtly and abruptly, "like now."

"But the baristas, or the bartenders, will kick you out."

"Not if I give them a big tip."

"You smoke pot when you study?" Olek asked.

"The caffeine in the coffee helps clear my mind."

"Except you're drinking a hard seltzer, which has alcohol and is technically a sedative."

"But you also bought me coffee, which counteracts its effect."

"But you're not drinking the coffee. It looks like your coffee is just getting cold. I can drink the coffee and get you another hard seltzer, if you like." He bought a hard seltzer for her while she rolled another joint.

Unknown to Anastasia, her dealer had laced the dried marijuana sheaves with a synthetic opioid, at a dose that caused hallucinations and delusions. This drug combination distorted Anastasia's perception of time and she believed she still had sufficient time to deliver the medications to her grandmother's house. Anastasia thought the stranger was smooth and initially she liked the tone and seductive timbre of his voice, but now he gave her the impression he was mentally ill. Still, Anastasia thought he was handsome; he was well-built, with a lean body, and possessed distinctive, chiselled facial features, which reminded her of her favorite movie actor, whose name she couldn't remember now that she was stoned.

Then she remembered he said he was bipolar. She told him her family physician suggested she was bipolar, and her counselor said she had borderline personality disorder, but she ignored their diagnoses and advice, skipped her appointments, and stopped taking the medication because the pills made her feel drugged. Considering her drug habits, the irony of that statement did not register with Anastasia.

Looking out the picture window of the café, she saw the steady downpour of rain showed no signs of abating, so she started smoking the laced cigarette. This time, the barista insisted Anastasia couldn't smoke in the café. The barista added that she smoked herself, outdoors, many meters away from the doors to the establishment, in Greektown Park. Anastasia told the barista that she just wanted to piss her off, make her miffed, and spoil her day, and, anyway, it was technically illegal to smoke in the park as well. The barista grew exasperated, so Anastasia stepped outside and smoked the weed on the sidewalk across the street.

Olek headed outdoors with her and stood alongside. She offered Olek a puff, but he urged her to stop smoking or she would damage her lungs. After she told him about her grandmother, Olek's mind went into overdrive. He felt a manic urge to help, and he urgently needed to leave, albeit he didn't want to seem abrupt. He figured Anastasia was an alcoholic, cute, and a bit narcissistic, although he thought any vanity she possessed about her appearance was justified. She looked sexy in her leggings, her sheepskin boots, and a lacy pushup bra beneath her open red parka.

He said he should leave, that he needed to hurry home for supper or his mother would worry. He went inside the café and took the medication from her handbag, while she smoked pot outside in the park, found her nonna's address on the label, and donned his rain coat and rubber boots. A man on a mission, to do good, he headed along the pathway to her grandmother's house in East York. When the rain finally stopped, Anastasia was stoned, and under the influence of more than marijuana.

Walking along the path to her grandmother's house, Anastasia paused when she saw a red fox sniffing its way through the park. She pulled biscotti from the café from her parka's pockets and tossed pieces towards the fox, who shyly ate the crumbs from the lawn and sidewalk. When she noticed Black-eyed Susan flowers blossoming along the trail, she stopped to pick a bunch. Anastasia thought Nonna would be delighted by the gift of a fresh bouquet of flowers growing wild.

Her flower picking suddenly stopped when a rushed, energetic by-law enforcement officer quickly approached her, waving his arms. As he came towards her, she spit tobacco on the cement sidewalk, even though she knew spitting in public places was a violation of Toronto by-laws. The officer cited her for an infraction and accused her of vandalizing the park.

Belligerent, Anastasia threw down her leather handbag, stomped her foot, and argued with the enforcement officer, who called for backup. Reinforcements came in the form of the Toronto police bike patrol, a uniformed officer patrolling the neighbourhood and wearing bicycle gear arrived furiously peddling his mountain bike. Realizing she could be arrested and charged criminally, she apologized, but a police cruiser also arrived as backup. She again apologized profusely to the crew of police officers and the by-law enforcement officer. Anastasia said she was coming down from a bad trip, a green out, after a stranger gave her some pot, which, she said, she believed was laced with PCP.

The police officers gazed at each other at the mention of phencyclidine and became suspicious. The officer in the police cruiser asked for her valid photo identification, emphasizing "valid." As he doubled checked her identification, consulting the dispatcher over his two-way radio, tightly gripping her student's card in his beefy hand, the officer claimed she had an outstanding warrant for her arrest on impaired driving charges.

Meanwhile, Olek hurried to Nonna's house and anxiously knocked at her door. Anastasia's grandmother asked who was at the door. Olek told her he was the pharmacy delivery person. He had her water pills and her blood pressure medication. Nonna invited him inside, saying she was too weak and tired to answer the door, which was unlocked. Nonna sat at her cluttered kitchen table, sipping tea, eating dry toast. Her housecoat was worn, tattered, and stained, and smelled faintly of perspiration and urine. Nonna looked haggard and tired. Seeing her kitchen untidy, Olek believed he saw the opportunity to do more good.

"Your daughter and granddaughter don't help you clean the house?"

"No. They can't wait for me to die soon, so they can inherit the house quick. And I can't clean the house myself because of my heart problems."

Olek literally leapt into action. He swept the kitchen floor, vacuumed the carpets in the living room, and tidied the clutter on the table and countertops. He polished the surfaces and then washed, rinsed, and towel dried her dishes. He cleaned the cupboards, swept the porch, vacuumed the carpets on the stairwell, and took out the garbage before then cleaning her washroom, including the toilet, sink, and mirror. He even tossed out expired medication. As he worked, Olek revealed to Nonna he had been a hospital cleaner, but he was fired because of his bipolar condition. Too many nurses complained about him trying to help their patients. Nonna just nodded in fascination, too tired to do much else.

When Nonna complained about her poor television reception, Olek set a neighbour's ladder against the side of her house, climbed up the roof, and adjusted and fine-tuned the position of her satellite dish. He also reconnected and tightened the cables, which had become loose from the signal splitter. Immediately noticing improved satellite TV reception, Nonna thanked him profusely.

Then Olek couldn't help noticing her kitchen cupboards were bare. The food on which she subsisted seemed stale and bland, basic staples, tea and marmalade and toast, hardly nutritious. Olek asked if she needed any food and Nonna shrugged. With his encouragement, she compiled a grocery list on the back of an envelope for an unpaid telephone bill.

First, Olek walked to the strip mall and paid the overdue bill at the bank branch. Then, he went into the drugstore, and, concerned about her nutritional status, he bought a bottle of multi-vitamins and mineral supplements. He debated with himself over the protein powder, since she seemed frail, undernourished, and could probably use nutritional supplementation. Despite the hefty price tag, he tossed the container of whey protein powder in his shopping basket. Then he visited the supermarket, at the other end of the strip mall, and, again with his own cash, bought her fresh fruit and vegetables and fresh cuts of meat and chicken and, for convenience, frozen TV dinners.

In her backyard, Olek discovered she had a ridiculously photogenic Pomeranian, but its sheer white coat looked soiled. He offered to wash the Pomeranian and gave it a bath and gentle scrubbing outside with the garden hose. Still, the dog looked neglected or restless to the overly friendly stranger, so he offered to take the dog for a walk. While Nonna ate Greek yoghurt straight from the container, which he bought at the supermarket, he took the Pomeranian for a walk along Park Street outside her house. Then he headed uphill towards the strip mall. He bought doggie biscuits and organic dog food from the pet supply store. He returned to Anastasia's grandmother's house with the deliriously happy dog in tow.

When he returned, Anastasia was there, steaming, tearing apart the house interior, searching for where she left her vaping cartridges. She looked up at Olek with amazement. "What the hell are you doing here?"

Olek shrugged and said, "You said she needed her meds and you weren't going to make it on time. I saw the chance to do good, so I took the medication and brought it to her." He looked around. "And did a few other things for her. Why don't you help your grandmother out, she needs help!"

Anastasia ignored him. Instead, she berated her grandmother, "Nonna, your ankles are so swollen and your feet and legs look like an elephant's."

"That's a symptom of congestive heart failure," Olek said, "it's not a good sign. She's retaining fluids."

"And your flesh is grey."

"Another ominous symptom," he said.

"And there's blue around your eyes, lips, and fingernails."

"Cyanosis. Another worrying sign."

Noticing Olek sounded like a doctor, Anastasia demanded to know what business he had in Nonna's house, which, she indignantly reminded him, was private property. Olek pointed out there wasn't a "No Trespassing" sign posted outside the house or yard. Beside the mailbox a sign merely warned no junk mail, which Anastasia insisted on taping to the window frame to stop kids delivering flyers to her door. Lonely, isolated, Nonna actually enjoyed the neighbourhood kids dropping by, even when they pranked her, playing practical jokes, or were up to mischief. Olek said he merely visited her grandmother's house to deliver her prescription drugs.

"But I didn't give you permission to take the medication."

"You did," Olek insisted, "but I think you were so stoned and high you don't remember."

"I did not consent," Anastasia insisted louder, in a cutting voice.

"But you did," Olek insisted.

Anastasia grabbed Nonna's boning knife from a wooden block above the cutlery cupboard and lunged towards him. "Get out."

Olek initially resisted the urge to intervene with physical force at this melodramatic gesture, but he also feared the fierce look in her eyes and her angry facial expression. Young, naïve, under the influence of illicit drugs, Olek thought, Anastasia posed a threat and a danger to herself and others. He thought she could harm herself, her grandmother, or even him. Olek tried to seize the knife from her clenched hands, with their pretty, painted nails, but she looked determined and possessed a strong grip. Anastasia slashed at his hand, cutting his fingers, slicing the flesh, slashing the flesh between his thumb and finger.

"Fuck," Olek said. "Ouch."

In school and even the workplace, Olek had been bullied and beat up, punched in the head, kicked in the rear and stomach, slapped in the face, socked in the mouth, but he had never been stabbed or slashed with a knife.

"Leave," Big Red shouted, as her grandmother started to sob.

Nonna called the police on her cordless telephone with its keypad of huge oversized numbers. Olek realized he should indeed leave before Anastasia became more erratic and violent. In the steady rain, he clutched his wrist and nursed his slashed and bloodied hand. As he walked hurriedly along Park Street, stooped in the rain, hurting, he continued to bleed profusely from the gash in his hairy hand.

A police cruiser, searching the neighbourhood for a potentially rabid fox sighted in the park, and then an animal control officer in a van, sped past, splashing Olek with muddied water from the puddles alongside the curbs. Another police cruiser with flashing lights, raced towards Nonna's house and stopped in front of Olek at a pedestrian crosswalk.

Ya'el Chaikind, MPH, MA, LPCC is a licensed psychotherapist in private practice and a certified practitioner of Brainspotting, a brain-body trauma healing system. She holds a Master of Arts in Clinical Counseling from Highlands University and a Master of Public Health from Rutgers University. To date, Ya'el has published eight nonfiction books and numerous poems, essays, articles, and short fiction in various anthologies and literary journals. As a psychotherapist, Ya'el supports clients in re-writing the stories that no longer serve them to create a life of more connection, meaning, and belonging. As a book consultant, she shares her craft with aspiring authors to help them achieve their writing and publishing dreams. She lives in beautiful Santa Fe, NM. Visit her website at www.yaelchaikind.com.

Barry M. Panter, MD, PhD graduated from Rutgers University and Temple University School of Medicine. He did his pediatric residency at Cedars of Lebanon Hospital in Hollywood, California and a psychiatric residency at Yale University, New Haven, Connecticut. He is a clinical professor of psychiatry (Emeritus) at the USC school of medicine and a training and supervising analyst at the Southern California Psychoanalytic Institute (Emeritus) and the Institute for Contemporary Psychoanalysis in Los Angeles. (Emeritus). He is a Life Fellow of the American Psychiatric Association. He is board-certified in Pediatrics and in Psychiatry and Neurology. He has co-authored and co-edited *Creativity and Madness – Psychological Studies of Art and Artists*, volumes 1, 2, and 3. He is the author of *Thirty-Three Poems for Mary Lou*. Jacqueline, his wife, is the founder and co-director of the Women of Resilience Conferences. They reside in Rancho Mirage with their Italian water dog Pucci (Puccini), whom they consider to be Best of family.

www.ingramcontent.com/pod-product-compliance
Lightning Source LLC
Chambersburg PA
CBHW030408130626
46549CB00004B/1679